D0365509

CHILDREN AND YOUTH
Social Problems and Social Policy

CHILDREN AND YOUTH
Social Problems and Social Policy

EMIC

(Emergency Maternity and Infant Care)

A Study of

ADMINISTRATIVE EXPERIENCE

Nathan Sinai

and

Odin W. Anderson

ARNO PRESS
A New York Times Company
New York — 1974

Reprint Edition 1974 by Arno Press Inc.

CHILDREN AND YOUTH
Social Problems and Social Policy
ISBN for complete set: 0-405-05940-X
See last pages of this volume for titles.

Manufactured in the United States of America

Library of Congress Cataloging in Publication Data

Sinai, Nathan, 1894-
EMIC (Emergency maternity and infant care).

(Children and youth: social problems and social policy)
Reprint of the ed. published by the School of Public Health, University of Michigan, Ann Arbor, which was issued as no. 3 of Bureau of Public Health Economics research series.
1. United States--Armed Forces--Medical care --History. 2. Maternal health services--United States --History. I. Anderson, Odin Waldemar, 1914- joint author. II. Title. III. Series. IV. Series: Michigan. University. Bureau of Public Health Economics. Research series, no. 3.
[DNLM: 1. Emergency health services. 2. Infant care. 3. Maternal welfare. W1BU951 no. 3 1948a / WA310 S615e 1948]
UB403.S57 1974 353.008'41'982 74-1704
ISBN 0-405-05981-7

BUREAU OF PUBLIC HEALTH ECONOMICS

RESEARCH SERIES No. 3

EMIC

(Emergency Maternity and Infant Care)

A STUDY OF

ADMINISTRATIVE EXPERIENCE

NATHAN SINAI, DR. PH.

ODIN W. ANDERSON, PH. D.

SCHOOL OF PUBLIC HEALTH

UNIVERSITY OF MICHIGAN

Ann Arbor, Michigan

1948

Printed in U.S.A.

Table of Contents

PART ONE

EMIC, Background, Development and Scope

PART TWO

Current Health Economic Problems and the Experience of EMIC

TABLE OF CONTENTS (continued)

PART ONE

EMIC

Background, Development and Scope

Chapter I

INTRODUCTION

Few will question that the distribution of the health services—medical care, dental care, nursing, hospitalization and others—comprises a broad social movement in the United States and over the world. The movement has assumed such large proportions that, accompanying it, there has developed a new field of study. By some it is called "social medicine;" by others, "medical economics" or "public health economics" and, as with other movements, this one has evolved in the United States to a point where its issues must be re-defined.

The question of how a social idea, such as a national health plan, may work when transformed into a social institution can never be settled by conflicting theoretical charts. Such charts have certain of the touches and devices used by the ancient cartographers. There are areas of unknowns; by some they may be drawn in dark and forbidding colors, inhabited by monsters; by others they may be pictured in attractive pastel shades. It is little wonder that confusion results.

Too much of the discussion of a national health plan has about it an air of unreality. The comparable picture is somewhat like that of the old philosophers, who, probably sitting on the sunny side of the Tower of Pisa, debated the subject of whether a heavier body would fall a given distance faster than a lighter one. "Pure logic" provided the answer that it would, so it was absurd to subject the conclusion to any test—and climbing towers is very tiring. The tower was there, light and heavy objects were available but why bother—until Galileo demonstrated by the experimental method.

The experimental method is both the product and the pride of modern science and attracts strong professional and popular support. Is it possible to use it in connection with a national health plan; to subject proposals and methods to critical test as a means of reducing the area of unknowns? At first thought the application of the experimental method to a national health plan appears to be fanciful. Trial and especially error on such a grand scale would result in confusing conflicts. When, however, the issues and problems of a national health plan are organized and classified and when they are examined in the light of what has been happening in the United States the possibilities of the experimental method become real and within reach.

Over the country there are, literally, dozens of "experimental laboratories" in which there are rich collections of information. While a national health plan is being discussed in theory, on all sides there are to be found the elements of a national health plan, in fact. Blue Cross hospital plans, medical society plans, relief plans, rural plans—these and many others contain partial answers to questions that are being discussed as if no experience exists.

More significant, while theoretical discussions of a national health plan have been taking place, at least *six actual national health plans have been started and three of these are operating now.* All this has occurred within the decade when the debate has been most vigorous. It makes little difference that three of the national health plans were launched as emergency measures; all presented many answers to many questions that are being discussed currently—questions of centralized or decentralized governmental authority, of professional relations, of actuarial experience, of facilities, the quality of services, the form of payment and others.

With six national health programs in a little over a decade what was learned? The first undertaking was the huge relief program that was financed by the Federal Government for over twenty million people in every part of the country. Under Rules and Regulations No. 7 issued by the Federal Emergency Relief Administration "Governing Medical Care Provided in the Home to Recipients of Unemployment Relief" what were the details of organization and administration in the states and local communities? Where did the system work well, where did it prove defective—and why? What were the expressed needs of the people, what services were given, how well did the various forms of payment work? As with other missed opportunities there are no answers to these, the same questions being asked now and for which answers supported by experience could have been obtained. Thus, a national health plan that involved professional personnel and patients was in operation for about eighteen months and it ended with virtually nothing added to the knowledge of public health economics.

The next two national health plans were started in 1936. One was the program of the Farm Security Administration for low-income farmers. The rural health problem has been a perennial subject of discussion with emphasis on the lack of facilities and personnel, the needs of the people and the difficulties of arranging for the payment for services. But here was a program that, eventually, was to provide, within the limits of available facilities and personnel, services in over a third of the counties of the country to a total of more than seventy-thousand families in 1944. Here, too, was a program that should have excited the critical attention of every agency that claims to have an interest in public health economics. The opportunity to analyze the possibilities: the strengths and the defects of local control, rather than state or national; and of local organization and administration, including the utilization of facilities and personnel; costs and other pertinent subjects was made to order. But, except for those studies made within the administrative agency itself, the Farm Security Administration program grew to a peak and declined without exciting more than ripples of sporadic interest in a few of its controversial elements. The laboratory for the study of rural health organization and administration by independent agencies was not utilized.

The other program established in 1936 was the one for crippled children authorized by the Social Security Act and administered by the Children's Bureau. This program is continuing and the policies and procedures developed for carrying it on deserve close study from many standpoints. Some of these are Federal-state administrative relationships, state-local administrative relationships, development of cooperation between public and private agencies, determination and maintenance of standards, and many others. The evidence is there and only awaits analysis.

The fourth national health plan is the one that forms the foundation of this report. At its peak the Emergency Maternity and Infant Care program exerted its influence upon virtually every community in the country. Despite the sharpened interest in a national health plan little attention was given to EMIC, probably because of its "emergency" aspects. But, emergency or not, valuable current experience was accumulating. The program included a wide variety of administrative techniques; it faced the development of national, state and local policies; it involved much of the subject of payment, including the basis, the method and the amount; it established procedures for professional and public relations and it offered valuable material on the problems of standards and the quality of services. This is not to say that in all of these aspects of organization and administration the EMIC contributions were positive and satisfactory. Errors were made, certain ambitions exceeded accomplishments but the experience, whether positive or negative, offers much of value to those interested in a national health plan.

While this report is being prepared a fifth national health plan, that of the Veterans Administration, is developing. The Veterans Administration has provided health services for many years but the reason for classifying its program as a national health plan is the introduction of a new element in 1946. The element is "home town care" for veterans with service-connected disabilities. The care is provided by private practitioners, hospitals, etc., in local areas in accordance with agreements arranged by the Administration. All evidence points to the rapid spread of the program until, like EMIC, it covers the country. Many of the problems to be solved are comparable to those of EMIC or any national health plan. Once again a laboratory is being created.

Finally, a sixth national plan, that of Vocational Rehabilitation, is expanding and using, more and more, the health facilities of the nation. Here, too, is a laboratory with problems comparable to those of EMIC and the Veterans Administration. It is not an unreasonable conclusion that what these laboratories produce should be given tangible weight in evaluating any future proposals that may be made.

The EMIC Study

It was during 1944 that the possibilities of the EMIC program as a research laboratory in public health economics became self-evident. Two obstacles, neither minor, stood in the way of an acceptable critical study. The first was the financing of such a study; the second was the possible attitude of a government agency toward an analysis of its administration.

As a rule Federal agencies exhibit a restrained enthusiasm toward any proposed analysis of their activities. This is especially true when the study involves a controversial subject and when the research is in the control of a non-governmental organization. It is, therefore, to the high credit of the Children's Bureau that when the proposal for study was presented the response was one of complete approval. And during the course of the study the approval was supported by the actions and the attitude of the staff. The research workers were given complete freedom; the files of correspondence, including recommendations, complaints and criticisms were open to review, and stenographic reports of intra-agency conferences on the operation of the EMIC program were made available.

Financial support of the research project was granted by two foundations, the New York Foundation and the Marshall Field Foundation. To both foundations the project was presented as a study intended to contribute to the chief issue in public health economics, the organization and administration of a national health plan. Following favorable action by the foundations the preliminary preparations for the study began in the late fall of 1944.

The methods of study included an analysis of the enormous amount of material in the office of the Children's Bureau—Congressional hearings and actions, financial data, plans from the states, administrative rules and regulations, correspondence, reports, and statistical data. But the primary emphasis of the study was upon the field work. Maternity and infant care are services provided to people living in local communities within states and how the program worked could be learned only by visiting a cross section of states and communities. It was here that the answers to vital questions would be found.

The selected states included Massachusetts, New York, Michigan, Illinois, Georgia, Mississippi, Nebraska, and California—north, south, east and west. Within the areas selected there were to be found virtually all of the variables that may be expected to influence the organization and administration of a national health plan—social extremes, economic extremes, professional extremes, with each set of extremes showing the in-between gradations that make up the average.

Much of the work in the field was devoted to interviews. Whether 55 or 110 babies had been delivered in a particular community was a secondary matter but the attitudes, the opinions, the experiences, the suggestions and the recommendations of those whose lives had been touched by the EMIC program were important. And an amazing number of people were in this category. Physicians, dentists, nurses, public health workers, social workers, hospital administrators—these, aside from over a million patients in the country, make up the groups to whom EMIC was more than four letters of the alphabet. In preparation for the study the field staff discussed and revised the patterns of the interviews and agreed upon the type of data that would be sought. It was and is recognized that such an approach, except for the factual supporting data, is a subjective one. Within the study the only method of controlling errors was to check the conclusions of field staff, wherever possible, through discussions of their findings and comparisons with views expressed in the medical journals and with the opinions of administrators. A much better control would have been possible if two or three other agencies with an interest in public health economics had undertaken a comparable study.

Throughout the report the phrase "national health plan" will appear. This has no reference to any single proposal that has been presented. The major problems that are discussed are problems that attend the process of organization and administration. It is a grave mistake to interpret these problems as less weighty for a voluntary national health plan than for a compulsory one. Whatever the auspices the plan requires organization and administration.

Attention is directed, also, to the important fact that in the presentation of problems the phrase "state health plan" might well replace "national health plan" if one has in mind such states as California, New York, Ohio, Illinois, Michigan and many others. Within the populous states are found the majority of the administrative problems that face the nation; what differences exist are variations in degree.

In the succeeding chapters of Part I descriptions of the Children's Bureau and the EMIC program are presented. These are intended to provide the atmosphere and the setting within which the organization and administration of a national health plan developed. Left for Part II are the interpretations and evaluations of the experience gained.

Chapter II

THE CHILDREN'S BUREAU

The Establishment of the Bureau, 1912

There are many lessons contained in the series of events that led to the establishment of the Children's Bureau by an act of Congress in 1912. Viewed in retrospect the events preceding and during 1912 form the pattern of action that, then and now, culminates in a new law or a new agency.

One of the standard criticisms that attends any proposal for social legislation is that it was inspired by "small interested groups" or by "professional social workers." The question is usually asked: Where is the evidence of widespread public demand? It is implied that public demand is something that has a spontaneous origin and that unless a proposal originates in an upsurge, a tidal wave, of public opinion its validity is in question.

Social legislation and for that matter other types as well, develops in successive stages. Individuals or small groups become aware of a particular situation; they write, they speak, they recommend, they begin to focus public attention upon what they conceive to be the need. To them this becomes the "most important" problem that calls for public action and by their activities they arouse the interest of more and more people. Organizations take action in favor of the proposals to solve a problem; public polls are used both to obtain a measure of public opinion and to educate; sponsoring committees are organized and funds are collected to acquaint greater and greater numbers with the need for action.

While this is going on members of a state legislature or of Congress become a part of the sphere of interest and translate the proposals into the tangible form of recommended legislation. Thus, what started as the interest of a small group finally emerges as a legislative act. And the progress from interest and support by a restricted group to strong public demand does not differ markedly whether the proposal has to do with enabling legislation to organize voluntary medical and hospital plans, a new medical practice act or the organization of a new government agency.*

*The same description would apply to the "build-up" of opposition to a proposal.

An important event leading to the creation of the Children's Bureau is reported to be the suggestion of Lillian D. Wald, founder of the Henry Street Settlement in New York City, to President Theodore Roosevelt in 1906 that such a governmental agency be established.[1] As stated by Julia C. Lathrop, the first chief of the Children's Bureau, it is no mere coincidence that "this Bureau was first urged by women who have lived long in settlements and who by that experience have learned to know as well as any persons in this country certain aspects of dumb misery which they desired through some governmental agency to make articulate and intelligible."[2] Some of the dumb misery referred to was, of course, the need as seen in the city slums for an effective program of maternal and child welfare.

Mrs. Florence Kelley, head of the National Consumers League and Miss Wald were influential in bringing the National Child Labor Committee into the struggle. This committee drafted the first bill for the creation of the Bureau which was first presented to Congress in 1906 and 1907 and also maintained a lobbying and pressure office in Washington until the proposal was approved.[3]

The proponents for the institution of a bureau began to increase in number and influence. They argued for a center of research and information concerning the welfare of mothers and children. Obviously without a sound basis of information no intelligent and effective maternal and child welfare program could be formulated. Information and statistics on maternal and infant mortality and morbidity, juvenile delinquency, nutrition, and child labor and related problems were sorely lacking. It was argued pointedly that the Federal Government had already established agencies to serve as centers of research and information in other fields, such as agriculture, and it might well look to the welfare of one of the more important resources of the country—children.

Finally, success was achieved in enlisting the active interest of Congress. Many bills directed toward the creation of the Children's Bureau were introduced from 1909 to 1912, and extensive hearings were held on each one.[4] As an indication of the strong support that

1U S. Children's Bureau, *Yesterday, Today and Tomorrow*. Washington, Government Printing Office, 1937. p. 1.

2Julia C. Lathrop, "Children's Bureau," *American Journal of Sociology*. 18:318, November, 1912.

3Ibid.

4U. S. Congress. House. Committee on Expenditures in the Interior Department. Hearings on HR. 24148 for the Establishment of the Children's Bureau in the Interior Department. 60th Congress 2nd Session. January 27–28, 1909.

U. S. Congress. Senate. Committee on Education and Labor. Hearings on had been mustered, an imposing array of organizations and influential individuals appeared before the Congressional committee to testify in favor of the provisions of the bills. Among them were the late Jane Addams of Hull House of Chicago, Judge Ben Lindsey of juvenile court fame, and the representatives of many powerful organizations such as the National Consumer's League, the State Charities Aid Association, the American Association for Labor Legislation, and the Russell Sage Foundation. All stressed the pressing need for information and statistics stating that while there would be no compulsion on the states to utilize the information they would be encouraged to enact sound child welfare laws on the basis of such information. One interesting argument proposed was that it "would multiply the efficiency of private philanthropy." There seemed to be little evidence of opposition to the bills; the task at hand was apparently one of bringing pressure upon Congress to take concrete and final action. President Theodore Roosevelt and, later President Taft lent their prestige and influence.

Although there was unanimity of purpose as to the functions of the proposed bureau, considerable disagreement arose as to where it should be placed in the governmental administrative machinery. The three alternatives suggested at the time were the Bureau of Labor and the Bureau of the Census, both in the Department of Commerce and Labor, and the third, the Bureau of Education in the Department of the Interior. It was apparent that the work of the proposed bureau would perhaps overlap all these agencies. The Bureau of Labor was concerned primarily with working conditions which would also relate to the working conditions of women and children; the Bureau of the Census collected vital statistics concerning mothers and infants; and the Bureau of Education dealt with the education and school environment of the child. The United States Public Health Service, then a part of the Treasury Department, was not considered, at least not in the records of the hearings. This may have been due to the broad social service aspects of the proposed bureau overshadowing the health aspects. In any case, the three bureaus mentioned above were reluctant to accept respon-

S. 8323 (Same as H.R. 24148 above) for the Establishment of the Children's Bureau in the Interior Department. 60th Congress 2nd Session. February 4, 1909.

U. S. Congress. House. Committee on Expenditures in the Department of Commerce and Labor. Hearings on H.R. 23259 to Establish in the Department of Commerce and Labor a Bureau to be known as the Children's Bureau. 61st Congress 2nd Session. April 13, 1910.

U. S. Congress. House. Committee on Labor. Hearings on H.R. 4694 for the Establishment of Children's Bureau in the Department of Commerce and Labor. 62nd Congress 1st Session. May 12, 1911.

sibility for the work of the proposed bureau, and their chiefs admitted as much in the hearings on the bills. They did, however, offer to cooperate with the new bureau wherever it might be placed.

The 62nd Congress passed the measure sponsored by Senator Borah, and it was approved by President Taft on April 9, 1912. The Children's Bureau, as it was originally named, was placed as a separate agency in the Department of Commerce and Labor. When this department was split into the respective Departments of Commerce and of Labor in 1913, the Bureau was retained by the Department of Labor where it remained until transferred to the Federal Security Agency in 1946. In 1920 a close associate of Lillian Wald and a strong supporter of the Bureau expressed her gratitude over the Bureau's placement in the Department of Labor: "Had the Bureau in its inception been limited by the outlook either of a department of health or a department of education—assuming that both of these departments were led by the wisest and most generous of statesmen—there would of necessity have been lost much of the very fine work of the division. Its activities have traversed many fields and in particular they have thrown great light on the so-called borderland of science, the undefined region which has belonged assuredly to none. Under its present direction in the Department of Labor, the department which par excellence is concerned with broad considerations of human well-being, the Bureau has had the untrammeled right freely to serve the Nation."[5] Granted the organic and integrative approach of the Bureau to its problems it, nevertheless, has had several struggles to keep the health aspects of its program from being transferred to the United States Public Health Service—but more of that later.

The Sheppard-Towner Act, 1922

The Act establishing the Children's Bureau reads in part, "That said Bureau shall investigate and report . . . upon all matters pertaining to the welfare of children and child life among all classes of our people, and shall especially investigate the questions of infant mortality, the birth rate, orphanages, juvenile courts, desertion, dangerous occupations, accidents and diseases of children, employment, legislation affecting children in the several States and Territories."[6] It will be noted that the Bureau was originally established solely to *investigate* and *report,* but as it gained in experience and

[5]Florence Kelley, "The Children's Bureau in Its Niche," *Survey* 43:455 January 24, 1920.

[6]37 Stat. 79 (1912).

had assembled and trained a small but highly technical staff of persons who had become experts in the problems of maternal and child welfare, it became the natural agency to be entrusted with new programs of this nature. Such was the case when the Bureau was designated by Congress as the agency to administer the first Federal Child-Labor Law effective from 1917 to 1918 and subsequently declared unconstitutional by the Supreme Court. The later programs that expanded the original functions of the Bureau, each new program being larger than the previous ones, were the Federal Maternity and Infancy Act in effect from 1922 to 1929, popularly known as the Sheppard-Towner Act, the maternal and child welfare provisions of Title V of the Social Security Act passed in 1935, and the present Emergency Maternity and Infant Care program which grew out of the war emergency and was made possible through a very liberal interpretation of Title V by Congress.

Thus the expanding functions of the Bureau have reflected the growing needs in a dynamic society and the attempts to meet them. It is a truism to state that no government agency exists in a vacuum; it is too frequently forgotten that a government agency is an effect and not a cause of attempts to cope with social problems.

During the first nine years of the Bureau's existence, from 1912 to 1921, it laid a firm foundation for scientific research and the dissemination of scientific information to the people of the country. These services were maintained as the Bureau undertook the administration of new programs. The early studies of infant mortality, which placed major emphasis on income, housing, employment of the mother, and other factors affecting the infant death rate, were made under the direction of a staff which included physicians, social workers, and statisticians. "Baby Weeks" in 1916 and 1917, "Children's Year" in 1918, and the White House Conference of 1919 all brought out important facts as to maternal and child health in this country and added to the data accumulated by the Bureau. Evidence gathered concerning conditions under which children were employed plus the campaign by the National Child Labor Committee led to the passage of the Federal Child Labor Law in 1916. The studies of maternal and infant care in rural areas and the analyses of other data led to the adoption of the Sheppard-Towner Act in 1921, which through grants-in-aid to the states was intended to encourage greater interest and action in maternal and child welfare programs.

The provisions embodied in this act were first recommended by Miss Lathrop in her fifth annual report in 1917. They were based upon the principle of extending maternal and child health services to local communities through the leadership and assistance of state health agencies aided by grants of funds from the Federal Government, these grants being matched by the states. Thus precedents that had been developed extensively for the improvement of agriculture through Federal aid were applied to the promotion of maternal and child health. Interesting also is the fact that the research and reporting functions outlined in the act that created the Children's Bureau in 1912 had been suggested by similar work in the Department of Agriculture. These are excellent illustrations of how precedents established in one field of activity are applied to other fields. Law making bodies are much more likely to authorize an activity if it or something like it has been done before.

The expansion of the functions of the Bureau from investigating and reporting to administrative and supervisory activities in health matters caused bitter controversy. The hearings on the bills introduced in Congress in 1919, 1920, and 1921 were contests between opposing factions, with the Congressional committee members conducting the hearings caught between the verbal cross-fire.[7] It is of interest to note that many of the issues discussed and the general tenor of the hearings with respect to the Sheppard-Towner Bill are practically the same as for the later EMIC proposals. In fact, if names of people and events were deleted from the records of the hearings during the two periods, 22 years apart, they could hardly be differentiated from each other.

The opponents of the Sheppard-Towner Bill argued that its adoption would be another step toward "socialized medicine;" it would provide the "entering wedge;" too much power would be centralized in Washington; States' rights would be violated. The proponents countered by pointing out that no state would be forced to accept grants-in-aid; no physician would be forced to participate; the actual administration of the program would be left entirely to the states, the Children's Bureau would serve only in a consultative and supervisory capacity; no medical services, as such, would be rendered by the agency; state and local initiative would be strengthened instead of weakened by grants-in-aid. The opponents appearing at the hearings were individual physicians, representatives of the American Medical Association, the Woman Patriot

7U. S. Congress. House. Committee on Labor. Hearings on H.R. 12634 on Hygiene of Maternity and Infancy. 65th Congress 3d Session. January 15, 28, 1919.

U. S. Congress. Senate. Committee on Public Health and National Quarantine. Hearings on S. 3259 for the Protection of Maternity and Infancy. 66th Congress 2nd Session. May 12, 1920.

U. S. Congress. House. Committee on Interstate and Foreign Commerce. Hearings on H.R. 2366 for the Public Protection of Maternity and Infancy. 67th Congress 1st Session. July 12–16, 18–23, 1921.

(official organ of the National Association Opposed to Woman Suffrage), Sentinels of the Republic, and the Catholic women's organization in Massachusetts. The proponents appearing were from various women's organizations, child welfare organizations, the president of the American Public Health Association, and representatives of other organizations.

The inter-agency controversy between the United States Public Health Service and the Children's Bureau reached an acute stage in the hearings on the bill. There was some testimony favoring the administration of the provisions of the bill by the Public Health Service instead of the Children's Bureau. The question was asked whether the bill was chiefly concerned with health or with general child welfare; if with health the Public Health Service should be designated as the administrative agency; if with general child welfare the Children's Bureau would be the logical choice. The competition between the two agencies was brought to a temporary end in a last minute conference called by the respective cabinet chiefs (Treasury and Labor), as a result of which the Children's Bureau retained control over the maternal and child health program.[8] In this regard it is the opinion of a student of the grants-in-aid principle that the Bureau gained control over this program "by right of discovery and occupation and that the Public Health Service had been derelict in not promoting this type of work with sufficient vigor to maintain its belated claim to jurisdiction."[9] This quotation deserves reading and re-reading by public health officials today. When the subject of a governmental health plan arises one of the first concerns is the agency of administration. Control "by right of occupation" is a phenomenon that repeats itself many, many times in governmental activities.

A further reason for the Bureau's retention of this program was expressed by an authority on Federal health activities: "The Children's Bureau is based not only upon the administrative theory of the special population group, but also upon the political conviction held by large groups of women and social workers that child and maternal welfare problems were, before its creation, suffering from comparative neglect, and since its creation have obtained at the hands of its essentially feminine personnel a sympathetic and progressive development."[10] In the evolution of the function of the

8Robert D. Leigh, *Federal Health Administration in the United States.* New York, Harper, 1927. p. 418.

9V. O. Key, *The Administration of Federal Grants to States.* Chicago, Public Administration Service, 1937. p. 208.

10Leigh, op. cit., p. 528.

Bureau, the health aspects of its program have become its most important features, hence the inevitable clash with another government agency dealing exclusively with health matters.

The Sheppard-Towner Act set the pattern for later maternal and child health programs. Its chief features were: (1) Federal financial aid to the states, (2) administration by the Children's Bureau, (3) the application of grants-in-aid to the problem of reducing maternal and infant mortality and its use in protecting the health of mothers and infants, and (4) the vesting in the states of authority to initiate and to administer plans, subject to approval by the Federal Board of Maternity and Infant Hygiene.[11] Further, the Federal government granted $1,240,000 a year to the Children's Bureau to be used in grants-in-aid to states, and $50,000 a year for Federal administration. The states could accept or reject aid as they saw fit, but in order to secure the benefits of the act each state legislature was obliged to accept its general provisions, and designate a state administrative agency. In the actual initiation and operation of the state plans each state had to submit descriptions of programs to the Federal Board of Maternal and Infant Hygiene for approval and make reports of operations. The board was composed of the Chief of the Children's Bureau, the Surgeon General of the Public Health Service, and the Commissioner of Education, the chairman being chosen by the board from among its own membership. The Chief of the Children's Bureau acted as chairman for the duration of the act. The powers of the board consisted of approving or disapproving the state plans submitted, and of withholding Federal funds from any state whose program was not being operated as agreed upon between the state and the board. The duties vested in the Children's Bureau were the general administration of the act—formulating rules and regulations and consulting with the states, certifying payments to the Secretary of the Treasury and making studies and investigations.

Thus, Congress authorized the first grants-in-aid program in the broad field of maternal and child health.* It is argued that the grants-in-aid principle lends itself to the American constitutional system because of the separation of state and Federal functions and the taxing power of the Federal Government. Furthermore, "the grant system builds on and utilizes existing institutions to cope with

*The first grants-in-aid program for health was the short-lived Kahn-Chamberlain Act of 1917 to combat venereal diseases.

11U. S. Children's Bureau, Publication No. 137, *Promotion of the Welfare and Hygiene of Maternity and Infancy*. Washington, Government Printing Office, 1924. p. 1.

national problems. Under it the states are welded into national machinery of sorts and the establishment of costly, parallel, direct Federal services is made unnecessary. A virtue of no mean importance is that administrators in actual charge of operations remain amenable to local control. In that way the supposed formality, the regularity, and the cold-blooded efficiency of a national hierarchy is avoided."[12] When the Supreme Court of the United States declared the present Social Security Act constitutional, the grants-in-aid was given a firm, legal basis.

During the seven years of the Sheppard-Towner program the groundwork was laid for a national maternal and child health program administered by the states. From 1912 to 1920, 32 states had established divisions or bureaus of child hygiene. From 1921, the year of the passage of the act, to 1923 an additional 15 states had created agencies.[13] It is difficult, if not impossible, to determine to what extent the act stimulated the states to create new child hygiene agencies. But it is of interest that the expansion of the functions of the Children's Bureau and the creation of state agencies of child hygiene go hand in hand. The Federal and state activities in this field are part of the same context and it is reasonable to assume that this reflects the growing popular interest in maternal and child welfare. The Children's Bureau program, therefore, can be given credit for the expansion of the work of the current maternal and child welfare projects carried on by the states.

Under the Sheppard-Towner Act 45 states submitted programs to the Federal Government for approval. Three states, Illinois, Massachusetts, and Connecticut, refused to avail themselves of Federal funds. However they did have their own programs. The staff immediately added to the Bureau for the administration of the act consisted of a medical director, a public health nurse, an accountant, a secretary, and a stenographer, but the Bureau felt that this staff was insufficient for effective field work.[14] Later more members were added.

In 1926 a bill was introduced in Congress to extend the Sheppard-Towner Act from five years to seven years. This also aroused vigorous debate. Opponents of the original act seemed to have assumed that it was a temporary measure to give the states a "lift", so to speak, until they could carry the full expenses of their own pro-

12Key, op. cit., p. 383.

13Committee on Economic Security, *Social Security in America*. Washington, Government Printing Office, 1937. p. 270 (U. S. Social Security Board. Pub. No. 20).

14U. S. Children's Bureau, Publication No. 137, op. cit., p. 27.

grams.[15] The proponents of the bill contended that the state programs were still not strong enough to be continued by the states alone. Upon being asked how much time would be needed, of course no definite answers could be given. In any case, the act was extended for another two years, and efforts to continue its provisions beyond 1929 were to no avail.[16] Following the expiration of the act, the legislatures in a few of the states increased their appropriations for maternal and child health, in some instances to an amount that exceeded the previous combined Federal and state funds. However, the net effect of the withdrawal of Federal aid to the states and the District of Columbia was that five states reported increases over amounts expended in 1928 and 35 reported decreases; nine reported no appropriation at all. Significantly, 22 of the states and Hawaii reported expenditures for the depression year 1934 which were less than 50 percent of those expended in 1928 under the act.[17]

In its first comprehensive report of the operation of the Sheppard-Towner Act the Children's Bureau stated that, "In a few States where the initial work has not been outstandingly successful it is largely due to lack of understanding of the purposes and plans of the State program. In order that medical cooperation might be assured, a number of State plans definitely stipulated that the State health department should not undertake work in any county or community, even though a demand existed for it, until the project had been placed before and endorsed by the local or county medical society. Thus, the responsibility of fulfilling a recognized local need, demanded by the public, was placed entirely upon the local medical profession."[18]

A sympathetic observer of the program who had interviewed many state health officers and directors of child hygiene divisions was of the opinion that the Bureau adopted a "laissez-faire policy" in the administration of the act, a policy which naturally received widespread approval of the state officials cooperating in the program. He added that "no other Federal law has been so consistently misrepresented, nor so frequently accused of making possible Federal domination."[19]

15U. S. Congress. House. Committee on Interstate and Foreign Commerce. Hearings on H.R. 7555 for the Extension of the Public Protection of the Maternity and Infancy Act. 69th Congress. 1st Session. January 14, 1926.

16U. S. Congress. House. Committee on Interstate and Foreign Commerce. Hearings on H.R. 14070 to Provide a Child Welfare Extension Service and for other Purposes. 70th Congress 2d Session. January 24–25, 1929.

17Committee on Economic Security, op. cit., p. 272–273.

18U. S. Children's Bureau, Publication No. 137, op. cit., p. 25.

19Austin F. Macdonald, *Federal Aid.* New York, Crowell, 1928. p. 223.

Unsuccessful attempts were made in 1931 and 1932 to revive the Sheppard-Towner Act.[20] Thereafter no further movement was made in this direction until the Social Security Act was adopted in 1935 with provisions for maternal and child health embodied in Title V.

It is difficult to assess the effect of the Sheppard-Towner Act on maternal and child health programs throughout the country, but it is true that a pattern of Federal-state administrative and fiscal relationships was established which was carried, for good or for ill, into the administration of the maternal and child health program inaugurated by the Social Security Act and the later expansion of this program to include EMIC.

The Social Security Act, 1935

With the adoption of the Social Security Act in 1935 the Children's Bureau regained and added to the functions it lost when the Sheppard-Towner Act was discontinued in 1929. From 1929 to 1935 the Bureau continued its research program and promotional work in the general field of maternal and child welfare. After the adoption of the Social Security Act direct administrative relations with the states were again established.

The Children's Bureau was given responsibility for the administration of Title V of the Social Security Act which provided for three programs of maternal and child welfare: (1) maternal and child health, (2) crippled children, and (3) child welfare services. By statute the Bureau was given an annual budget of $8,170,000 for grants-in-aid, exclusive of administration, allocated as follows: maternal and child health, $3,820,000; crippled children, $2,850,-000; and child welfare services, $1,500,000.

The beneficiaries of the programs are theoretically all mothers and children in the states who wish to avail themselves of the services. The usual services provided under maternal and child health by the state are: (1) to develop maternal and child health services in district or county public health units and in areas without full-time public health services; (2) to develop high standards of services in the maternal and child health field; (3) to enlist the cooperation of

20U. S. Congress. House. Committee on Interstate and Foreign Commerce. Hearings on S. 255 and H.R. 12995 for the Promotion of the Health and Welfare of Mothers and Infants and for other Purposes. 71st Congress 3d Session. January 20, 22, 1931.

U.S. Congress. Senate. Committee on Commerce. Hearings on S. 572 for the Welfare and Hygiene of Mothers and Children. 72d Congress 1st Session. February 4–5, 1932.

members of the medical and allied professions and of community groups in extending state-wide facilities for continuous medical and nursing care and health supervision through maternity, infancy, and childhood, and in maintaining high standards of care; and (4) through health education programs conducted by physicians, dentists, nurses, and nutritionists to inform parents and children of the practices essential for health.[21]

The crippled children's program deals with medical services and rehabilitation for crippled children, and the child welfare program with foster home care, juvenile delinquency, and many other child welfare problems.

The basis of allocation to the states varied with each type of program. For maternal and child health each state was entitled to $20,000. The sum of $1,800,000, called "Fund A", was to be shared among the states on the basis of the number of live births in each state in relation to the total number of live births in the United States, with the states matching their allotments from Fund A. Another sum of $980,000 was allocated to the states on the basis of financial need and the number of live births in the state. No matching of funds by the states was required. This was the "B Fund" to be described later since it was this money with which the emergency program that preceded EMIC was started.

For crippled children $20,000 was granted to each state, and the remaining sum of $1,830,000 was allotted according to the need of the state as determined by its number of crippled children in need of services and the cost of furnishing such services.*

Lastly, each state was granted $10,000 for child welfare services and the remainder, $990,000, went to the states on the basis of plans submitted and the proportion of the population that was rural.

In 1939 the total appropriation to the Children's Bureau for grants-in-aid was increased from $8,170,000 to $11,000,000. The maternal and child health program received an additional $2,000,000 divided equally between its matched and unmatched funds, the crippled children's program received an increase of $1,020,000, and the child welfare program $10,000. In 1946 Congress amended Title V again providing for an over-all increase in appropriations from $11,000,000 to $22,000,000 plus an increase in the amount for administrative expenses.

Within 10 months after the appropriations under the Social

*There was no B Fund under this program until 1939.

21U. S. Children's Bureau, Publication No. 259, *Maternal and Child-Health Services under the Social Security Act; Development of Programs, 1936–39.* Washington, Government Printing Office, 1941. p. 12.

Security Act became available on February 1, 1936, all the 48 states, the District of Columbia, Alaska, and Hawaii had submitted plans for maternal and child health services for approval by the Children's Bureau and had qualified for grants. The total grants to states for maternal and child health services increased from almost $3,000,000 in 1937 to $5,820,000 in 1941, the latter being the entire amount appropriated by Congress. The control that the Children's Bureau has over the programs is vested primarily in its power to withhold funds from the states if they do not submit plans for programs which meet the requirements established by the Bureau in accordance with the conditions of the Social Security Act, or if a state does not maintain the program satisfactorily once it is established.

During 1942 when the problem of the care of the wives and infants of servicemen first arose, more than 160,000 mothers received prenatal care under the maternal and child health program. About 185,000 babies and some 300,000 young children were given health examinations at medical conferences; more than 1,600,000 school-age children were examined by physicians; over 2,000,000 children were vaccinated against smallpox, and more than 1,600,000 were immunized against diphtheria, and approximately 1,500,000 mothers and children were given care by public health nurses. The report for 1942 shows the progress that was being made with grants-in-aid administered by the Children's Bureau and matched in part by state funds.

When the problem of the maternity and infant care of the wives and infants of servicemen came before Congress in 1943 the Children's Bureau seemed the natural Federal agency to be entrusted with a program of this nature. In the Federal office it had a staff trained and experienced in the problems of maternal and infant health and crippled children's services; in each of the state departments of health the Bureau had worked through divisions of maternal and child health since 1936, which agencies were the only ones in the states with experience and training in this field; the Bureau could legally, as was proven later, expand the interpretation of Title V of the Social Security Act to include the program for wives and infants of servicemen; and the Bureau could finance the beginning of the program by resorting to Fund B which could be allocated to the states on the basis of financial need. After Fund B was exhausted, Congress had the power to authorize a deficiency appropriation even though the Social Security Act had established a statutory limit. Such action was subject to a point of order, but during the war period emergency appropriations were made without points of order being raised. This was an emergency, and actions to meet emergencies do not usually wait for legal niceties!

Thus, from 1912, when the Children's Bureau was established, to 1942 the groundwork was unwittingly laid for the administration of the Emergency Maternity and Infant Care program for the wives and infants of servicemen. The strengths and weaknesses of the administration of the maternal and child health and crippled children's program would very readily become apparent in the administration of the new program.

CHAPTER III

THE ESTABLISHMENT OF THE EMIC PROGRAM

The Problem Emerges, 1941-1942

In October, 1940 the first compulsory military training act in peacetime was passed by Congress. From that time until the Japanese attack on Pearl Harbor on December 7, 1941, the military forces of the country grew constantly. In the years following Pearl Harbor and the declaration of war on Japan and Germany, the number of men in the armed forces increased to approximately 12 million.

By the latter part of 1941 the number of wives who followed their husbands to many parts of the country increased to a point where the areas around military camps and installations became badly congested, taxing the service facilities of the camps and the surrounding communities beyond their capacity. To many of these women children were born under sub-standard conditions because of inadequate funds to procure the services of the medical personnel and facilities that existed. In a very short time the acute nature of the problem became obvious.

The needs were easily definable, the people requiring assistance were easily identified, and the particular geographical areas where the greatest needs existed could be delineated. The needs were for financial assistance and the provision of services for obstetrical, hospital and pediatric care. The persons involved were the wives and infants of servicemen, and the areas in which their needs attracted attention were around military training camps and installations. It was this attention, first concentrated about the military areas, that led to action involving the wives and dependents of servicemen throughout the nation.

The first direct appeal for help came from Ft. Lewis, Washington in August, 1941, after the medical staff in the camp hospitals found itself overwhelmed with the problem of providing maternity services for the wives of servicemen stationed at the camp. The military authorities turned to the Washington State Department of Health for assistance. The division of maternal and child health in the department had approximately $14,000 of unexpended funds from the B Fund which, as previously described, was an outright

Federal grant to the state on the basis of need. The division asked the Children's Bureau for permission to use this fund for the purpose of providing obstetrical and hospital services for the wives of servicemen, and approval was granted. From August, 1941 until July, 1942, 677 women in the area were registered for care.[1]

As early as March 27, 1942 the Committee on Maternal and Child-Health of the Association of State and Territorial Health Officers in consideration of the above experience recommended "that state health agencies develop plans to finance from MCH (maternal and child health) funds the medical and hospital care needed by wives and children of men in military service unable to purchase such care, and to make more readily available medical and nursing services for mothers and children in critical areas."[2]

In the light of this early experience and action it is discomfortingly significant that in seven of the eight states in which the study of EMIC was made, it was reported that there were no direct appeals for assistance to the state health departments from servicemen or their wives or from agencies which had occasion to handle hardship cases among them, such as Red Cross chapters and public welfare agencies. Yet, American Red Cross representatives at 240 Army posts reported that in the one month from July 15 to August 15, 1942, 3,262 servicemen requested help in securing maternity care for their wives; 39 percent of these were for assistance in obtaining care for wives living near the Army post, and 61 percent were requests for assistance in obtaining care for wives living in another state. Furthermore, the American Red Cross reported that it received 2,601 requests from wives of men in service for help in obtaining maternity care or care for their sick children during the month of August, 1942. This report was based on a study of a 10 percent cross-section of the chapters in 46 states.[3] Investigations were also made by the Children's Bureau in the defense areas and great need for assistance was found.

Not until the EMIC program was launched officially in March, 1943, and publicity concerning it reached the newspapers, did an avalanche of demand descend upon the state departments of health. This effect is too often ascribed to an artificially stimulated demand for a program of this nature by the Children's Bureau rather than

[1] U. S. Congress. House. Committee on Appropriations. Hearings before the Subcommittee on the First Deficiency Appropriation Bill for 1943. 78th Congress 1st session. February 11, 1943. p. 326.

[2] U. S. Children's Bureau. Recommendations of the Committee on Maternal and Child Health of the State and Territorial Health Officers, March 27, 1942. 2p. (mimeographed).

[3] Hearings. February 11, 1943. op. cit., p. 325.

to a real demand based upon a real need. Though the appeal for assistance from Ft. Lewis, Washington, was direct and insistent, and similar assistance was necessary around other military training camps and installations, it is frequently contended that the acute conditions in these areas could have been alleviated without eventually involving every health department in the United States and the majority of physicians and hospitals. Neither argument carries weight in the face of the Red Cross reports and the later support of the American Legion, based upon the experience during and following World War I when its members struggled with problems of paying for obstetrical care. The accelerating demand for obstetrical and pediatric care after the EMIC program was launched should indicate beyond a reasonable doubt that real need existed.

Rarely do unorganized potential beneficiaries of any social program make their desires and needs known to government agencies directly. Usually needs are recognized by individuals, groups, and agencies which are in a position to identify them and marshall the community resources. The fact that state health departments were not approached by servicemen and their wives indicates only one thing with certainty—the lack of an association in the public mind between the need for maternal and child care and the functions of a division of maternal and child health. After the EMIC program was launched the departments of health became much more real to servicemen and their wives since they then had a government agency to which they could make their needs known and from which they could expect help.

Such, in brief, is the story of the beginning and the recognition of a social problem which aroused the interest of the general public, government agencies, and Congress. Once the problem was recognized the next steps were concerned with its solution.

Appeals to Congress, 1943-1946

By July, 1942 the program in the state of Washington had attracted the attention of divisions of maternal and child health in other state health departments. When the Federal allocations for the fiscal year beginning July 1, 1942 were made, 27 states had received approval to use B Funds to provide maternity, obstetrical, hospital, and pediatric care for the wives and infants of servicemen. Of the total Fund B, amounting to $1,980,000, the Children's Bureau allocated $198,000 for this program. Actually, however, the Bureau had received requests totalling $544,000 from 38 state health departments.

Later, the Children's Bureau dug deeper into Fund B during the six months period of July to December, 1942, and allotted

$319,295. In addition eight state health departments were able to use unexpended balances in the amount of $70,882.[4] Thus, a total of $390,177 was made available. The Children's Bureau felt that this was the maximum amount possible without seriously interrupting existing state and local maternal and child health services. Since the B Fund would be exhausted long before the end of the fiscal year ending in June, 1943, the Children's Bureau believed that $1,817,200 would be necessary as a supplementary appropriation until June 30, 1943.

On February 1, 1943 Congress received a recommendation from the President for $1,200,000 instead of the $1,817,200 desired by the Children's Bureau.* The request was referred to the Committee on Appropriations of the House of Representatives two days later and it became part of the First Deficiency Appropriation Bill of 1943, H.R. 1975.* The Subcommittee of the Committee on Appropriations held hearings on the bill dealing with the request for funds by the Children's Bureau on February 11, 1943. Miss Katharine F. Lenroot, Chief of the Children's Bureau, and Dr. Martha M. Eliot, Associate Chief, were present to justify the request for additional funds.

The budget requests, the hearings, and Congressional actions are presented in some detail. In the Federal Government the usual procedure for requesting funds is as follows: The government agency submits an estimate of need to the Bureau of the Budget; the Bureau approves, rejects, or modifies the amount requested; the amount thus recommended is transmitted to the President for his consideration and he, in turn, submits the budget request to Congress. Thus are seen examples of the legislative process, examples that are healthy antidotes to the dangerously prevalent concept of the government agencies and Congress as centers of political chess where few moves are made on a basis of merit. They serve, too, as examples of the manner in which public servants are required to fulfill their responsibilities and justify their actions.

Miss Lenroot stated at the hearing that up to February 9, 1943 requests and estimates from state health departments for the period January to June, 1943, totalled $2,291,492. Concerning the need Miss Lenroot testified as follows:

"Experience during the past 5 months shows that the demand for this service is very great, the sums available have not been suffi-

*See appendix for chronological table of appropriations for EMIC.

**It should be noted that all bills dealing with appropriations must originate in the House.

4Ibid., p. 318.

cient to enable some States to accept all of the cases for which application has been made. Exact data on waiting lists are not available from all States, but it is known that one State had in December 1942, a waiting list of 300, another of 400. Still another is receiving applications at the rate of 12 a day and estimates an increase to 20 a day shortly. In this State funds are exhausted. Another State is receiving applications at the rate of 25 a week but reports that funds are exhausted. Many State health agencies are not accepting all requests for care since they know they cannot care for them with existing funds."[5]

The members of the Subcommittee apparently did not question the need for additional funds since the discussion turned quickly to the details of administration and finance. Miss Lenroot explained that the states would not be expected to provide funds; their contribution would be the existing administrative machinery in the divisions of maternal and child health in the states.[6] The chairman of the Subcommittee expressed some concern as to whether or not the program was a continuation of an already established one: "This then is not initiating a new program or starting a new project. It is going on at the present time. The proposition before us is not to provide a new activity but to continue your present activity." Dr. Eliot answered: "Yes."[7]

The chairman wished to know the requirements specified by the Children's Bureau of a state department of health before a program is approved. The requirements were expressed in the following testimony:

"Acceptance of cases regardless of legal residence, the establishment of methods of authorization for medical or hospital care, methods of referral of cases to public health nursing and social services as needed, the establishment of fixed rates of reimbursement for services rendered under the plan, safeguards of the quality of medical and hospital care.

"Grants-in-aid will be made quarterly to the States on the basis of (1) current experience in each State with respect to the number of birth certificates issued showing the father to be in military service, (2) the cost of the service per case within limits based on average cost of care for the area, and (3) the number of authorizations per month."[8]

[5]Ibid., p. 319.
[6]Ibid., p. 321.
[7]Ibid., p. 323.
[8]Ibid., p. 324.

With the information as given to this point, representative Wigglesworth, Massachusetts, inquired:[9]

Mr. Wigglesworth: What persons in a given State were eligible to similar medical care or help through your funds before you started this new project?

Miss Lenroot: There were in certain counties in certain States demonstration projects.

Mr. Wigglesworth: Haven't you had a maternity and child health program?

Miss Lenroot: Our maternal and child health program in the main was not used for hospital costs and medical care at the time of confinement. It is used for the cost of prenatal care and postnatal supervision and nursing care.

Mr. Wigglesworth: What were the conditions for prenatal and postnatal care?

Miss Lenroot: Prenatal and postnatal care were available as part of the general public health program without qualifications as to indigency.

Mr. Wigglesworth: Wouldn't a girl whether she was a soldier's wife or not be eligible to either program?

Miss Lenroot: She would be eligible to prenatal and postnatal care.

Mr. Wigglesworth: Why do you want this new program?

Dr. Eliot: Because the funds that have been available so far to the States, and the State and local funds were not adequate for the States to set up programs of obstetric care, paying the doctor and the hospital for care. In order to do that more funds are needed.

Mr. Wigglesworth: Haven't you had that all along? That is what my question is directed to.

Dr. Eliot: Not obstetric and hospital care at confinement; only prenatal care by doctors and nurses, which costs much less than delivery care.

Mr. Wigglesworth: And I thought postnatal care was included there also.

Dr. Eliot: Yes; postnatal care also.

Miss Lenroot: That would be patients' visits to a clinic 6 weeks after delivery.

Dr. Eliot: That is right.

Miss Lenroot: But the major cost, you see, is the care of the mother during the 10-day to 2-week period around the time of the birth of the baby either in the hospital or at home and funds have not been available for that except for a few demonstrations.

9Ibid., p. 327.

Dr. Eliot: Of course, there is a great need for a broad program.

Mr. Wigglesworth: This program is open to anybody regardless of financial position and is open to any State without a cent's contribution by any State?

Dr. Eliot: The basic program that the States are now providing is the foundation for this program. A considerable proportion of the cost of this is provided by the States and localities.

Despite the seemingly favorable response by the members of the Subcommittee in the hearing on the request for $1,200,000 submitted by the Children's Bureau, the Committee on Appropriations in House Report No. 170 on February 24, 1943 denied it. The need for the program was not questioned, but there were certain technicalities which the Committee members felt were serious enough to block even an emergency measure. They were:[10]

(1) Basic enabling legislation should be enacted for a program of this nature. The Committee felt that the proposal "needs more consideration than can be given it by merely dealing with a sum of money in an urgent appropriation bill." It was felt that some authority existed in the Social Security Act, "but the funds requested are not predicated upon any existing law but are left entirely to the discretion of the Secretary of Labor and the Chief of the Children's Bureau." (2) The other issue was the "lack of financial ability* as a prerequisite to the benefits."

When the Deficiency Appropriation Bill reached the floor of the House on February 26, Mr. Keefe, Wisconsin, attempted to put the $1,200,000 back in the bill rejected by the Committee on Appropriations.[11] Mr. Starnes, Alabama, opposed the amendment on a point of order since he thought that the Committee was neither a legislative nor policy-making Committee. He saw no legislative authority for the appropriation, but he offered to help draft the necessary enabling legislation.[12] Mr. Keefe introduced an enabling law, H.R. 2041, but it died in Committee.

In any case the First Deficiency Appropriation Bill for 1943, H.R. 1975, passed the House and was referred to the Senate Committee on Appropriations minus the request of the Children's Bureau. On March 2, 1943 the Subcommittee held a hearing on the section dealing with the Children's Bureau request. Miss Lenroot and Dr. Eliot appeared again to justify their request and attempt

*Ability to pay, as determined by a means test.

10H.R. Report 170 p. 6.

11*Congressional Record,* 89:1405 February 26, 1943.

12Ibid., p. 1408.

to have it put back in the bill. Secretary of Labor Perkins also attended the hearing to lend her support.

The members of the Senate Subcommittee were concerned with the same issues as the Subcommittee of the House, namely, whether or not it was a new program, that it was entirely a Federally financed program, and that it provided no means test. Miss Lenroot and Dr. Eliot repeated the assertions they had made at the hearing before the Subcommittee of the House as to the legality of the program. Senator McCarran, Nevada, stated: "This item itself, however, as it comes before this Committee and as it came before the House Committee, is a new activity." Miss Lenroot answered: "No, Senator, it is not a new activity; but it is an item that was felt by the House Committee not to be covered by basic legislation. Although the amount of money to be appropriated was in excess of that authorized in Title V, Pt. I, of the Social Security Act, the activity is covered by the legislative authority under Title V, part I."[13] Miss Lenroot testified further that after the exhaustion of the $1,200,000 requested in the present deficiency appropriations bill the Bureau would need an estimated $6,000,000 to carry the program for a full year.

As of March, 1943 Miss Lenroot reported that 28 states* had approved plans under which they were providing this special service, one more since the hearing before the House committee in February. However, 10 of these states had exhausted their funds, and in a number of other states the funds would be exhausted very shortly. "So, if additional funds are not made available, the programs will have to be discontinued in the 28 states where they are now in operation, and no additional states will be able to set up their programs."[14] Dr. Eliot added that "The State health departments would organize the program if they had funds. They are not asking for any administrative funds in this picture at all; they are asking only for the hospitalization and medical care of the patient."[15]

Presented with such an accomplished fact the senators were placed under a weighty responsibility if they should insist on re-

*Alabama, Arizona, Arkansas, California, Connecticut, Hawaii, Idaho, Illinois, Indiana, Maine, Maryland, Minnesota, Missouri, Nebraska, New Hampshire, New Jersey, New Mexico, North Carolina, Oklahoma, Rhode Island, South Carolina, South Dakota, Texas, Utah, Vermont, Washington, Wisconsin, and Wyoming.

13U. S. Senate. Committee on Appropriations. Hearings before a Subcommittee on the First Deficiency Appropriation Bill for 1943, H.R. 1975. 78th Congress 1st Session. March 2, 1943. p. 128.

14Ibid., p. 129.

15Ibid., p. 136.

jecting the Children's Bureau request on a basis of technicality. In the discussion ensuing on the floor of the Senate on March 12 it was decided to amend the appropriations bill as submitted from the House and put back the $1,200,000 for the Children's Bureau.[16] In the Joint House and Senate Committee considering this bill on March 15 it was decided to permit the inclusion of the Children's Bureau request since, as reported by Representative Cannon, Missouri, there was no difference of opinion as to its merits.[17] On the same day the House passed the bill as amended. Thus, on March 18 the first Deficiency Appropriation Bill for 1943 became Public Law 11. The Emergency Maternity and Infant Care program which had begun as an expansion of Title V of the Social Security Act now had the official sanction of Congress.

In summary, the chief issues of concern to the members of the Subcommittee were: (1) whether this was a new program or a continuation of one already established, (2) no contribution was required from the states other than administrative machinery, and (3) no means test would be applied. These represent a search for precedents. Even if the members of the Subcommittee were satisfied that the program was the expansion of one already in existence, they still had to wrestle with issues (2) and (3). Outright grants to states without state matching was at variance with the usual grants-in-aid pattern established by the Social Security Act in 1935. The absence of a means test to determine eligibility before persons are given assistance from public funds to which they have not contributed directly, ran counter to long established public welfare traditions. The fact that these precedents were disregarded in the appropriation bill which became law indicated the emergency conditions under which Congress was working. Although these issues were ostensibly settled as far as Congress and the Children's Bureau were concerned they were not readily accepted by organized medicine in the application of the law. This will be noted when the responses of recipients of services, state health departments, physicians, and hospitals to the program are discussed.

On March 24, 1943 less than a week after EMIC became law the Children's Bureau expressed a need for $6,000,000 to cover the program for the next fiscal year, July, 1943 through June, 1944. By the time it reached the Committee on Appropriations of the House of Representatives on April 13 the amount had been reduced to $4,800,000. The House committee reduced this sum further to

[16] *Congressional Record,* 89:1988 March 12, 1943.

[17] *Congressional Record,* 89:2063 March 15, 1943.

$4,000,000 which was the amount included in the appropriations bill for 1944, H.R. 2935. The Subcommittee of the Committee on Appropriations held a hearing at the Children's Bureau request. Miss Lenroot and Dr. Eliot represented the Bureau.

Dr. Eliot stated that the original request of $6,000,000 was based on an estimate of at least 72,000 applications during the fiscal year at about $85 per case. It was presumed, however, that the total number of cases would be higher.

An issue from the previous hearing, the desirability of a means test, was raised again by the chairman of the Subcommittee, Representative Hare of South Carolina. He was still concerned about its omission in the original act, but he seemed to resolve the problem to his own satisfaction, saying: "I have the strong conviction that the regulations should limit these expenditures to those who are actually in need of this assistance, or put a definite limitation on, as to the amount for each one, unless you are going to say this is a contribution to the family as an expression of gratitude to those in the armed forces who are actually offering their lives in the service. If you put it on that basis, it is an entirely different proposition."[18] Miss Lenroot answered: "I think we have to assume that that was the basis Congress put it on, because of the language of the act."[19] This seemed to settle the issue of the means test as far as Congress was concerned, because the subject was not discussed by the members of that body again.

The exclusion of the means test was a logical development stemming from the philosophy and the activity of the Children's Bureau since its inception in 1912. This was perhaps particularly true when the Bureau entering the health administration field in 1922, stressed the public health philosophy of service to the entire community for the benefit of the entire community regardless of income. The inclusion of a means test in the EMIC program would have meant a reversal of a fundamental Bureau policy. Furthermore, state health departments would have had to create new administrative machinery to apply the means test or would have had to work in cooperation with state welfare agencies.

On June 14, 1943 the Committee on Appropriations of the House of Representatives recommended the sum of $4,000,000 to

[18] U. S. Congress. House. Committee on Appropriations. Hearings before the Subcommittee on the Department of Labor. Federal Security Agency Appropriations Bill for 1944, H.R. 2935, Part I. 78th Congress 1st Session. April 17, 1943. p. 250.

[19] Ibid.

cover the 4th, 5th, 6th, and 7th pay grades.* However, it was recommended that the Children's Bureau should render assistance where circumstances required to wives of men in the first three pay grades.[20]

The Committee also recommended a reduction of $28,000 of the $350,000 requested annually by the Children's Bureau for salaries and expenses in administering the maternal and child health, crippled children, and child welfare programs. The Committee was of the opinion that these appropriations for the three programs "are in the same amounts as have been appropriated for the past four years. As the program progresses, it should be possible to reduce the amount necessary for administrative expenses."[21] This naturally was of great concern to the Children's Bureau because it had undertaken the EMIC program without an increase in the general budget for administration. In the states the Bureau had hoped that the state health departments would augment their budgets for administration from their own funds. It appears that the Committee on Appropriations had taken seriously the testimony of the Children's Bureau when Miss Lenroot and Dr. Eliot stated in the hearings on the initial request for appropriations in March that funds for administration were not needed, at least not at that time.

On June 19, 1943 Miss Lenroot and Dr. Eliot appeared before the Subcommittee on Appropriations of the Senate asking for the $28,000 refused by the House Committee and also for the $800,000 deducted from the request of $4,800,000 for the EMIC program. The Senate Committee was receptive to the Bureau's request and recommended the restitution of both items in its report to the Senate on June 24, 1943.

The Senate Committee recommended further that the following proviso be stricken from the bill: "Provided, that no part of any appropriation contained in this title shall be used to promulgate or carry out any instruction, order, or regulation relating to care of obstetrical cases which discriminate between persons licensed under state law to practice obstetrics."[22] Dr. Eliot had opposed this

*Army: Private; Private, 1c; Corporal; Technician, 5th grade; Technician, 4th grade; Sergeant, 4th grade. Marine Corps: Private; Private, 1c; Corporal; Sergeant, 4th grade; Assistant cook; Cook, 3c; Field cook; Field music; Field music, 1c; Field music corporal; Field music sergeant; Steward's assistant, 3c, 2c, 1c; Steward, 3c. Navy and Coast Guard: Apprentice seaman; Bugler, 2c, 1c; Coxswain; Fireman, 2c, 1c; Hospital apprentice, 2c, 1c; Seaman, 2c, 1c; Steward's mate, 2c, 1c.

20U. S. Congress. House. Committee on Appropriations. Report No. 540, June 14, 1943, p. 6.

21Ibid.

22U. S. Congress. Senate. Committee on Appropriations. Report 342. June 24, 1943. p. 2.

proviso as submitted by the House Committee because it would jeopardize the power of the Children's Bureau to establish and maintain standards for persons rendering obstetric care.[23] Apparently the Senate Committee agreed with her.

When the appropriations bill reached the House on July 1, 1943, the debate centered completely on whether or not the Children's Bureau might designate standards for practitioners participating in the EMIC program. The issue was Federal interference with state matters. Representative Keefe, Wisconsin, a strong supporter of EMIC, wished to leave the determination of standards to the states.[24] The bill passed the House with the amendment leaving the matter to the states.

The next day, July 2, when the appropriations bill was in the Senate, chief attention was paid to the issue of whether or not the Children's Bureau should have the power to determine standards of practitioners in the states.[25] Senator LaFollette, Wisconsin, was in favor of Federal determination of standards. He saw no issues involving Federal-state rights.

The final outcome was in favor of state determination of standards when the appropriation bill, H.R. 2935, became Public Law 135 on July 12, 1943. The appropriation for EMIC for the fiscal year 1944 was set at $4,400,000, $400,000 more than was originally recommended by the House Committee and $400,000 less than that recommended by the Senate Committee and the Bureau of the Budget, a perfect compromise. The Bureau had requestd $378,000 for the cost of administering its programs, including EMIC. The House Committee reduced this by $28,000, but in the final appropriations bill the House and Senate Committees had apparently compromised in a reduction of a little over $15,000. Thus, the Children's Bureau received no funds for the administration of EMIC.

The Children's Bureau had $4,400,000 for EMIC grants to the states for the fiscal year, July, 1943 through June, 1944. By the middle of August, 1943 the Bureau realized that it had greatly underestimated the demand for services and on August 25 reported the need for a supplement of $20,076,235, with $622,799 or about 3 percent to be allotted to states for the cost of administration. In his recommendation to the Committee on Appropriations of the House of Representatives on September 16, the President reduced

23U. S. Congress. Senate. Committee on Appropriations. Hearings before the Subcommittee on Labor-Federal Security Appropriations Bill for 1944, H.R. 2935. 78th Congress 1st Session. June 29, 1943. p. 12.

24*Congressional Record* 89:7014-21 July 1, 1943.

25Ibid., 89:7095-7103 July 2, 1943.

the original figure to $18,600,000 with nothing earmarked for state administration. Very quickly the House reported and passed a bill for the same amount on September 22, but the discussion in the hearings the previous day brought out some pertinent issues.

At the hearings held before the Subcommittee of the Committee on Appropriations of the House Miss Lenroot stated: "The Children's Bureau had greatly underestimated the number of cases which would require care under the program. It was thought that 25 percent of the total anticipated deliveries would apply for assistance. The actual experience of the first two months of the fiscal year indicates that about 50 percent of the eligible cases will apply for care."[26]

Miss Lenroot stated, further, that the request for $18,600,000 would provide for 9 1/3 months. She felt that she should have asked for $24,000,000 in June. In addition $33,000 was requested for the administrative expenses of the Children's Bureau to offset the reduction of $15,000 in the previous appropriation bill.

The EMIC program provided specified services to the wives and infants of servicemen rather than direct cash payments. The physicians and hospitals rendered the services at established rates paid by EMIC funds through state departments of health. This procedure was of great concern to some physicians who preferred that the patient receive a cash allotment and make her own arrangements for care, leaving the financial settlement to the physician and patient as was customary in private practice. In this way the physician would avoid dealing with a government agency.

The chairman of the subcommittee asked Miss Lenroot:

"Do you not think, Miss Lenroot, if it was understood that this was government assistance and was granted on a standardized plan, that a physician would bring upon himself considerable criticism if he attempted to charge more, to charge the wife of some soldier fighting for his country in a distant land more than the standard price? Do you not think from the very nature of the situation it would be self-policing?"

Miss Lenroot: "I do not think it would be completely self-policing. I think perhaps there would be a number of instances where there would be an attempt to make an additional charge. Already there is evidence that physicians wish to be allowed to

26U. S. Congress. Committee on Appropriations. Hearings before the Subcommittee on the First Supplemental National Defense Appropriations Bill for 1944, H. J. Resolution No. 159. 78th Congress 1st Session. September 21, 1943. p. 458.

charge an additional fee and to negotiate these fees directly with the serviceman's wife.

"Moreover, I want to point out, if this policy were adopted, practically every wife would apply for care under the program. My view is that the amount required would be increased perhaps 85 or 90 percent if it were in the form of a cash allowance."[27] The issue of cash allowance did not come up again during this hearing.

As the members of the Subcommittee went more deeply into discussion of administrative details such as fees, rules and regulations, and forms and records they appeared to want a standardized program throughout the country—this was especially true of fees to physicians. Representative Ludlow, Indiana, asked: "Now, everything connected with the Army and Navy is all tied in with the military effort and patriotic aspect, and everything connected with the Army and Navy, the soldiers, sailors, WACS and WAVES, is all standardized. What would be your thought, Miss Lenroot, about removing the variable factor from the allowances and, as Mr. Cannon (Missouri) I think, asked, make a standard allowance."[28]

Miss Lenroot: "We have canvassed that situation in the staff and I think the feeling in the staff is that it would greatly limit the program in some States; because there is a wide range of cost and it would probably be impossible to get enough doctors in some areas to cooperate in the program. We already have complaints; we have complaints from Members of Congress that the amount allowed for the doctor is so low that there are not enough doctors in the locality to serve the mothers."[29]

It was brought out that the variation in fees to physicians for complete maternity care ranged in the states from $35 to $50, the latter figure being the maximum permitted by the Children's Bureau. Representative Hare, South Carolina, revealed that two physicians in his district refused to cooperate not because of the fee, "but upon the universal, abnormal, and what they considered unjustified number of requests and blanks giving information that they had to furnish in connection with the work. In other words, they said that the administrative work required by the Bureau was much more than the professional work required; therefore, they did not care to be bothered with it at any price."[30]

27Ibid., p. 471.
28Ibid., p. 475.
29Ibid.
30Ibid.

At this point Dr. Eliot stated that while requirements regarding reports from physicians were matters for the state to decide the Children's Bureau needed reports as to the number of cases and the costs upon which to base its estimates and reports to Congress. The Bureau had prepared suggested application forms to be used by the prospective patient, but no specific form had been required for the physician to report the care given.

After a discussion of the details of administration the hearing ended with some comments regarding the future implications of the program. Representative Lambertson, Kansas, was in full sympathy with the program, and thought it was serving a very good purpose. At the same time he saw how it could be easily enlarged. He said: "The only thing I can see about it is that it is drifting to socialized medicine and in the direction of the Wagner-Murray bill." Miss Lenroot answered: "This is a war program, and consideration of what happens next will have to be something else."[31] Mr. Lambertson was not satisfied, however: "This is just an argument for the Wagner-Murray socialized medicine bill. It is just a leverage."

On September 22 the House passed the First Supplemental National Defense Appropriation Bill for 1944 with some change in the original law covering the EMIC program. Families of men in grades 1, 2, and 3 were not eligible under any circumstances; grades 4, 5, 6, and 7 were now the only pay grades eligible. The House passed a request for $18,600,000, plus $20,000 for Federal administration though the Bureau had originally asked for $33,000. The Committee reduced the amount by eliminating the proviso for two medical administrative consultants and assuming a somewhat shorter period of employment for auditors and clerks.

At the hearing before the Subcommittee of the Committee of Appropriations of the Senate on September 24, 1943 Miss Lenroot recommended that the Senate act on the basis of the appropriations made by the House. She was willing to accept the House provision of $20,000 for administration, stating that it would be very difficult to get along without it.[32]

As in the House Committee fear of "socialized medicine" was expressed by Senator Holman, Oregon: "At the outset let me say that I am opposed to socialized medicine, and I don't know from my

31Ibid., p. 495.

32U. S. Congress. Senate. Committe on Appropriations. Hearings before the Subcommittee on H. J. Resolution 159, a Joint Resolution Making Additional Appropriations for the Fiscal Year 1944 for Emergency Maternal and Infant Care for Wives of Enlisted Men in the Armed Forces. 78th Congress 1st Session. September 24, 1943. p. 10.

immediate knowledge whether that subject is involved in the present joint resolution or not. But when Congress, as it presumably will, makes this appropriation, are there restrictions on the use of the appropriation within the States which tend to Federal control of State practice?"

Miss Lenroot: "The plan is a state plan, and the state health agencies are responsible for developing the procedures under the plan. We have required certain conditions before we would approve a plan, inasmuch as the program is related to Title V, part 1, of the Social Security Act, and the appropriation itself required that the Chief of the Children's Bureau should approve plans."[33] On October 1, 1943 H. J. Resolution 159 became Public Law 156, and the Children's Bureau received an increased appropriation of $18,620,000.

The fear of socialized medicine and the influence of the Wagner-Murray Bill was the context in which the EMIC program emerged, but in spite of the fears expressed regarding its implications the program had the support of Congress and, as is seen, appropriations were made unstintingly. The emergency of war stimulated action regardless of future implications. The program also had public support, some evidence of which was presented by Representative Bradley, Pennsylvania, who stated, when the appropriation for EMIC was discussed on the floor of the House: "I would like to make the observation that . . . it took the power of the public press, the American Legion, and the Veterans of Foreign Wars to compel the Republican Governor of Pennsylvania to make these benefits eligible to the servicemen of our state."[34] Apparently the Governor had at first refused to let the state health department accept grants-in-aid from the Federal Government for this purpose.

Not until the spring of 1944 was EMIC given consideration again by Congress. In the meantime the Children's Bureau, the state health departments, the physicians, the hospitals, and the wives and infants of servicemen were experiencing the full effects of the program. In the six months that had elapsed since the last appropriation the administrators, those who provided services, and the recipients of services had time to express their satisfaction or dissatisfaction. The succeeding Congressional hearings reflected the heightened feeling regarding the program.

The last appropriation bill for the EMIC program had been passed on October 1, 1943. In order to prepare for the fiscal year

[33]Ibid., p. 12.

[34]*Congressional Record* 89:7843. September 22, 1943.

beginning July 1, 1944, the Children's Bureau indicated need for $24,100,000 plus $104,200 for Federal administration. Congress received a Presidential recommendation for $20,000,000 and $43,000 on January 10, 1944. On March 31 the President sent to Congress amendments to the proposed appropriation to include Army aviation cadets, who had formerly been excluded, and a recommendation that not more than 4 percent of the appropriation be allotted for state administration, and that the whole appropriation be made available immediately. The states were appealing for assistance to meet the costs of administration and the case load was mounting so rapidly as to exhaust even the supplemental funds of $18,600,000 for the current fiscal year.

Instead of the proposal that the $20,000,000 be made available immediately it was decided to present a separate request for another supplement of $6,763,600 to carry through until July 1, 1944. The supplemental budget was reduced to $6,700,000 and submitted to Congress on April 29. In two weeks this amount was approved by both the House and the Senate without debate and became Public Law 303 on May 12, 1944. The House Committee held a hearing but the Senate Committee did not.

In the meantime the request for $20,000,000 for the next fiscal year was still under consideration and on April 20, 1944 the Children's Bureau expressed a desire for another supplement of that sum amounting to $22,810,400. Four percent of the total was for state administration. On April 29 Congress received a recommendation from the President for the round figure of $22,800,000.

On May 27, 1944, when House Bill No. 4899 was reported, the House Committee had considered the two requests and the total sum acted upon was $42,800,000. Two percent was to be set aside for state administration and Army aviation cadets were excluded from EMIC benefits. On June 1, 1944 the House passed the bill in this form. On June 13 the Senate Committee reported the same amount but had stipulated 3 percent for administration and the inclusion of Army aviation cadets. The bill was passed by the Senate in this form on June 15. Since the House and the Senate disagreed, committees of both houses met and worked out a compromise of 2½ percent for state administration and the inclusion of Army aviation cadets. On June 28 the bill became Public Law 373. Congress also appropriated $43,000 to the Children's Bureau for Federal administration. Within 15 months, from March 18, 1943 to the above date, Congress had appropriated a total of $72,693,000 for the costs of maternal and pediatric care, $1,070,000 for state administration, and $63,000 for Federal administration.

The hearings conducted during the spring of 1944 represent the high point of discussion and debate in the Congressional appropriation committees. As will be seen the later hearings conducted on appropriation bills in 1945 and 1946 were quite routine and perfunctory. But in 1944 there was much discussion; some issues were resolved and others were brushed aside.

Although the issue of cash or service benefits had been settled by Congress it remained a source of controversy within the medical profession. Representative Hare, South Carolina, Chairman of the Subcommittee on Appropriations said: "I have been bombarded recently by communications from medical associations, here, there, and elsewhere, insisting that the next appropriation carry a provision to the effect that the allotment should be made directly to the beneficiary; that is, to the mother of the child, in order that she might use the funds as she may see fit."[35]

Dr. Eliot again presented arguments against any provision for cash benefit adding as follows, to her statement made during the previous hearing in September, 1943:

"Furthermore, under a plan based on cash allowances there would be no way to assure the enlisted man that care, and the kind and amount of care needed, will be available for either his wife or his infant. In many cases a wife might not know what the community resources are and there would be no State or local public agency to which she could go to ask how to work out a plan for her own care or care of her baby.

"A plan for cash allotment to cover the costs of sickness in the case of the baby would be more unsatisfactory than in the case of maternity care for the wife of an enlisted man. The costs of care of individual sick infants would vary even more than the costs of maternity care and there would be no way to determine in advance the amount of a cash allotment necessary to meet these needs.

"The wife could have no assurance in advance that a cash allotment would meet the hospital and physician's bills that it may be necessary for her to incur. Nor could the hospital or doctor be sure that bills would be paid since they would not receive payment directly from an agency of government. The wife who is pressed for cash to meet living expenses might not be able to save the cash given her until the time comes to pay her doctor and hospital bills. Hospi-

[35]U. S. Congress. House. Committee on Appropriations. Hearings before the Subcommittee on Appropriations on the Department of Labor-Federal Security Agency Appropriation Bill for 1945, Part I. 78th Congress 2nd Session. March 25, 1944, p. 312.

talization for these wives would not be assured to the extent it is under the present program that guarantees hospital payment.

"The board of trustees of the American Hospital Association on March 17, 1944, passed the following resolution: '*Resolved*, That the American Hospital Association approve the system adopted by the Children's Bureau of the United States Department of Labor which provides for the purchase of hospital care by direct payment to hospitals on a cost basis. The American Hospital Association further recommends that the Children's Bureau continue this policy in future purchases of hospital care. . . .' "[36]

Apparently the Subcommittee was satisfied with the existing system of service benefits since the discussion turned to a maternity case in Georgia described by Representative Tarver from the same state. According to the Congressman the expectant mother, a wife of a serviceman, had delivered her child prematurely and therefore had not had an opportunity to apply for care under the EMIC program. She had fully intended to do so. Consequently her application was denied by the Georgia State Health Department because of a regulation that the prospective beneficiary must apply for care prior to the time care is to be given.

Representative Tarver was quite disturbed over this case; he felt the regulation was unjust since this mother could not give the notice because she had no reason to believe that she was going to be confined prematurely. As far as he knew there was no provision in the law passed by Congress requiring such a regulation. Therefore, as he stated it: "I do not know of any reason why your Bureau (speaking to Miss Lenroot and Dr. Eliot) should permit any state organization to set up any such requirement which would prevent according consideration in such a case, and the payment of the expenses of the mother that is prematurely confined. If there is anything that you or Miss Lenroot would care to say in exculpation of the procedure followed in that case, I would be glad to hear you."[37]

Dr Eliot replied that the Children's Bureau had corresponded with the state health department regarding this particular case suggesting that an exception might be made to the rule that was set up in the state plan.

Mr. Tarver: "And the State health department refused to do that?"

Dr. Eliot: "The State health department replied to us that they were unable to find circumstances that would warrant approval of

36Ibid., p. 313.

37Ibid., p. 314.

maternity care in this case. We believe, however, that the State health departments must, under the conditions of this program, take the responsibility for allowing a certain flexibility within the rules, and make exceptions where exceptions are desirable."

Mr. Tarver: "It ought not to be necessary to make any exceptions in that sort of case. You are spending Federal money. You are not spending State money. And when you permit a State health department to deny relief under the circumstances of a case such as I have detailed, you are certainly not acting according to the wishes of Congress in the appropriation of these funds.

"I do not understand how you can undertake to justify it at all; or why you try to put the responsibility on the State health department. It is an outrageous thing. I expect to discuss it on the floor, and I suggest, if you have anything further you want to say in excuse of this very flagrant misinterpretation of the law and the purposes of the law, I should be glad to have you say it for the record."[38]

Other members of the Subcommittee took up the discussion regarding Federal-state relationships. Representatives Keefe and Hare disagreed with Tarver as to the extent of control the Children's Bureau should have over the state departments of health. Representative Tarver, however, was so perturbed over the case he knew about in Georgia that he thought the rules and regulations should be changed so that notice would not be required of the mother prior to the delivery of the child. Furthermore, he suggested: "I say that before you approve these regulations—and it is your responsibility to approve the regulations—you ought to require a provision not that it might be done, but that it shall be done."[39] Miss Lenrott replied to the Subcommittee: "Mr. Chairman, I think we would be glad to be more strict in our requirements as to this point of discretion. I think all the plans permit the discretion. We have felt that it was a State-administered program and that, after the money was paid to the State, we had to leave to the State the responsibility as to individual cases, with such direction as we could give. However, we will be glad to make more stringent our requirements with reference to exceptional cases."[40] Also during the discussion Miss Lenroot stated: "Mr. Chairman, may I say that if it is the desire of the Committee and the Congress that we administer this as a Federal program, we are perfectly willing to do so."[41] Mr. Tar-

38Ibid.
39Ibid., p. 320.
40Ibid., p. 321.
41Ibid., p. 315.

ver did not see the problem as one of Federal or state administration, but as he expressed it: "The trouble comes not with granting to the States authority to administer the program under your supervision, but of the failure on your part, as I see it, to exercise proper discretion in the approval of State plans. Wherever you approve a State plan which does not adequately care for situations . . . I have described, I think you are not exercising the proper supervisory discretion."[42] Later the rules and regulations were changed requiring state health departments to provide benefits to wives who failed to apply in time, if good reason is given.

During the same hearing the results of the proviso in the earlier EMIC appropriation law forbidding the Children's Bureau to determine standards for practitioners in obstetrics participating in the EMIC program in the state was discussed.[43] The apparent reason for the proviso, as interpreted by the Attorney General of the United States and the Solicitor of the Department of Labor, was to limit the power of the Children's Bureau over the states. The states were to follow their own laws, many of them permitting practitioners other than Doctors of Medicine to practice obstetrics. It was found that some state health departments, acting under state laws giving such authority to the department, established their own standards excluding practitioners without a degree of Doctor of Medicine apparently in violation of the state licensing laws. The Children's Bureau was, of course, in no position to force the state health departments to comply with their state licensing laws when other state laws permitted the departments of health to establish their own standards. Representative Keefe, Wisconsin, stated that this completely nullified the intention of Congress which in his mind was to give all pregnant wives of servicemen access to any practitioner they desired, but he thought the Children's Bureau had acted correctly and in good faith. Since he had brought up the issue of States' rights in September as a reason for preventing the Children's Bureau from establishing standards in the states contrary to the state licensing laws he did not suggest that the law be changed so that state health departments would be forced by the Children's Bureau to comply with the laws of the state. He saw it as an example of the complexity of drafting laws so that they could be applied in the manner intended by the legislative body. The comments of Representatives Keefe and Tarver, both strong supporters of the EMIC program and of States' rights, indicate the difficulties that arise when

[42]Ibid.

[43]Ibid., p. 343–350.

philosophies must be transformed into the day-to-day realities of administration.

When hearings were held on the appropriation bill, H. R. 4899, for the fiscal year 1945 on April 27 and May 3 the members of the Subcommittee brought up three problems with Miss Lenroot and Dr. Eliot: payments to physicians, payments to hospitals, and the extent of state control over the EMIC program. Representative Andersen, Minnesota, asked Miss Lenroot: "Do you feel the government is liberal or otherwise in its payments to hospitals and doctors that take care of a serviceman's wife and child?"[44] Miss Lenroot thought that the hospital rate was entirely fair. As for physicians, "Our advisory committee, in the beginning, felt that for this program of service to men in the armed services and their families, it was fair to take a reasonable rate for the general practitioner, since the greatest percentage of the cases are handled by general practitioners; and that there would be difficulties in setting up a differential for specialists."[45]

Representative Hare, chairman, had received the complaint that it was unfair to hospitals to receive only the average per diem cost of ward care for EMIC patients because these patients are almost all maternity patients. It was stated that the actual cost per day for maternity cases is higher than for other cases. Miss Lenroot answered that she would be glad to consider per diem costs for maternity patients only if hospitals could give data and isolate the costs of maternity patients and general patients.[46] Representative Hare continued: "If you are going to arrive at your hospital cost on the basis of the average cost per person to the hospital, why would it not be fair, then, to arrive at the medical fee, the physician's fee, on the basis of the average charge in that vicinity or in that community or in that hospital for births?"[47] Dr. Eliot replied: "We recognize the fact that the charges made, the average charges made by general practitioners in different parts of the country, vary to some extent. In an original recommendation to the state agencies we said that it was their responsibility to set the medical fee, provided it did not exceed a certain maximum which we felt must be established as a

[44]U. S. Congress. House Committee on Appropriations. Hearings before the Subcommittee on H. J. Resolution 271, a Joint Resolution Making an Additional Appropriation for the Fiscal Year 1944 for Emergency Maternity and Infant Care for Wives of Enlisted Men in the Armed Forces. 78th Congress 2d Session. May 3, 1944. p. 17.

[45]Ibid., p. 18.

[46]Ibid., p. 20.

[47]Ibid.

ceiling; we thought we were recognizing that very differential in different parts of the country.

"I think you may be interested to know, in a recent conference with the Children's Bureau, that the Association of State Health Officers made a recommendation to the Bureau that the Bureau set a uniform fee for the country, and that a similar recommendation was made to us last September by the same body of State health officers."[48]

Representative Tarver of Georgia who previously had brought up the case of the woman in Georgia who was denied services under EMIC because of failure to apply for care in time, took the Children's Bureau to task for not allowing the states any discretion in setting up their plans. He maintained: "So that instead of the states developing these plans, you develop the plans for the states and simply send them out instructions as to the type of plans which they must develop in order to receive approval of the Children's Bureau."[49] Dr. Eliot answered that the Bureau outlines the administrative policy, but not the details of administration. Mr. Tarver apparently did not see the contradiction in his current position and the one he took on March 25, six weeks previously, when he thought that the Bureau should have made the state health department of Georgia take care of an exceptional case. At that time he urged the Bureau to prepare rules and regulations for every contingency which might arise in the states. Now he said: "And the idea that you have state-administered plans and state discretion is fallacious; because, while that is nominally true and the language of the appropriations act would seem to so contemplate, as a matter of actuality you have instructed them in regard to the minutest detail of their program."[50] Because of this he believed that the Children's Bureau and not the Georgia State Health Department was responsible for the manner in which the maternity care in his state was handled.

During the hearings on April 27 and May 3 testimony on the program was heard from the American Medical Association, a few state medical associations, the American Legion, women's organizations, and citizens' groups. The chief issues brought forward were direct cash allotment, low fees to physicians, "socialized medicine," and Federal encroachment on the states.

The organized medical profession was represented by the Amer-

48Ibid.

49U. S. Congress. House. Hearings before the Subcommittee on the Department of Labor-Federal Security Agency Appropriation Bill for 1945. Part I. 78th Congress 2d Session. May 3, 1944, p. 454.

50Ibid., p. 455.

ican Medical Association, the state medical associations of Minnesota, New York, New Jersey, Iowa, Louisiana, and California, and the Committee of Physicians for the Improvement of Medical Care. One physician represented himself. Other organizations represented were: State and Territorial Health Officers' Association, the National Child Welfare Division of the American Legion, the National Women's Christian Temperance Union, Congress of Women's Auxiliaries of the C.I.O., the National Women's Trade Union League of America, the National Board of the Young Women's Christian Association of America, and the National Congress of Parents and Teachers.

Dr. W. W. Bauer testified for the American Medical Association and presented the resolution of the House of Delegates of that organization recommending that cash allotments be made to the expectant mother to defray the hospital and medical expense of her illness.[51] He did not think the amount of the fees to the physicians was an issue; adding that $75 or $100 or any other sum in excess of that specified would not solve the problem. He continued: "The problem in the mind of the medical profession is the problem of Federal control and a feeling that there is not sufficient opportunity for the program to be controlled in the States which it serves and where the needs of the locality are best known."[52] If direct cash allotments were made to the wives of servicemen he did not believe physicians would charge any more for their services than the cash allotment given to the wives. His viewpoint, which was the viewpoint of the House of Delegates, was reiterated by representatives of the state societies.

Dr. William B. Thompson representing the California Medical Association voiced the general opinion of the organized profession but he also added his own personal opinion. Excerpts from his testimony follow:

"It distresses us practicing physicians, that we should be cleverly placed in the light of antagonism to a program beneficial to and needed by the wives and children of men fighting to preserve the free institutions of free America. We are not so opposed; it is the administration of the program that has aroused our ire."[53]

"The plan of the Bureau was presented at a meeting of its advisory committee, but the committee was enjoined against offering any advice. Next, the plan was sent out to State boards of health, presumably for criticism, but any suggested modifications were

51Ibid., p. 516.
52Ibid., p. 508.
53Ibid., p. 488.

ignored. It was then presented to Congress as a program worked out in cooperation with the medical profession. Not until the Bureau's press release flooded the country did the rank and file of medical men have any intimation of Federal participation in this service."[54]

"We resent that implication that we would not give these dependents every necessary care, unless bound by contract to render certain specified services."[55]

"I think that the medical association would be glad to work out a plan whereby those of us who are caring for these women would agree among ourselves to take care of the situation without signing a contract with a government hereon; that we could charge these women so much money, and that we would not exceed that amount."[56]

Dr. Thompson stated that the physicians were losing money on the program; upon being asked what would be a fair price he answered: "$100 for specialists in a large city, $75 in a small city, and $50 to $60 for general practitioners in small towns."[57]

After Dr. Thompson had spoken at length on the bad features of the rules and regulations, Representative Keefe, Wisconsin, asked him what he would like to have eliminated in these regulations. His reply was: "I would like to have the contract eliminated."[58] Then Representative Thomas, Texas, queried: "Would the profession like to see the subsidy part of the program withdrawn too?" Dr. Thompson: "I think we would be very happy not to have any provision made for payment, although we feel that the dependent's circumstances are such that she probably needs it. But as far as we are concerned, that would free us from the Children's Bureau supervision, and we then would be left with our own conscience to deal with these people."

Mr. Thomas: "It is your opinion, then, that the medical profession as a whole would like to see the payment end of the program, or the subsidy end of it withdrawn, too; do I understand you to say that?"

Dr. Thompson: "That is my personal feeling about it, that we would be very happy to forget the fact that certain payments would be made by the government."

[54]Ibid.
[55]Ibid., p. 489.
[56]Ibid., p. 494.
[57]Ibid., p. 499.
[58]Ibid., p. 503

Mr. Thomas: "And put it right back as a purely contractual basis between the patient and the doctor?"

Dr. Thompson: "Yes, sir."[59]

Dr. George C. Ruhland, Secretary of the State and Territorial Health Officers Association speaking for the state health officers complained of the lack of administrative funds. On behalf of the association he presented a resolution recommending that funds be provided each state and territorial department of health for administrative purposes, and also, that as far as possible a uniform fee for prenatal and obstetric service be established in all of the states and territories on a basis of $15 for prenatal and $35 for obstetric delivery services.[60]

The other organizations presented a solid front in support of the current program and in strong opposition to the direct cash allotment principle. Congress did not grant the request of organized medicine for the cash allotment and the appropriation bill for the EMIC program was passed leaving intact the principle of the service benefit. Thus ended the stormiest sessions through which the EMIC program passed either before this time or later.

On October 7, 1944 the Children's Bureau indicated it needed $44,189,500 for the fiscal year beginning on July 1, 1945. This amount was approved and sent to the Committee on Appropriations of the House of Representatives on January 9, 1945. Two and one-half percent or $1,104,700 was to be earmarked for the costs of state administration. The bill was approved by both houses and became law July 3, 1945 (Public Law No. 124, 1945).

Compared with previous hearings, those held before the Subcommittee on March 14, 1945 had reached a perfunctory stage. Broad philosophies and policies were no longer under discussion and only representatives of the Children's Bureau and members of the Subcommittee were present. Miss Lenroot and Dr. Eliot reviewed the program up to that time. In speaking of the general program of the Children's Bureau Miss Lenroot requested funds to increase the number of personnel in regional offices. It was the purpose of the Bureau to place more responsibility upon regional staffs and thereby make progress toward the decentralization of the administration.[61]

The administrative problems in the EMIC program which came

59Ibid., p. 507.

60Ibid., p. 486.

61U. S. Congress. House. Committee on Appropriations. Hearings before the Subcommittee on the Department of Labor-Federal Security Agency Appropriation Bill for 1946, Part I. 79th Congress 1st Session. March 14, 1945. p. 261.

up for discussion were the provision of care for wives and children of discharged veterans and the possibility of the application for maternity care automatically serving as an application for the care of the expected child. Under existing regulations two applications had to be made.

Regarding the care of wives and children of discharged veterans Miss Lenroot stated that the Children's Bureau recommended to the states that "if the application for care were made and accepted before the husband was discharged from the service, care could be continued through completion. But we have not felt under the language of the act we were in position to authorize care after the discharge of the husband from service."[62] This procedure was agreeable to the Subcommittee and Representative Keefe thought that the policy was important enough to publicize because of the increase in the discharge rate. He thought also, that it should be discussed on the floor of the House so that all members of Congress would be advised of it.

The other administrative problem was raised by Representative Keefe. He did not see the need for the mother applying for care twice, once for herself during pregnancy, and the second time for her child after it has been born. He stated: ". . . . it seems to me it is putting an unwarranted burden on the mother so that she has to go and fill out another application in case the baby is sick. Why isn't the original application sufficient to cover the care of the child for the year following delivery?"[63] Dr. Eliot agreed that the original application should be sufficient. She mentioned that the matter had already been taken up with the Solicitor's Office for drafting.

In May, 1945 Germany capitulated to the Allies and in August, 1945 the Japanese surrendered to the Americans in the Pacific. These events naturally affected the future of the EMIC program since it was established to meet a war emergency. Before the Japanese surrender the national budget for the prosecution of the war for the fiscal year 1946 had been approved by Congress. With the war's end the President requested a review of the entire budget for possible reductions. The Subcommittee on Deficincy Appropriations of the House held hearings and the EMIC program came up for review on October 2, 1945.

Dr. Eliot stated that on the basis of new estimates the budget for the EMIC program could be reduced by $8,000,000. Representative Johnson, Oklahoma, was astonished at a government

62Ibid., p. 265.
63Ibid., p. 291.

agency offering, on its own volition, to suggest that it's budget be reduced; "Mr. Chairman, do you mean to say that somebody has come up here voluntarily and said that their agency was a wartime agency and need not be continued in peacetime? It is most unusual for anyone to appear before this Committee and make such a statement.

"Do I understand from the witness that you have voluntarily returned money and ask that it not be continued for this service?"

Dr. Eliot: "In response to that question, I would like to say that the Children's Bureau has accepted the fact that this is a wartime service. We realize that it has been a very great service to the wives and infants of servicemen in this country. We also appreciate very fully that in peacetime as well as in wartime there are many mothers in this country and many children who are in need of the kind of service that has been provided in this program.

"I believe it is a question for the Congress to decide as to whether or not the Federal Government will in the future make it possible for the mothers and children of this country to have the kind of care that they should have during the maternity period and during the period of childhood when proper growth, development, and health means so much to the health of future citizens of this country."[64] Later she said: "Now, we have made mistakes in the past with respect to our estimates. Those mistakes were in the other direction. We estimated a figure that was far too low for the fiscal year 1944 and we had to come back to your Committee for deficiency appropriations. In 1945 we underestimated the requirement of the program by a small amount and we had to come back for a smaller deficiency appropriation. I would hope that the Committee, if it does decide to reduce the amount of the appropriation by $8,000,000, will make it possible for the Bureau to come back should it be shown as the year goes along that we have overestimated the reduction."

Representative Johnson: ". . . Mr. Chairman, may I add that most departments know their way back to this Committee."[65]

The Subcommittee on Deficiency Appropriations was in high spirits, as well it migh be, since the enormous government expenditures could now be reduced considerably. Representative Cannon, Missouri, Chairman, addressed Dr. Eliot: "I want to congratulate you on the splendid way in which you have administered this fund and the results you have secured. I do not think any money we have spent has been better invested than the money spent for this purpose."[66]

64Ibid.. p. 593.
65Ibid., p. 594.
66Ibid.

Mr. Ludlow, Indiana: "I want to express my unqualified admiration for the witness and the presentation she has made."

Mr. Johnson: "Mr. Chairman, I tried to express my unqualified approval of the program, in addition to my admiration for the witness and her statement.

"Let me say, seriously, that no witness has appeared before this Committee for a long time who has given us a more straightforward story or talked in a more intelligent manner about the program."[67]

On February 18, 1946 when the First Supplemental Surplus Rescission Bill for 1946 was passed (Public Law 301) the appropriation for the EMIC program was reduced by $8,113,600. However, the Children's Bureau overestimated the decreasing demand for services and on April 26, 1946 reported a need for $2,148,800 to supplement the appropriation for the fiscal year. This amount was approved, sent to Congress on May 3, and passed on June 12, 1945 (Public Law 83).

On October 8, 1945, to prepare for the fiscal year beginning in July, 1946, the Children's Bureau believed it needed $18,548,400. A month later on the basis of new data this was reduced to $17,-593,000. Congress received a recommendation for $17,593,000 of which $649,000 was to be expended for state administration. On July 26, 1946, Congress passed an appropriation bill of $16,664,000 of which $649,000 was to be allotted to the states for administrative expenses (Public Law 549, 1946).

While this appropriation was under discussion the Children's Bureau submitted a request for $929,000 on April 29, 1946 to study the experience under the EMIC program. This sum was to be taken from the $17,593,000 requested by the Children's Bureau at that time. The proposed study excited much discussion in the hearings held on May 20, 1946.

Representatives Hare and Keefe asked if the study was an entirely new activity. Miss Lenroot said it was. Mr. Keefe stated: ". . . I think it should be noted that there is no authorization at all for this appropriation. You concede that, do you not?"[68*]

Miss Lenroot answered: "Well, Mr. Chairman, as far as a study is concerned, I would think the act of 1912 would be sufficient authorizaiton, directing us to investigate and report on all matters

*It will be recalled that Mr. Keefe at the beginning of the EMIC program was concerned with proper authorization. He did not think that the Social Security Act Title V was sufficient although he supported the objectives of the program.

67Ibid., p. 595.

68U. S. Congress. House Committee on Appropriations. Hearings before the Subcommittee on the Department of Labor. Federal Security Agency Appropriation Bill for 1947, Part I. 79th Congress 2d Session. May 20, 1946. p. 291.

pertaining to children, child welfare and child life, and mentioning infant mortality specifically."[69] This justification seemed to satisfy the Subcommittee; the members then wished to hear about "the wisdom, possibility, and advisability" of the proposed study.

Miss Lenroot: "Mr. Chairman, the Emergency Maternity and Infant Care Program has now been in operation for 3 years. This, as you know, is a unique program. Under that program, about one out of every seven births has been provided with care and all necessary arrangements.

"The Children's Bureau, from its earliest days, has been interested in infant mortality, which was mentioned specifically in the act creating the Bureau, and maternity mortality, and has made very important studies of maternal and infant mortality which have been widely used as a basis not only for public effort, but also for private effort.

"Many people have expressed a desire to have a study made of the experience under the Emergency Maternity and Infant Care Program in order that we may know whether the mortality rates and the general results of care under that program compare favorably or unfavorably with the general experience in the total population. State health departments have wanted that information and have talked to us about their desire to know what their own experience showed. They have been unable to get conclusive information on the basis of State experience, because those mothers and babies move across State lines so much and you cannot decide what the infant mortality is, for example, for a series of births in the State of South Carolina . . . unless the Government follows those babies to wherever their mothers go and sees whether the baby lived or died."[70]

Representatives Hare and Keefe doubted that a valid statistical study could be made, going into the details of research procedure to prove their point. They discussed comparability of data in different areas, experimental control groups, and so on, displaying a general knowledge of statistical research techniques. They thought the same result could be obtained on a much smaller scale. It was agreed that the program had been of great benefit to the young women who had received care. That did not need proof. "On the other hand," said Dr. Eliot, "I believe it exceedingly important from many points of view, to have a careful review and a careful study of the effect of this program, and of a series of factors that are involved in this program in order that we may analyze it effectively

69Ibid.
70Ibid., p. 292.

and know whether such a program as this is the way in which the States should proceed themselves, in their localities and on a State-wide basis, for the future."[71]

Mr. Keefe: "That brings us right to the very nub of the situation—and I intended to go into that at some time. There are people in this country who have discussed this matter with me, who believe that this program should be adopted as a permanent program of government. And I want to ask the blunt, plain question, whether or not this so-called statistical information that you are seeking to get as a result of this appropriation does not find its genesis in the thought that you will be able to show an experience which will justify the adoption of a national policy in this field, to continue this program on a national basis.

"Let us be perfectly fair about it. If that is the situation; I think the Congress is entitled to know it, and I say that as one, as you know, of the original sponsors of this program and one who has defended it and believes in it and has fought for appropriations for it.

"There is not any use of having any window dressing for this. I have had these people come into my office and discuss this matter with me, and they have indicated that they desire to have this investigation made for one specific purpose that outdistances everything else; namely, that it can be used as the foundation and the groundwork of a national health program. And they speak with great assurance, that the results will demonstrate so conclusively that this had been such a success, that it should be continued and adopted on a nation-wide basis, as part of a national policy."[72]

Mr. Hare: "This is just what I am afraid of, that this is going to be a lever to make it a national program. If you were to put me in charge, or put anyone else who is familiar with statistical methods in charge of this program, we could prove conclusively what they want to be proved, by the figures. There would be no doubt about it. It would be so convincing that we could not be excused from taking any position but that it should become a national program. And I don't know whether it should or not."[73]

Mr. Keefe repeated his question as to the motives behind the proposed study. Miss Lenroot answered: "In the first place I think the Bureau has stated the fact that it can make studies and desires to know the facts, whatever those facts may be and for whatever purpose they may be used as argument for or against a certain pol-

[71]Ibid., p. 294.

[72]Ibid.

[73]Ibid.

icy. That is what our infant mortality studies through the years have been—an effort to obtain the facts through the best statistical procedures we could develop.

"When the Emergency Maternity and Infant Care Program was a new program, I recall a conference where we had representatives of certain organizations that were fearful of the possible extension on a permanent basis of a program of this kind, who raised the question as to what my attitude would be in the future. At that time I said that I thought this experience, which was a wartime program, should be evaluated; and the results might be used by those who were against extension, or they might be used by those who were for a permanent public program for maternity and infancy care; but in either case I thought the facts would be valuable in determining what should be done in the future. I do not know just what this will show. I have talked with some people who tell me that the conditions of babies in some of these cases are below the average of the general population, because the mothers are young and have moved around and have lived under poor conditions; sometimes have not had the right diet, and it may show in certain cases excessive mortality among certain groups. But it seems to me that just as we would not be afraid of having the facts show whatever they may show, so the opponents of any permanent policy for maternity and infant care also should not be afraid to have the facts made known.

"In fact, we have been asked sometimes why we did not make a study and have been asked whether we were afraid to have the facts known, as to what was happening."[74]

Mr. Keefe: "Do you advocate a national program at this time?"

Miss Lenroot: ". . . the Children's Bureau has been on record since 1917 as being in favor of a public program for the protection of maternity and infancy. That is what the Sheppard-Towner Act was in a small way. That is what Title V, part 1 of the Social Security Act is. We believe that those programs should be expanded as soon as possible, so that there would be everywhere available, in every State, a service for the protection of the health of mothers at the time of childbirth, and the health of the children.

"We do not think this maternity and infant care program, just as it is, should be the permanent program, because it had to be developed very hastily. The States need time to work out methods by which more adequate standards of care can be assured and by which all of the experience under this program and other programs can be assessed to determine the best way of organizing services. But

[74]Ibid., p. 295-6.

I can frankly say that the Children's Bureau believes and has always advocated the extension of public care for maternity and infancy and childhood."[75]

Mr. Keefe: "Along the same general lines as has been provided in this?"

Miss Lenroot: "No. There will be differences in the program and different methods of administration. Our administration of this program had to be very much more in the direction of Federal determination of procedures, because there was not time for the long, slow process of gradually developing with the States standards and policies. I would think of a longtime, continuing program, being much more flexible, with much greater variations within the States and much less detailed prescription by the Federal Government than was the case with the Emergency Maternity and Infant Care Program."

Mr. Keefe: "But is it anticipated in the request for this money that the experience and the facts which you hope to develop may disclose a situation that would favorably dispose the Congress to adopt a permanent policy of Government in extending aid in some manner, in this field of maternity and child protection and obstetrical care?"[76]

Miss Lenroot: "Mr. Keefe, I do not know what the results will show, but I think that the people of the country are entitled to as much information as they can get concerning what care, such as that provided under the program, results in. I do not know whether it will be negative or positive in all respects. I think in many respects we could probably believe that it would be positive. But I know there are some people who think in some of these aspects there may be a negative finding. But I think the people of the United States are entitled to know after an investment of the amount of money that is represented in this program, what the program resulted in."[77]

Mr. Keefe was still not satisfied as to the motives behind the proposed study, and he repeated his question. Miss Lenroot: "As to your direct question, Mr. Keefe, the Children's Bureau from the time that it was created has had as its guiding motive the production of facts, but the fact-finding studies—and I have been with the Bureau since 1915, and a great part of that time not as head of the Bureau—I would say were not biased, or deflected according to any

[75]Ibid., p. 296.
[76]Ibid., p. 297
[77]Ibid.

particular policy that the Bureau wished to advocate. The Bureau was created at a time when the public generally felt that if we could know the facts there would then be a basis for public action in determining what ought to be done. I still think that this is a valid purpose of Government and the first duty of the Children's Bureau."[78] As was noted earlier, the request of $929,000 for a study of the EMIC program was not included in the final appropriation bill.

This testimony indicates that the members of the Committee on Appropriations of the House and Congress supported the EMIC program largely because it was designed to meet an emergency. As revealed in earlier hearings, there was fear of "socialized medicine" and the future extension of this type of program during peacetime. Another fact that the testimony reveals is the fear of ulterior motives in social research which will bias the results in a desired direction, especially when the research is sponsored and conducted by a government agency in its own program.

From March, 1943 until the last appropriation bill passed on July 26, 1946 Congress had appropriated over $130,500,000 for the EMIC program. This program was channeled through a government agency which before this time was expending only around $11,000,000 under Title V of the Social Security Act.

During the short period of three years almost all members of Congress received communications from their constituents praising, condemning or simply requesting information about EMIC. They were from physicians, hospital administrators, servicemen and their wives. Communications were reported by the senators from 41 states and by the representatives from 48 states. The Children's Bureau and its regional offices received over 4,500 letters during one year alone, July, 1943 to July, 1944. It is clear that the EMIC program was close to the people; new policies and rules and regulations had an almost instant response.

[78]Ibid., p. 299.

CHAPTER IV

THE DEVELOPMENT OF RULES AND REGULATIONS

August, 1941 - March, 1943

Prior to May, 1942, the Children's Bureau had approved plans submitted by the states for maternity and infant care for the wives and infants of servicemen on an individual state basis. On May 1, 1942 the Bureau drew up a formal set of policies which it sent to the state health departments to be used as a guide in the preparation of programs for the fiscal year beginning in July, 1942.[1] The Bureau suggested that the plans and the request for funds for this supplemental service be submitted at the same time that the regular annual maternal and child health plan was submitted to the regional offices of the Bureau.

The Children's Bureau, it will be recalled, had set aside 10 percent of the B Fund of the maternal and child health appropriation for the fiscal year 1943, amounting to $198,000, for allotment to state departments of health wishing to finance this type of care. It was recommended that state health departments limit their budgets to the first quarter or the first and second quarters of the fiscal year. The Bureau expressed the hope that additional resources would be made available to continue the program after the exhaustion of the B Fund early in the fiscal year. To conserve the limited funds and to make sure they would be used where most needed the Bureau asked that they be used for the cost of medical or hospital services not readily available to the families eligible for these services.

The suggested policies, according to the Children's Bureau, were "prepared in an effort to assist the State agencies in drafting workable eligibility determinations and authorization procedures, establishing standards of medical and hospital care, and simplifying the methods of payment for care." It was hoped that the plans of all the states would follow similar general policies in order to expedite the transfer of records from one state to another if the patient moved

1U. S. Children's Bureau. Memorandum to State Health Agencies from the Director of the Division of Health Services on the Subject of Medical and Hospital Obstetric and Pediatric Care for Wives and Infants of Men in Military Service. May 1, 1942.

after care had been authorized. This indicates the national scope of the problem, necessitating the formulation of many policies which would have nation-wide application. Services administered to beneficiaries who were on the move tended to minimize local and state characteristics and autonomy. Thus arose the issues of "centralization," "control from Washington," and so on.

The following principles were suggested as a guide in the development of the program for the wives and infants of men in military service:[2]

I. BENEFICIARIES.

A. All expectant mothers in the state, irrespective of legal residence, who state that the father of the expected child is in military service and not a commissioned officer.

B. Any child under one year of age whose father is in military service, but not a commissioned officer.

II. APPLICATION AND AUTHORIZATION FOR CARE.

A suggested form or one similar to it (form M*) should be widely distributed to wives of men in military service by public health and welfare agencies, the American Red Cross, and military authorities. Part 1 of this form should be filled out by the patient and part 2 by the attending physician, who should then send it to the state maternal and child health director. The director should immediately notify the patient, the attending physician, the hospital (if hospital care is recommended by the attending physician), and the local health department or local public health nursing service.

Similar procedures should be established for authorization of medical and hospital care of infants eligible for these services.

III. SERVICES.

A. A complete medical service for the wife during the prenatal period, including at least five prenatal examinations, delivery, puerperium (including care of newborn infant) and postpartum examinations. A minimum of ten days hospital care after delivery.

B. Home, office, and hospital care for the sick child under one year of age. Child health supervision should be given

* See Appendix page iii.

[2]Ibid.

in existing child health conferences already operating under or in cooperation with divisions of maternal and child health in state and local health departments.

IV. Rates of Payment.

A. Physicians' Services.

1. The suggested fee of $35 to obtain statewide to physicians for the complete maternity care described above. If prenatal care was provided in a prenatal clinic, or if less than five prenatal examinations were made by the attending physician, $25 might be paid for services during labor, the puerperium (including care of the newborn infant), and postpartum examinations.
2. For sick children it was suggested that the first medical visit might be paid for without prior authorization, but subsequent care should be authorized on a case basis ,not on a fee per visit basis, the cost depending on the type and dufation of the illness. The example given was: Pneumonia care authorization of $10 for home or hospital care during the first week of illness, with a minimum of three visits, or $5 each succeeding week of illness. Cost of pediatric care in excess of $20 per case should not be authorized without review of the case and recommendation by a pediatric consultant.

B. Hospital Services.

The actual per diem cost of operating the hospital, to embrace all costs of care while mother and newborn infant are in the hospital, including delivery room, laboratory services, drugs, and so forth, except the medical services of the attending physician. Hospital care for sick children should also be paid on a per diem cost basis.

V. Standards of Care.

A. Physicians.

1. Must be a graduate of a medical school approved by the Council on Medical Education of the American Medical Association and be licensed to practice in the state.
2. Prenatal care should be of a quality comparable to that recommended in the Children's Bureau publication, *Standards of Prenatal Care.*

3. Obstetricians and pediatricians who are certified by the American Specialty Boards, or whose training and experience meet the requirements of such boards, should be appointed consultants by the state health departments and, wherever possible, be made available for consultation with the general practitioners participating in the plan.

B. Hospitals.

1. Hospitals must either have been approved by the American College of Surgeons or inspected and approved by the state health agency as meeting the standards, established by the state health agency, for obstetric and pediatric service. There should be a minimum of ten days hospital care after delivery.

VI. OTHER.

A. The patients are to have free choice of physicians and hospitals participating in the program; however, where the case load is concentrated in certain areas the employment of full-time or part-time qualified obstetricians and pediatricians was suggested. It was felt that this arrangement would assure high standards of medical care, and payment on a salary basis would eliminate the difficulties of fee schedules.

B. The fees and rates paid to physicians and hospitals by the state health departments are to cover the entire cost of the services. The patient is not to pay anything.

On January 1, 1943 the rules and regulations were modified and expanded superseding the first rules and regulations issued on May 1, 1942.[3] Hospital payment was limited to the cost of ward care. It was suggested that all patients should be referred immediately to local health departments for nursing services in the home, including bedside-nursing care if necessary, before, during, and after delivery. Care could be purchased from a local visiting-nurse agency when it could not be made available by the public health nursing service of the local health department. Special nursing care in the hospital might be authorized upon the request of the attending physician for maternity patients or infants who were seriously ill. Rates of payment to nurses were not mentioned.

3U. S. Children's Bureau. Memorandum from the Director of the division of Health Services to the State Health Agencies on General Policies Recommended for Medical and Hospital Care of Maternity Cases and Children When the Father is in Military Service. January 1, 1943.

It was recommended that, for patients needing assistance in dealing with personal problems, referrals should be made to the appropriate state or local welfare agency. Also, the inclusive rate for complete maternity service should include the care of complications and operations. In other words the physician would receive the same fee for complicated cases as for uncomplicated ones. It was felt that the established fee was an average for all types of cases which the physician might encounter over a period of time.

The definition of per diem hospital cost was clarified on July 23, 1942 and incorporated in the current memorandum. The policies adopted at this time were to be effective a year later so as to enable the hospitals to acquire the data needed. The policies included:[4]

1. Hospital care shall be at a rate not to exceed the ward cost per patient day calculated by each hospital according to the formula presented by the Children's Bureau.

2. Each hospital participating in the program shall prepare for the state health department, before May 1 each year, a statement of its operating expenses for its most recent accounting year.

3. Payments per patient day for ward care, after 14 days' hospitalization of any individual, shall not exceed 75 percent of the calculated ward cost per patient day.

4. For the purpose of computing the cost of ward care it was estimated that the cost of such care approximated 85 percent of the cost per patient day for all types of in-patient services.

It is apparent that a few of the administrative problems were beginning to appear even though the number of cases handled each month was still only in the hundreds. The program was becoming large enough so that exceptional cases were creating a problem in the determination of fees. The flat fee for maternity cases was not designed to cover exceptional cases needing unusually skillful and long care. The same fee was to cover both uncomplicated and complicated cases.

The determination of hospital costs was also becoming a larger problem as more EMIC patients were hospitalized. Since a government agency paid nonprofit hospitals only the actual cost per patient day of operating the hospitals, it became the hospitals' responsibility to make an accurate determination of what constituted cost. A great many hospitals were not prepared to do this because they

4U. S. Children's Bureau. Memorandum from the Chief to the State Health Agencies on Purchase of Hospital Care under Crippled Children's or Maternal and Child Health Programs. July 23, 1942.

had not established standard accounting systems. Hence the state health departments were notified by the Children's Bureau on February 1, 1943 that hospitial administrators should be advised that regional auditors of the bureau would verify the hospital statements by actual audit of hospital expenditures each year in a spot check of a few hosiptals in each state.[5] However, this was never put in effect. Hospitals which were paid less than $100 a year by the state health department did not need to submit an operating statement.

Again on March 15, 1943 a memorandum on the purchase of hospital care was issued superseding the two previous memoranda.[6] A more explicit statement of what should be included in the ward cost of a hospital was prepared; the other memoranda had left too many unknowns. Hospitals receiving payments for care totaling less than $500 a year were given the choice of submitting a statement of their operating costs or accepting the inclusive per diem rate established by the state department of health.

March, 1943 - December, 1943

On March 18, 1943 the first EMIC appropriation act was passed by Congress. The Children's Bureau drew up another set of policies, *MCH Information Circular No. 13*, issued on March 29, 1943 superseding all other memoranda in order to comply with the act and the intent of Congress.

The text of the act reads in part, ". . . to provide, in addition to similar services otherwise available, medical, nursing, and hospital maternity and infant care for wives and infants of enlisted men in the armed forces of the United States of the fourth, fifth, sixth, or seventh grades, under allotments by the Secretary of Labor and plans developed and administered by State health agencies and approved by the Chief of the Children's Bureau."[7] The Bureau was empowered to administer the programs in accordance with the procedures, policies, and regulations relating to the maternal and child health program, Title V, part 1, of the Social Security Act.

5U. S. Children's Bureau. Memorandum from the Chief to the State Health Agencies on Purchase of Hospital Care under the Cripled Children and Maternal Child Health Programs. February 1, 1943.

6U. S. Children's Bureau. Memorandum from the Chief to the State Health Officers on Purchase of Hospital Care under the Crippled Children and Maternal and Child Health Programs. March 15, 1943.

7U. S. Children's Bureau, MCH Information Circular No. 13, Revised, March 29, 1943. Instructions to State Health Agencies with Regard to Plans and Financial Reports Related to Emergency Appropriations for Maternity and Infant Care. 12p.

In the *MCH Information Circular No. 13* the Children's Bureau presented in detail the information required of the state health departments before their plans would be approved. The states were required to indicate eligibility, methods of application for care, methods and policies of authorizations for payment of services, referrals for medical services, nursing services and social services, rates of payments for medical services and hospital care, standards to be followed for all services, and all pertinent statistical and financial data. The Bureau established requirements on all these items with which the states had to comply in order to receive approval of their plans. Since this was an emergency program and financed completely by Federal funds, and since the services provided were to be made available to eligible wives and infants even though they moved from state to state, the Bureau felt and assumed a great deal of responsibility in the formulation of detailed policy.

Three items in the act itself conditioned the seeming rigidity of the policies formulated by the Bureau. These items contained the apparent intent of Congress and had a great bearing on the nature of the administrative process down to the local level. The services to be provided were clearly stated; the fact that the benefits were to be in the form of service and not cash was implied; and the exclusion of a means test was easily interpreted. The immediate provision of medical, nursing, and hospital care for maternity patients and infants was made mandatory. The personnel and facilities had to be marshalled and these were to be utilized for the benefit of the group designated in the law, regardless of income. From the conditions established by the law there flowed many policies to implement and apply it. Only by following the administrative process from the basic law to the persons who receive the ultimate benefits can the process be understood and evaluated.

The chief changes in the policies after the first EMIC appropriation act will be described in some detail. Whereas, using B funds, care had been given to needy wives and infants of men in service below commissioned officers, the new law designated the fourth, fifth, sixth and seventh grades in the Army, Navy, Marine Corps, or Coast Guard as the eligible ones. This excluded the families of commissioned officers, of master, major, first, technical, staff, and platoon sergeants, and of chief, first, and second-class petty officers. On the application form for care the wife was to indicate the husband's serial number and rank, verified by the attending physician from the applicant's allowance card or a letter from the husband.

Subjects covered by the policies are shown in the following brief resume:

1. Application for authorization for hospital care in case of emergency should be submitted by the hospital or attending physician within 24 hours of admission to a hospital. These applications may be retroactive to cover the emergency period while authorization was pending.

2. Initial authorization for hospital maternity care should not be for more than 14 days, and a minimum stay of 10 days postpartum should be arranged if at all feasible. Previous rules and regulations had not designated a limit on the number of days.

3. The attending physician and the hospital are to understand that they may accept no payments from the patient or family for services rendered. Payment from the state department of health is to constitute payment in full.

4. Hospital out-patient departments or health department clinics that have arrangements for complete maternity care should be utilized as well as the services of physicians in their own offices.

5. Complete maternity care was further defined to include routine blood tests for syphilis, hemoglobin determinations, and urinalyses.

6. Differential rates of payment to general practitioners and specialists were suggested. Specialists may receive approximately one-fourth to one-third higher fees than general practitioners. To be designated a specialist and to qualify for a higher rate an obstetrician had to be certified by the American Board of Obstetrics and Gynecology. Assistant consultants had to have one or more years of graduate training in obstetrics in an approved residency.

7. As the need arose, it was suggested that the fee schedules for nonobstetric surgery and specialized consultants services should be considered by the state health agency in conference with a technical advisory committee selected and appointed by the state health agency. These fee schedules should be submitted to the Children's Bureau for approval.

8. Rates of payment to physicians for the care of sick infants were made more explicit. It was recommended that such care be financed on a case basis if more than three visits were required; for example, $10 for home and hospital medical care during the first week of illness and $5 for home, office, and hospital medical care for succeeding weeks, with a minimum of three visits per week and for periods of not longer than three weeks. Renewal of authorization for more prolonged medical care should be given only after review of the case by the maternal and child health director or a pediatric consultant appointed by the state health agency.

Higher rates of payment were suggested for medical services rendered by pediatricians certified by the American Board of Pediatrics or for assistant consultants who have had one or more years of graduate training in pediatrics in an approved residency. These rates could be from one-fourth to one-third higher than those paid physicians who have not had the additional graduate training and experience.

As the need arose, fee schedules for minor or major surgery for infants, specialized consultant services, and rates of payment for care of sick infants for periods of longer than three weeks should be considered by the state health agency in conference with a technical advisory committee selected and appointed by the agency. These fee schedules should be submitted to the Children's Bureau for approval.

9. When review of the maternity or pediatric records submitted shows that the standards of care recommended have not been provided, the state health agency should not authorize further care by such physicians.

10. Provision may be made for reimbursing physicians for the cost of long-distance telephone calls for consultation for patients when bedside consultation is not feasible.

11. Further refinement in the determination of per diem hospital cost for ward case was required. Since the services of intern and resident staff are included in the hospital ward cost per patient day, the intern and resident staff may not receive extra remuneration from the state health department. Also, payments may not be made to attending physicians for services customarily provided to ward patients in hospital without reimbursement.

12. The services usually provided by hospitals were expanded to include the cost of blood for transfusions and similar exceptional services. These were to be paid for at the customary ward rate and were not part of the per diem ward cost.

13. Some changes were made in the original qualifications for physicians who could participate in the program in order to provide for exceptions and to assure as many eligible physicians as possible. Originally the only physicians eligible to participate were those who were graduates of a medical school approved by the Council on Medical Education and Hospitals of the American Medical Association. The new ruling provided that individual exceptions may be made when a person with the degree of Doctor of Medicine who is a graduate of a medical school not approved by the American Medical Association has completed postgraduate training in obstetrics

and/or pediatrics which, in the opinion of the state health officer and his technical advisory committee, makes him competent to participate.

14. Regarding hospital standards it was recommended that those employing intern and resident staff and meeting the standards for institutions approved for internships or residencies should be selected. Hospitals having an obstetrician and a pediatrician, certified or otherwise fully qualified on the attending staff should be preferred over those which do not.

Thus, as the program expanded and administrative problems increased the need for revisions and expansions of the rules and regulations became apparent. The emergency nature of the program and the limited experience with medical administration prevented the formulation of policies and rules and regulations which would be adequate for a rapidly expanding program without frequent and sometimes confusing revisions.

The policies were called "information circulars" and the frequent interpretations of the information circulars were usually called "memoranda." Between the issuance of the *MCH Information Circular* No. 13 on March 29, 1943 and *EMIC Information Circular* No. 1 in December, 1943 superseding all previous policies and memoranda, the Children's Bureau released 10 memoranda to the state health departments interpreting the policies set forth in March, 1943. Four of these were occasioned by the results of hearings before the Committee Appropriations of the House of Representatives.

On April 10, 1943 the Children's Bureau as a result of a conference with its advisory committee of obstetricians and pediatricians issued a memorandum amending the policy in regard to physicians' fees for sick infants.[8] For initial home visits the fee could be $4 a visit and for initial office and hospital visits, $2. Subsequent visits could be $2 and $1, respectively. In the same memorandum it was suggested that the funds under the regular maternal and child health program could be used for the employment of medical social workers.

The ruling relating to the non-payment of physicians for medical care in hospital wards if the physicians customarily contributed their services in the wards was changed on April 14, 1943 when instances were found where patients under the program were not in the same category as patients previously accepted for ward serv-

8U. S. Children's Bureau. Memorandum to the State Health Agencies on MCH Information Circular No. 13. April 10, 1943.

ices.[9] The new rule permitted the payment of the attending physicians for services to private patients occupying ward or other accommodations. It was also explained why the provision for the differential fee for specialists was omitted. This was done on the recommendation of the obstetricians and the pediatricians of the advisory committee to the Bureau, the recommendation stating that at the request of the states, not at the suggesion of the Bureau, differential fees might be included and approved.

In answer to inquiries from the states asking if funds for the EMIC program might be paid directly to the wives of enlisted men, the Children's Bureau on July 6, 1943 issued a memorandum stating explicitly that this could not be done.[10] This was also the opinion the Solicitor of Labor in the Department of Labor, the legal consultant for the department, in a discussion held on December 8 and 9, 1943.[11] The EMIC plan of the State Department of Health of North Dakota was refused approval because of the inclusion of cash grants to the patients. The Solicitor ruled against the North Dakota proposal on December 16, 1943.

When the appropriation bill for 1944 was passed on July 12, 1943, the state health departments received instructions two days later that the Children's Bureau was prohibited by a proviso, added to the appropriation act for the fiscal year 1944, from establishing standards which would discriminate between persons licensed under state law to practice obstetrics. The Attorney General of the United States advised the Secretary of Labor and the Children's Bureau on July 14 that this was the meaning and intent of the law. On July 28 another memorandum was sent to the state health agencies interpreting the instructions sent them two weeks previously regarding discrimination between practitioners. Many states had not understood the new ruling fully. The Wisconsin State Department of Health insisted upon limiting EMIC payments for obstetrics to Doctors of Medicine and it had the support of the Attorney General of that state. In such a situation, even if it had wished to do so, the Children's Bureau could not force the state health department to open the program to all who might be licensed to prac-

9U. S. Children's Bureau. Memorandum from Dr. Daily to Regional Medical Consultants on the Memorandum of April 10, 1943 to State Health Agencies Relating to Maternal and Child Health Information Circular No. 13. April 14, 1943.

10U. S. Children's Bureau. Memorandum from Dr. Daily to Regional Medical Consultants on the Memorandum of April 10, 1943 to state Health Agencies Relating to Maternal and Child Health Information Circular No. 13. April 14, 1943.

11U. S. Children's Bureau. Memorandum to State Health Officers and Maternal and Child Health Directors. July 6, 1943.

tice obstetrics in the state, because, according to the Federal interpretation, that would have been an interference with the right of a state.

To comply with the language of the appropriation act passed on July 12 for the fiscal year 1944 the Bureau notified the states that although services should be limited to wives and infants of enlisted men in the fourth, fifth, sixth, and seventh pay grades, certain hardship cases in the first three pay grades could be included.[12]

After considering many recommendations made by state health departments and hospital administrators the Children's Bureau revised some of the policies relating to the determination of per diem hospital costs on September 1, 1943. When hospitals did not or could not submit an acceptable statement of operating expenses, an inclusive per diem ward rate not to exceed $4.25 a day was to be paid during the fiscal year.

Many inquiries had been received by the Children's Bureau as to whether a patient under the EMIC program might pay for a portion of the care rendered. The patient might wish to pay the physician's bill or the hospital bill herself. The Children's Bureau recommended that the patient may be permitted to pay a portion of the bill provided such payment is made to the state health department and credited to the EMIC account.[13]

In September supplemental funds were provided by Congress and the law governing the EMIC program was amended striking out the inclusion of the first three pay grades even if they were hardship cases. The states were notified to this effect on September 29, but they had to be renotified on November 17.

December, 1943 - March, 1945

In December 1943 all the information circulars and memoranda on the EMIC program were consolidated and expanded to comprise *EMIC Information Circular No. 1.*[14]

The following changes were made:

1. The effective date of authorization from which the state health department assumes responsibility for payment for services

[12]U. S. Children's Bureau. Memorandum from the Chief to the State Health Agencies. July 20, 1943.

[13]U. S. Children's Bureau. Memorandum from the Chief to the State Health Agencies. September 7, 1943.

[14]U. S. Children's Bureau. EMIC Information Circular No. 1. December, 1943. Administrative Policies; Emergency Maternity and Infant Care Program. 21 p.

shall be the date during pregnancy when the wife first requested care from physician, clinic, or hospital, provided the application, signed by physician, is received by the state or local health agency within six weeks after the date when the wife first requested care under the program.[15] The effective date of authorization for medical care of a sick infant shall be the date when the physician, clinic, or hospital agreed to give care provided it is not more than ten days prior to the date when the application was received in the state or local health agency.[16]

2. Ward care should be provided but the hospitals must provide whatever accommodations are indicated by the patient's medical condition at the per diem ward rate paid by the state health department. Authorizations may be made for a maximum of 14 days with extension of care when necessary for two-week periods after review by the state or local health agency. The same conditions apply to sick infants.

3. The number of prenatal visits required before the physician may receive the full fee established for complete maternity care was increased from five to seven. The rate of payment could be set by the state health department, but not in excess of $50.

4. The problem of paying for services rendered during pregnancy for conditions which were not due to pregnancy had arisen. Supported by the legal opinion of the Solicitor of the Department of Labor the Children's Bureau ruled that additional payments may be paid by the state health department for medical care and major surgery for "intercurrent nonobstetric conditions" in the home and hospital. Treatment in the office was to be considered as part of the complete maternity service with no extra payment. Major nonobstetric intercurrent surgical operations may be performed by physicians who qualify as consultants in a surgical specialty at a rate not to exceed $50 for preoperative, operative, and postoperative care. Additional payments may also be made for medical care of other intercurrent nonobstetric conditions in the home or hospital for a period of three weeks which do not require major surgery. The maximum rate of payment was to be $12 for the first week of illness for four visits. If fewer than four visits are made the rate of payment should be reduced proportionately. For succeeding weeks of illness the rate of payment should not exceed $6 a week.[17]

5. When only prenatal care is provided by the attending phy-

15Ibid., p. 5.
16Ibid., p. 6.
17Ibid., p. 7–8.

sician the rate of payment for seven visits should not exceed $15. If less than seven visits are made the rate of payment should be reduced proportionately. If the pregnancy terminates in spontaneous abortion not requiring an operation the fee should not exceed $15, plus proportionate payment for any prenatal examinations made. The rate of payment for therapeutic abortions or spontaneous abortions requiring an operation should be the rate established by the state health department for complete maternity care, and not in excess of $50.[18]

6. The rates of payment for medical care, including minor surgery, for infants under one year of age should not exceed $12 for the first week of illness, and should include at least five visits. For succeeding weeks $6 a week should be paid for at least three visits a week. The rate for complete major surgical care should not exceed $50.[19]

7. Immunizations may be provided infants in physicians' offices or at child health conferences or immunization clinics not conducted by state or local health departments. The rates of payment should not exceed $6 for immunization for smallpox, diptheria, and whooping cough plus the cost of biologicals if not furnished by the state or local health departments. These immunizations will usually require during the first year of life one procedure for smallpox, two or three for diptheria, and three for whooping cough.[20]

8. Bedside nursing in the hospital or home when requested by the attending physician should be authorized for a period not to exceed four days, with review by the state or local health agency before authorizing extension of care. The rate of payment should be the prevailing local hourly or per diem rates not to exceed the maximum rate established by the state health agency. [21]

Bedside nursing in the home may be authorized for care of mother and infant while the mother is receiving bed care during the puerperium. The number of visits should not exceed six, with review by the state health department before authorizing extension of care. Home visits for care of a sick mother or infant may be authorized but not to exceed 14 visits. Home nursing visits may be authorized for the period of labor and delivery. The rates of payment for these services should be at the prevailing local rates

18Ibid., p. 8.
19Ibid., p. 10–11.
20Ibid., p. 12–13.
21Ibid., p. 13.

but not to exceed the maximum established by the state health department.[22]

The policies covering the mechanics of administration remained substantially the same. It is seen that there were attempts to separate physicians' services, nurses' services, and the medical needs of mothers and infants into definable units. Thus, rates of payments, quality of care, and the need for care could more easily be placed within an administrative framework.

For a short time all the policies for the program could be found in a single source; then information circulars and memoranda began to flow again. From December, 1943 to October, 1944 around 30 revisions in the policies contained in *EMIC Information Circular No. 1* were issued.

On January 15, 1944 the Children's Bureau released a memorandum to the states regarding the review of hospital accounts. "It appears that some State agencies have gained the impression that they should take no responsibility with regard to review of statements of operating costs received from hospitals for the purpose of detecting possible accounting errors or departures from instructions for preparing the statement."[23] The state health departments were told that they have the responsibility. "However, it is recognized that this was not made clear in the instructions issued to the State agencies."

Many of the patients receiving care in the EMIC program carried hospital insurance covering maternity care. The Children's Bureau ruled that the patients might use their hospital insurance if they wished, but they were advised to use the EMIC benefits exclusively and save their hospital benefits—usually limited to a given number of days per year—for other purposes. If the hospital insurance was on a cash indemnity basis, the patients could receive that money as well as the service benefits from the EMIC program.[24]

In March, 1944 the Children's Bureau felt it necessary to write a letter signed by Miss Lenroot to all the state health officers dealing with exceptions and cases not specifically mentioned in the policies formulated by the Bureau. Apparently the state health departments had been hewing so closely to the letter of the rules and regulations that some potentially eligible patients were not receiving

22Ibid.

23U. S. Children's Bureau. Memorandum from the Division of Health Services to the State Agencies Administering MCH, EMIC, and CC Programs. January 15, 1944.

24U. S. Children's Bureau. Memorandum from Dr. Deitrick to the Regional Medical Consultants on Hospital Insurance Maternity Benefits. February 26, 1944.

care under the program because of technicalities. The letter read in part: ". . . the Children's Bureau . . . recognizes the fact that State plans for a program of this magnitude cannot describe the method of handling all situations involving occasional deviation from the established policies and that appropriate exceptions must necessarily be made in view of the circumstances in individual applications for care. These decisions must be made by the State health agencies in the light of the intent of the program which is primarily to see that care is provided for eligible individuals and to relieve enlisted men and their families of uncertainty or anxiety as to how the cost of care will be met. When in your judgment an eligible wife or infant of an enlisted man would be denied care to which they are entitled under the program, and hardship and injustice result, you must certainly act in the best interest of the patient concerned. . . ."[25]

During the course of the year important revisions were made in the length of time care could be authorized and in the rates of payment. The limitations on the length of medical and hospital authorizations in *EMIC Information Circular No. 1* were found unsuitable for certain patients, such as premature infants requiring long-term care. This was amended so that medical and hospital care might be authorized for a period not to exceed two months. If additional care were required, extension for a maximum of one month might be authorized after review of the case by the state or local health department.[26]

A policy established in April, 1944 provided that rates for medical care for sick infants, including minor surgery, should not exceed $24 for the first three weeks, and for succeeding weeks of illness not over $6 per week. The maximum rate of payment for a home visit should not exceed $3 and an office or hospital visit not over $2.[27] In the same amendment these rates were also recommended for medical care for intercurrent nonobstetrical conditions.

An amendment was added later to equalize the periods authorized for both hospital and medical care for sick infants. Hospital care for sick infants might be authorized for 21 days, with extension of care authorized when necessary for three-week periods after

[25] U. S. Children's Bureau. Letter from Miss Lenroot to State Health Officers, March 11, 1944.

[26] U. S. Children's Bureau. EMIC Information Circular No. 1 Amendment No. 1. March, 1944.

[27] U. S. Children's Bureau. EMIC Information Circular No. 1 Amendment No. 3. April, 1944.

review of the case by the state or local health department.[28] This ruling seems to overlap the other ruling dealing with long-term care for certain types of cases.

Another amendment gave the states greater latitude in adjusting payments to physicians on an individual case basis for extraordinarily severe cases that require an exceptional amount of care within the period of time covered by a single authorization.[29] The flat-fee basis for all types of cases was not considered as equitable payment for such exceptional cases.

A new policy in September, 1944 extended the services for infants by permitting office care during their first year of life instead of a new authorization every three weeks as had been the previous requirement. This would include the office care of infants when sick or for immunization, or for general advice on care. The rate of payment for such care should not exceed $16 a year with appropriate reductions on an equitable basis when the minimum services required by the state health department have not been provided. For health supervision, including immunization, provided at a child health conference, the rate for office medical care should not exceed $10 a year.[30] In the amendment of the same date it was stipulated that health supervision may be purchased through EMIC funds for infants from voluntary health agencies conducting child health conferences. Maximum payment for this service during the child's first year of life should not exceed $15. The same service in a physician's office should not exceed $24 a year.[31]

Differential rates of payment between specialists and general practitioners were not mentioned in *EMIC Information Circular No. 1* although the states could establish such rates if they wished to do so. In August, 1944 the Children's Bureau issued an amendment stating that rates of payment to specialists may be established at the option of the state health department but not to exceed by more than 50 percent the rates paid general practitioners.[32]

In the same amendment the Children's Bureau stated that if differential rates of payment for specialists in obstetrics are estab-

28U. S. Children's Bureau. EMIC Information Circular No. 1 Amendment No. 7. August, 1944.

29U. S. Children's Bureau. EMIC Information Circular No. 1 Amendment No. 9. August, 1944.

30U. S. Children's Bureau. EMIC Information Circular No. 1 Amendment No. 10. September 15, 1944.

31U. S. Children's Bureau. EMIC Information Circular No. 1 Amendment No. 10. September, 1944.

32U. S. Children's Bureau. EMIC Information Circular No. 1 Amendment No. 8. August, 1944.

lished, the state health department should determine the qualifications for specialists. In differentiating between specialists in obstetrics and general practitioners in the states, health departments should show that the group identified as specialists includes only physicians who have had superior training and customarily receive higher fees than general practitioners. Recommendations were also made for the determination of specialists other than those in obstetrics. These specialists were defined as physicians who are graduates of medical schools approved by the Council on Medical Education and Hospitals of the American Medical Association and who have been certified by their respective American Specialty Boards or have the training and experience for admission to the examinations of such boards.

March, 1945 - July, 1946

In March, 1945, all the amendments and memoranda relating to EMIC Information Circular No. 1 of December, 1943 were consolidated and a few new provisions were added.[33] The major change in administration was the provision that when an expectant mother applies for maternity care the same application will automatically authorize care for the infant for one year after birth. Thus, the mother is saved the trouble of applying twice. Other changes included the following:

1. In the earlier information circular seven prenatal visits were considered the minimum number of visits for complete maternity care. In the new circular this number was reduced to five.

2. Circumcision of an infant over two weeks of age on medical indication might be authorized at a rate of payment not to exceed $5 including aftercare, rather than payment on a visit basis, at the option of the state agency. Circumcision performed within two weeks after birth is considered part of the complete maternity service with no extra remuneration.

3. Additional payment for time in travel and for cost of travel for physicians may be authorized for attending seriously ill patients or for home or hospital deliveries and aftercare outside of city limits of physicians' residences. The rates are not to exceed 25 cents per mile each way traveled outside of the city limits, with a maximum payment of $25 to a physician for travel for any one case.

33U. S. Children's Bureau. Emergency Maternity and Infant Care Information Circular No. 1. Administrative Policies. Rev. March, 1945. 20 p. — see appendix.

4. Payment for cost of travel in addition to payment for services of a graduate nurse not employed by a public or voluntary health agency to the home of a patient may be allowed at the cost of transportation outside of the city limits on a public carrier or at the usual rate for mileage established for state employees.

5. At the option of the state health department drugs prescribed by the attending physician for patients not hospitalized may be purchased under the EMIC program. The policies and procedures are to be established by the state health department.

From March, 1945 until July, 1946 the Information Circular No. 1 (revised) was amended 12 times. There was a tendency to give the states more administrative discretion. Several state health department officials had requested that an interpretive policy statement be issued to clarify the recommendations of the Bureau regarding the use by recipients of the EMIC program of voluntary prepayment medical and hospital plan benefits. The Bureau ruled that "Prepaid medical and/or hospital service benefits for maternity or infant care are considered as payments made in behalf of the patient; however, cash-indemnity insurance benefits paid to the insured are not considered as payments made in behalf of the patient."[34] It will be recalled that any payments to attending physicians or to hospitals in behalf of the patient made her ineligible for the cost of care. The Bureau stated that the policy "is in conformity with the basic philosophy of the emergency maternity and infant-care program, that benefits are to be made available to all eligible wives and infants on the same basis and without regard to their economic resources. Use of prepaid service benefits for maternity and infant care would greatly reduce benefits available to servicemen's dependents for other illnesses, because many prepaid medical and/or hospital benefit contracts limit the care for which payment may be made in a given period of time."

On the recommendation of the Maternal and Child Health Committee of the Association of State and Territorial Health Officers the ruling regarding the maximum payment of $25 to a physician for travel on any one case was eliminated.[35]

Several state health departments had indicated that under the present policies difficulties were occasionally encountered in hospitals which have a limited resident staff and require the services

[34]U. S. Children's Bureau. EMIC Information Circular No. 1 (Revised March, 1945) Amendment No. 1. May, 1945.

[35]U. S. Children's Bureau. EMIC Information Circular No. 1 (Revised March. 1945) Amendment No. 2. May, 1945.

of a physician on the visiting staff to assist the surgeon. The Children's Bureau revised its policy so that payment to a physician assisting the surgeon in a surgical operation in hospitals without available resident staff might be authorized at a rate not to exceed $10 per operation.[36]

The Association of State and Territorial Health Officers recommended to the Children's Bureau that as an alternative to the procedure for adjusting the rate of payment to physicians for maternity care to cover only the services actually rendered, a state health department may pay physicians the maximum allowed for each maternity patient provided they can show proof that for three consecutive months complete maternity care has been rendered to 80 percent or more of the maternity cases in which patients are delivered.[37] The recommendation was accepted and the Information Circular was so amended. This was intended to reduce the amount of administrative detail in the states.

After the surrender of Germany the discharge rate from the armed forces increased considerably so that applications for maternity care by the wives of servicemen were made after their husbands had been discharged. This brought up the question of whether the applicants in such a circumstance were eligible for care. In accordance with the recommendations made by the Committee on Appropriations of the House in its report (No. 551) of May 14, 1945 the Children's Bureau ruled that if the wife became pregnant while the husband was in service even though he might have been dischargd before application was made for care, such applicant would be eligible.[38]

In July, 1946 a series of amendments were issued involving revisions in the policies which the state health departments could apply or not as they saw fit. These changes were part of an attempt to allow greater discretion in the formulation of administrative policies by the states.

The experience of the state health departments had shown that the majority of sick infant cases require relatively prolonged care, necessitating a large number of supplemental authorizations under the three-week period of authorization. The following optional amendments were issued: (1) The initial authorization for care of

36U. S. Children's Bureau. EMIC Information Circular No. 1 (Revised March, 1945) Amendment No. 3. May, 1945.

37U. S. Children's Bureau. EMIC Information Circular No. 1 (Revised March, 1945) Amendment No. 5. May, 1945.

38U. S. Children's Bureau. EMIC Information Circular No. 1 (Revised March, 1945) Amendment No. 6. May, 1945.

a sick infant by a physician might be for a period up to four weeks. (2) The rate of payment for this care should not exceed $30 for the first four weeks of illness, and for succeeding weeks $6 per week. The maximum rate of payment for a home visit should not exceed $3 and for an office or hospital visit $2.[39]

Although the definition of "complete maternity care" included care of the infant during the first two weeks of life, it was considered desirable to make some provision for additional payment to the physician in cases where the newborn child was ill and required special care continuing beyond the first two weeks of life. The Children's Bureau ruled in an optional amendment that if an infant becomes ill during the first two weeks of life and the illness extends beyond that time care of the infant might be authorized retroactively beginning with the first visit for the illness.[40]

Another amendment permitted the state health departments, if they wished, to use state funds to supplement Federal funds for the purpose of increasing the maximum rates for professional services. This would theoretically permit greater state variations in professional fees.[41]

Many state health departments had experienced difficulties in applying the policies regarding the qualifications for physicians performing surgery. This was especially true in sparsely settled and predominantly rural states. In these areas general practitioners had been accustomed to perform whatever surgery was needed. The Children's Bureau believed that wherever qualified surgeons were available they should be used. An optional amendment was issued to encourage consultation on the part of general practitioners before they performed a surgical operation. The amendment stipulated that additional payments might be authorized to the attending physicians for major or intermediate surgical operations performed by them during pregnancy and six weeks postpartum for conditions not attributable to pregnancy provided that a consultant approved by the state health department had examined the patient before the operation and there was agreement on the diagnosis and treatment planned. The same rule might apply to major or intermediate surgical operations on infants. In either case minor surgery

39U. S. Children's Bureau. EMIC Information Circular No. 1 (Revised March, 1945) Amendment No. 7. July, 1946.

40U. S. Children's Bureau. EMIC Information Circular No. 1 (Revised March, 1945) Amendment No. 9. July, 1946.

41U. S. Children's Bureau. EMIC Information Circular No. 1 (Revised March, 1945) Amendment No. 8. July, 1946.

might be authorized at a rate of payment not to exceed $5 inclusive of aftercare, rather than payment on a visit basis.[42]

The original information circular stated that if pregnancy terminates in spontaneous abortion not requiring an operation the rate of payment to the physician should not exceed $15, plus proportionate payment for prenatal examinations made. An optional amendment suggested was that if it is necessary for the patient to be hospitalized for complications such as hemorrhage or infection, the rate of payment might be increased depending on the amount of care given but not to exceed the amount established by the state health department for complete maternity care.[43]

The last amendment issued related to additional payment to anesthetists for prolonged services. If the patient is hospitalized in a hospital that does not employ an anesthetist or if the patient is delivered at home, the services of an anesthetist may be authorized at a rate not to exceed $10. However, in exceptional cases, when anesthesia is required for two hours or longer, additional payments to anesthetists may be authorized at rates established by the state health department and submitted to the Children's Bureau.[44]

Opinions of the Solicitor of the Department of Labor

In the administration of the EMIC program it is evident that the Children's Bureau never took an action which might lead to conflicting legal interpretations without first presenting the problem to the Solicitor of the Department of Labor for guidance.

Some of the major problems of legal interpretation and administrative prerogatives submitted to the Solicitor follow. On February 1, 1944 the Children's Bureau requested the Solicitor to review the legislative history of the EMIC program for the purpose of expressing an opinion as to whether the policies adopted by the Bureau concerning supplementary fees from the patients to the physicians and hositals were in conformity with the intent of Congress. The Solicitor concluded: "After reviewing the legislative history relating to the EMIC program, I adhere to the conclusion expressed in my memorandum of December 9, 1943 that the Chief of the Children's Bureau, as a condition to the approval of State plans, may require that physicians and hospitals participating therein be com-

42U. S. Children's Bureau. EMIC Information Circular No. 1 (Revised March, 1945) Amendment No. 10. July, 1946.

43U. S. Children's Bureau. EMIC Information Circular No. 1 (Revised March, 1945) Amendment No. 11. July, 1946.

44U. S. Children's Bureau. EMIC Information Circular No. 1 (Revised March, 1945) Amendment No. 12. July, 1946.

pensated for services and care by payments made by State health agencies exclusively."[45]

Early in 1944 the Michigan State Medical Society requested that the Michigan EMIC plan be amended so that the state health department could turn the EMIC funds over to the voluntary medical prepayment plan. This organization would then pay the physicians for services rendered in the EMIC program authorized by the state health department. The Michigan State Medical Society was attempting to free the physicians from direct contact with a government agency. During 1944 the Bureau submitted this problem to the Solicitor three times. Each time the Solicitor saw no justification for the procedure, and the Bureau withheld its approval. In substance the Solicitor said that under the Social Security Act, Title V, part 1, the Children's Bureau was under duty to provide for methods of administration necessary for the proper and efficient operations of its programs, and he thought the inclusion of the Michigan Medical Service would make the administration of the EMIC program cumbersome and slow. "The Service is a mere volunteer and not answerable legally for the extent to which it performs its undertakings nor for its efficiency."[46] Again on April 19, 1944 the Solicitor stated: "The consequence of putting into effect the proposal of the State of Michigan is to give recognition, publicity and the color of official status to a private and non-governmental agency. These are not among the objectives of the legislation."[47]

When the question of differential rates of payment to general practitioners and specialists in obstetrics came up the Children's Bureau asked the Solicitor if differential rates were legal since the Bureau was not permitted to designate who may practice obstetrics in the program. The Solicitor stated: "The legislative history of the obstetrical provision is sufficiently clear to justify the interpretation that it was intended to prohibit the Children's Bureau from discriminating between those who may be licensed to practice obstetrics in a State. It does not apply to discrimination in the payment of fees to obstetricians and general practitioners engaged in obstetrics. Under this view it would appear not to be in violation of

45Memorandum from the Solicitor of the Department of Labor to the Children's Bureau Concerning Payment of Supplementary Fees by Wives of Servicemen to Physicians and Hospitals. February 26, 1944.

46Memorandum from the Solicitor of the Department of Labor to Miss Lenroot on the Proposed Amendment to the Michigan EMIC Plan. January 25, 1944.

47Memorandum from the Solicitor to Dr. Daily on the Michigan Medical Service and the Michigan EMIC Plan. April 19, 1944.

the proviso for the Children's Bureau to suggest to the States that they may, if they so desire, establish a differential rate for payments to the obstetricians and to general practitioners performing obstetrical services."[48] It was added that this opinion did not represent the final judgment of the Solicitor's office, but only current thinking.

Another interesting problem came up regarding the legal relationships of patient, physician, and state health department, and physician's liability for malpractice and breach of contract under the EMIC program. The Solicitor felt that if the bilateral contract for the rendition of services was considered to exist between the state and the physician and not between the patient and the physician it "would not only be unfortunate in practical effect, but not in accord with my understanding of the legal relationship existing under the program. It would be unfortunate because it provides an opening for opponents of the program to contend that Government is contracting for medical care and services." Quoting the Solicitor at length on this question:

"The State agency does not enter into any contract with the physician for the performance of medical services. By 'authorizing' the care, it does no more than to agree that if the physician abides by the agreement entered into with the patient for medical services to be performed for her, it will compensate him in accordance with that agreement, on behalf of the patient.

"Thus, in terms familiar to the law, the physician is under a 'duty' (by reason of his express agreement with the patient) to perform medical services quantitatively described; he has an inchoate 'right' against the State (by reason of the 'authorization') to a fixed remuneration if he fulfills that obligation of the agreement; and the State owes 'duty' to him (by reason of the 'authorization') to remunerate him under those circumstances." In conclusion he states: "you will observe that in this triangular arrangement the only contract for the performance of medical services is entered into by the physician and the patient."[49]

In the question of malpractice, the Solicitor decided that even though the contract calls for "complete maternity care" the physician is no more liable to a malpractice suit than under ordinary

48Memorandum from Peter Seitz, Department of Labor, to Dr. Eliot on Differential Rates of Payment for Certain Services Rendered by General Practitioners and by Specialists in the EMIC Program. June 19, 1944.

49Memorandum from the Solicitor to Miss Lenroot on the Legal Relationships of Patients, Physicians, and State Health Agency under the EMIC Programs. June 28, 1944.

circumstances since, "a malpractice claim does not arise out of a contract; the claim rests on a duty imposed by law on physicians." However, the patient might sue the physician for breach of contract if the services listed are not rendered.

At a meeting of a small group of obstetricians, including several members of the Maternal and Child Health Advisory Committee, called by the Children's Bureau on June 5, 1944 a question arose as to whether the scope of liability for malpractice is enlarged when a physician agrees to perform the medical services authorized under the EMIC program. The contention was made by one of the physicians present that a physician who requests authorization under the program enters into an agreement to perform all the services called for by the authorization and consequently takes upon himself liabilities not ordinarily imposed by law. The Children's Bureau wanted to know whether the enhanced liability in question might arise both in an action for breach of contract as well as in a negligence suit for malpractice.

The opinion of the Solicitor was as follows: "Malpractice is a common law liability and the standard of care required is completely independent of any agreement made by the physician.

". . . there is nothing in the agreement entered into by a physician to perform the services authorized under the EMIC program which calls for the exercise of more than average care and diligence. The physician may depart, in some particular, from the prescribed treatment, in the exercise of his judgment, but such omission would not render him any more liable for negligence than if he had so departed in treating a private case. Such departure might give rise to a technical violation of a contract; but clearly, it would have to be shown in a suit based on contract (as well as a suit in negligence) that the omission was the proximate cause of some harm that otherwise might have been avoided."[50] The Solicitor believed, however, that the contract liability of the physicians may be enlarged under the program, because they are asked to give a greater quantity of services for maternity cases than many of them ordinarily render.

50Memorandum from the Solicitor to Miss Lenroot on Physicians' Liability for Malpractice and Breach of Contract under the EMIC Program. July 5, 1944.

Chapter V

THE SCOPE OF THE EMIC PROGRAM

Prior to March, 1943, the month in which the first appropriation for EMIC was approved by Congress, 28 states were already operating maternity and infant care programs on a small scale for the wives and infants of servicemen. Many of these states, however, had exhausted or were exhausting their funds. After the inauguration of EMIC the states submitted their programs and estimates of need for funds for approval by the Children's Bureau. The speed with which the states developed plans is shown in the following table:

Table 1

Month and Year	Number of States* Whose Plans Were Approved in Specified Month	Cumulative Total
1943		
April	13	13
May	16	29
June	10	39
July	3	42
August	3	45
September	2	47
October	0	47
November	1	48
December	2	50
1944		
January	0	50
February	1	51
March	1	52

Beginning with a few hundred maternity cases in the state of Washington in 1941, the monthly average load of new cases throughout the nation rose to a peak of over 42,000 maternity cases by June, 1944, and thereafter began to decline. In November,

*Includes the 48 states and Alaska, Hawaii, Puerto Rico and the District of Columbia.

Fig. I

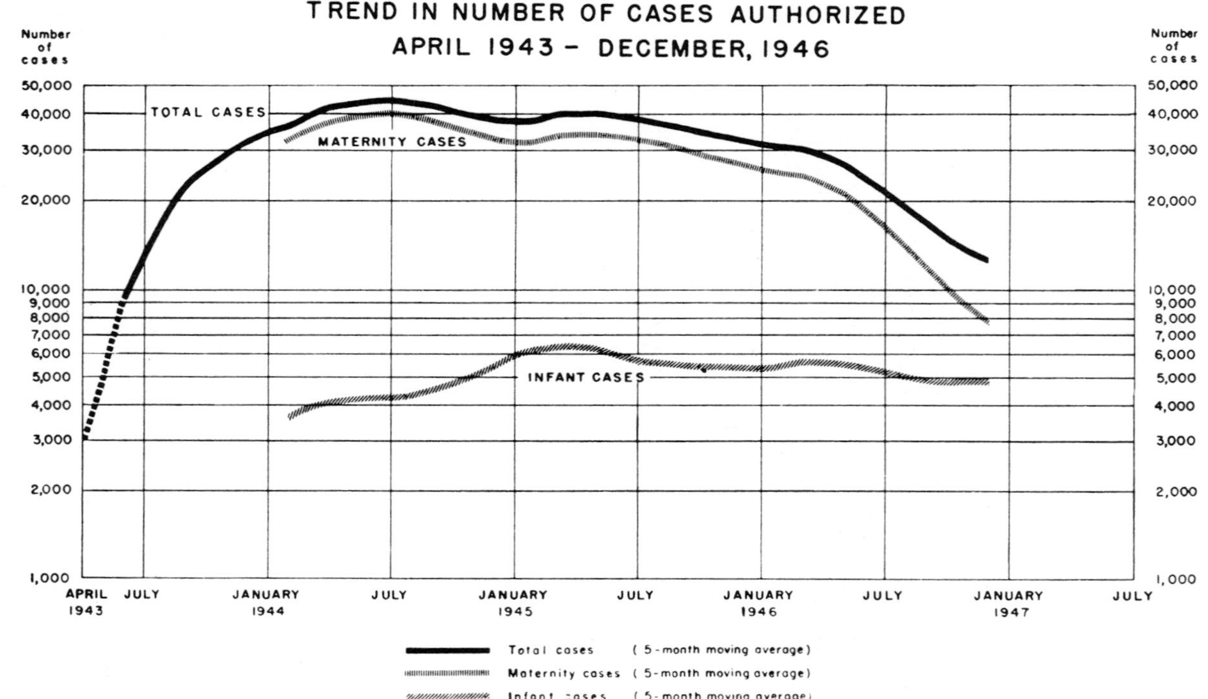

FEDERAL SECURITY AGENCY—Social Security Administration—U. S. Children's Bureau

1946 the new maternity case load was only about 8,000 (Fig. 1*). The total number of maternity cases authorized for care through November, 1946 was over 1,160,000; the number of infants authorized for care over 189,700. Through November, 1946, New York State alone authorized care for 100,407 maternity cases and California for 92,424. The eight states selected for the administrative analysis authorized care for almost 400,000 maternity cases or one-third of the national total at the end of 1946.

The Children's Bureau estimated that about 85 percent of the maternity cases eligible for care under the EMIC program applied for the services. It also estimated that at the height of the program one out of every seven births in the United States was cared for under the program. A study in Nebraska revealed that by 1946 slightly over 88 percent of the births to servicemen's wives were cared for by EMIC; and that 16 percent of all births in the state were under EMIC.[1]

Table 2 presents the average cost for physicians' services for completed maternity cases. The average has been computed on the basis of the total number of completed cases for whom physicians' care was purchased. The table reveals that the cost per maternity case for physicians' services, nationwide, rose from $37.52 in the quarter ending March 31, 1944, to $47.25 in the quarter ending June 30, 1946. The cost for hospital care per maternity case rose from $50.73 to $60.90 during the same period. The variations in the cost of physicians' services per maternity case among the eight states included in this study are also revealed in Table 2.

It will be noted that in the quarter ending March 31, 1944, of the eight states studied the lowest state had an average cost for physicians' services of $34.33 per maternity case and the highest state $47.69, a variation of $13.36. Over two years later, in June, 1946, the lowest average cost was $45.10, the highest $55.29, a variation of $10.19. Excluding New York State, the difference was only $4.12. A national program tends to standardize fees; at first the Children's Bureau attempted to promote state variations according to average prevailing physicians' fees for maternity care, but later left to the states the decision as to whether the medical fee paid should or should not be the maximum rate ($50) authorized by the Bureau for complete maternity care.

*See Appendix, Table 1.

[1]Roland H. Loder, *An Analysis of the Administrative Development; Procedures and Certain Statistical Trends in the Emergency-Maternity-Infant-Care Program for Servicemen's Families in the Nebraska Program during 1942–1946.* M.P.H. Thesis. Ann Arbor, School of Public Health, University of Michigan, June, 1946. Table IX, p. 51.

TABLE 2

Average Quarterly Cost of Physicians' Services Per Maternity Case Completed From January 1, 1944 to June 30, 1946

	QUARTERS									
	1944				1945				1946	
	FIRST	SECOND	THIRD	FOURTH	FIRST	SECOND	THIRD	FOURTH	FIRST	SECOND
United States	$37.52	$39.67	$42.30	$44.12	$45.18	$45.62	$45.48	$45.83	$46.54	$47.25
California	39.10	37.03	39.32	43.06	43.59	46.73	45.60	43.98	43.15	45.52
Georgia	34.50	36.73	36.91	41.79	45.65	47.31	47.07	47.54	46.71	47.53
Illinois	34.33	37.30	40.79	44.96	44.85	45.40	46.17	46.14	48.56	49.22
Massachusetts	42.53	45.61	47.21	47.86	47.87	48.28	47.67	47.43	47.58	47.69
Michigan	36.30	38.04	41.95	45.15	46.76	46.20	46.81	47.24	47.96	47.70
Mississippi	34.78	40.73	41.17	44.85	43.50	42.57	43.94	45.66	46.02	45.10
Nebraska	39.41	42.05	42.87	44.09	42.00	45.44	43.31	44.46	47.18	45.71
New York	47.69	48.21	48.60	48.54	48.55	50.92	51.35	52.76	54.06	55.29*

* Since the maximum fee that could be charged for a maternity case was limited to $50 it may be questioned why New York has an average of $55.29. This figure, as is also true of the other states, includes the extra permissable charges for complications whether or not attributable to pregnancy, during the the pre-natal and post-natal periods and delivery.

TABLE 3

Average Quarterly Cost of Hospital Care Per Maternity Case Completed From January 1, 1944 to June 30, 1946

	QUARTERS									
	1944				1945				1946	
	FIRST	SECOND	THIRD	FOURTH	FIRST	SECOND	THIRD	FOURTH	FIRST	SECOND
United States	$50.73	$52 09	$54.07	$52.84	$54.89	$56.30	$56.68	$58.34	$59.90	$60.90
California	72.07	67.66	71.91	68.65	71.73	72.82	70.07	70.01	71.82	73.23
Georgia	40.92	43.99	44.82	45.51	49.43	49.78	53.01	50.89	52.17	52.31
Illinois	51.28	55.22	56.47	56.86	57.23	58.12	59.46	60.69	62.79	63.59
Massachusetts	53.06	56.16	57.76	56.18	58.00	61.18	62.26	64.94	64.52	65.69
Michigan	54.85	57.45	57.06	57.34	59.76	62.30	64.07	65.35	68.16	68.24
Mississippi	37.38	37.50	39.52	43.36	43.97	46.41	49.41	48.41	49.84	52.75
Nebraska	41.35	47.57	48.37	48.46	48.82	49.53	48.71	52.30	52.49	55.07
New York	60.84	65.26	68.29	66.19	68.45	71.16	71.66	71.53	72.56	73.41

The variations in the average cost of hospital care per completed maternity case are shown in Table 3.

As in the case of the cost of physicians' services the average hospital costs are based on the total number of completed maternity cases for whom hospital care was purchased. The figures in both Tables 2 and 3 do not include payments to hospitals where a single combined payment was made to a hospital for both hospital care and physicians' services. However, by using the average based on all cases, the distribution of the total cost among the types of services can be seen.

The average payments per day for hospital care are presented in Table 4:

TABLE 4

Average Per Diem Payments for Hospital Care for Maternity Cases Completed in the Quarters Ending March 31, 1944 and June 30, 1946 for the United States and Selected States.

	Quarter Ending March 31, 1944	Quarter Ending June 30, 1946
United States	$5.38	$6.58
California	7.76	8.38
Georgia	4.46	6.65
Illinois	5.55	6.64
Massachusetts	5.23	6.61
Michigan	6.22	7.67
Mississippi	4.36	6.03
Nebraska	4.85	5.14
New York	6.19	7.43

These figures do not necessarily represent the actual per diem cost of the hospitals, but are the average payment to hospitals by the states in accordance with the policies and procedures established by the Children's Bureau.[2] During most of this period hospital care was purchased on a cost per patient day basis as determined by cost-accounting reports of the participating hospitals, taking into consideration the proportion of multiple-bed accommodations and subject to the maximum established per diem rates. Customarily, if no agreement was reached, the state paid a flat per diem rate. The figures do not show the range in each state within which there may be considerable variation.

The cost for hospital and physicians' services per infant case

[2] U. S. Children's Bureau, *Purchase of Hospital Care; a Bulletin for State Agencies Administering Services for Maternal and Child Health (including E.M.I.C.), Crippled Children and Vocational Rehabilitation, July, 1945* by U. S. Children's Bureau and Office of Vocational Rehabilitation. Washington, The Bureau, 1945. 34p.

fluctuated greatly from month to month and from state to state due in part to the small number of infant cases completed in some states. Also, the programs varied greatly from state to state in terms of number of cases, demand for services, and type or kind of service provided. California and New York authorized care for 8,494 and 28,202 infants, respectively, from the beginning of the program through November 30, 1946. Michigan authorized care for 7,106 and Georgia 1,508 infants from the beginning of the EMIC program through November, 1946. During this period in California the monthly average cost per completed infant case ranged between $33.10 and $123.07. In Georgia with a lower average cost than California the cost per completed infant case ranged from $10.26 to $147.27.

The effect of the EMIC program on the percentage of births in hospitals is clearly evident in Table 5. The states with an already high percent of births in hospitals, such as New York and California, could not go much higher, but like Nebraska and Georgia show a great increase in the percentage of hospital deliveries.

TABLE 5

Percentage of Hospital and Home Deliveries for Maternity Cases Completed in the Quarters Ending March 31, 1944 and June 30, 1946 for the United States and Selected States.

	Quarter Ending March 31, 1944		Quarter Ending June 30, 1946	
	Hospital	Home	Hospital	Home
United States	89.8	10.2	94.1	5.9
California	98.9	1.1	99.3	0.7
Georgia	75.9	24.1	86.8	13.2
Illinois	97.7	2.3	98.0	2.0
Massachusetts	99.6	0.4	98.6	1.4
Michigan	95.6	4.4	97.4	2.6
Mississippi	74.6	25.4	79.7	20.3
Nebraska	71.4	28.6	94.9	5.1
New York	99.0	1.0	98.9	1.1

The EMIC program also reveals the very high percent of deliveries attended by doctors of medicine in contrast to osteopaths and others. Fully 97 percent of the births were attended by licensed Doctors of Medicine, approximately 2.5 percent by osteopaths and a minor number by "others."

While this study was not planned to include any detailed statistical analysis of cases and costs, certain data have been presented to show the scope of the EMIC program. The tables include a review of cost and other experience through November, 1946. In a recent statement* from the Children's Bureau the following impressive totals for the program are reported:

Total maternity cases authorized	(May 1, 1948)	1,222,500
Total infant cases	(May 1, 1948)	230,000
Total grants of funds	(May 1, 1948)	$126,922,316

*Personal communication, June 4, 1948.

PART TWO

Current Health Economic Problems and the Experience of E M I C

By the time this report is published EMIC will be a part of the history of World War II. In the states and over the nation the discussion of state and national health plans for the distribution of medical and hospital care will occupy the minds of many who participated in EMIC. Many of the same questions that needed answers in EMIC need answers in existing or proposed plans. The questions are a part of the inherent nature of any plan, be it national or state, compulsory or voluntary. As products of an administrative laboratory the lessons from EMIC are of incalculable value. The problems of payment, the problems of quality and those that deal with the subjects of means tests, administrative controls and others are common to all organized plans to provide medical and hospital services. This is the reason for the study of EMIC.

Chapter VI

ORGANIZATION AND ADMINISTRATION

"Politics embraces the processes, procedures, and activities involved in the formation and declaration of public policy and the furnishing of the facilities and means with which to carry that policy into effect. Administration, on the other hand, is the carrying into effect of this will once it has been made clear by political processes."[1]

The statement of public administration describes a process and emphasizes a sequence of action. Both the process and sequence are fundamental to any plan or program for the distribution of health services, regardless of whether the "facilities and means" are public or private. In either case the distribution must be preceded by the adoption of public policy through processes that are political. If the policies are weak or hazy it is certain that these defects will be multiplied many times in the administrative activities that ensue.

EMIC serves as an example of the above sequence. It was created by Congress through a political process as an expression of public policy. The authority for and the technical tasks of administration were assigned to the Children's Bureau. In turn, the Bureau formulated administrative policies, using the general methods that it had established for existing programs. Thus, from the Congress to the Bureau to the states, each with its authority and its functions, the benefits of EMIC were distributed.

It cannot be over-emphasized that the preceding principles of public administration apply with equal validity and force to any national plan for distributing health services. For example, there is a significant political and administrative parallel between a Federal plan for medical service, such as EMIC under the Children's Bureau, and a national voluntary medical plan such as may be developed under the control of the medical profession. Necessary to the success of a voluntary national medical plan is the "formation and declaration" of public policy by a representative body in a position to form and declare. Next come the "facilities and means," i. e., a functioning agency, to carry the policy into effect. And then comes

[1]Pfiffner, John M., Ph.D. *Public Administration,* Ronald Press Co., New York. p.21.

the actual "carrying into effect" by the agency that has been given the necessary authority to fulfill its responsibilities.

More specifically, the principles would apply to the position of and the relationship between the American Medical Association, the state medical societies and the existing medical plans. The American Medical Association is a composite of the medical societies of the states and each state organization has a high degree of autonomy. The state societies, on a basis of proportional representation, elect their representatives to the national House of Delegates, the legislative body of the national organization. It is this body, the medical "Congress," that is in the position to adopt "political policy."

In almost all of the states there are medical insurance plans under the control of the state or local societies. During the past few years the national House of Delegates has adopted sets of principles intended to serve as the framework for these plans. In effect, the principles constitute political policy and, as was inevitable, the next step was the development of an administrative organization or mechanism to apply the policy. In 1945 the House of Delegates decided that the Board of Trustees and the Council on Medical Service "will proceed as promptly as possible with the development of a specific national health program with emphasis on the nationwide organization of locally administered prepayment medical plans sponsored by the medical societies."[2] To this end the Associated Medical Care Plans was incorporated in 1946 and the position of this agency as a central policy-making administrative unit might be considered as comparable to that of the Children's Bureau. However, the analogy ends at this point because whether the Associated Medical Care Plans, Inc., will be given the necessary administrative authority by the national body and the existing state plans remains to be seen. But, as will be noted throughout this report, many of the fundamental problems before an agency such as Associated Medical Care Plans, Inc., and those that faced the Children's Bureau are the same. They are the problems of administrative policy and administrative technique and without the power to choose solutions and the authority to act upon them no agency can be anything but innocuous.

The political structure of the country, with its divisions of power and its political checks and balances, expresses the traditional public fear of any too-great concentration of power. Especially rigid in concept but becoming more flexible in practice is the division of authority between the states and the central government. The fear of encroaching or appearing to encroach upon the rights of the states

2McVay, James R., M.D *Journal of the Tennessee Medical Association* December, 1947 p. 390.

has been responsible for the development by Federal agencies of the formalities that are a part of Federal-states relations. It is true that by one process or another the Federal Government has expanded its authority but the form of state autonomy remains despite the changes in its substance.

The chief medium through which the Federal Government influences programs and actions in the states is by the process of financial grants or grants-in-aid. Connected with a particular grant is a body of rules and regulations that govern the acceptance and expenditure of the funds by a state. No state is forced to accept a grant but if it does its plan to expend the funds must be approved. Thus, one of the chief sources of Federal authority lies in the power to reject or approve. In the normal chain of events there are negotiations, adjustments and compromises and only rarely is there the use of Federal power to withhold or withdraw funds. But the power is there to be used as a last resort; to reduce it would be incompatible with principles of good government and good administration.

Administrative or Advisory Boards

The urge to prevent too great a concentration of authority is the primary force behind the prevalent demand for boards. It strikes a responsive chord of public opinion when, with respect to administration, the charge is made that a proposal carries with it the power of dictation. Because the accusation stimulates a quick adverse reaction it is one of the most common devices used in political warfare.

The role of a board calls for some analysis in terms of the problems that attend the distribution of medical and other health services. The point is stressed that these are the only services under consideration and that what is said with respect to boards cannot be applied to all types of governmental activities. The reason for the emphasis is that, unlike certain other aspects of human relations, medical care is an intimate service that affects thousands of individuals and families daily and directly.

The application of public medical policy carries with it the principle of broad representation of the interests of all of the groups that are involved. If the administration is governmental it cannot represent only the consumer and pay little or no attention to the interests of the professions and institutions that provide care. Nor can a non-governmental administration represent a professional or institutional group and be inattentive to the interests of consumers. In short, where the health of the population is concerned no administrator, governmental or other, can be effective who works "for" one group and "against" others.

The organization of a board with regulatory powers at the national level of administration would hinder rather than further effective processes. To be adequately representative such a board would need to be large but, large or small, conflicting viewpoints would produce administrative confusion and an increasing tendency on the part of administrative personnel to dodge or shift responsibilities. Those who suggest a diffusion of administrative power as a safety measure give too little attention to the nature of medical care and to the technical processes of administration. Whatever policies are adopted have an almost immediate effect upon the lives of millions of people—professional and other. And in Part I the professional and public expressions with regard to these effects are presented in terms of the Congressional hearings and Congressional actions. In the chapters that follow the types of issues and decisions that would face a regulatory board, as they confronted the administrators of EMIC, will be described. It is in the light of these issues and decisions that realistic consideration must be given to the value of such a board. What has been said above does not imply that the advisory type of board functions automatically to concentrate rather than diffuse administrative responsibility. Given a weak and timid administration the tendency of an advisory board to usurp more and more administrative power is not a rare phenomenon.

The experience of the Children's Bureau in the use of advisory committees covers a period of nearly 30 years. The Pediatric Advisory Committee was appointed in 1919 to advise on publications dealing with child care. It comprised four pediatricians who were appointed, one each, by the following organizations:

American Academy of Pediatrics
Pediatric Section, American Medical Association
American Pediatric Association
American Child Health Association

A second committee, the Obstetric Advisory Committee was appointed in 1926 to advise on publications dealing with maternal care. The committee included only two members, both appointed by the Chief of the Bureau. Each of these committees was concerned with matters of a technical and professional nature.

Not until 1935, following the adoption of the Social Security Act, were large advisory committees representing varied professional interests appointed. The committee on maternal and child health included 58 members from the fields of general medicine, obstetrics, pediatrics, psychiatry, dentistry, nursing, public health administration and hospital administration. Subcommittees, one on maternal and one on child health, were appointed from the medical members of the main committee. The second advisory committee, that to deal with programs for crippled children, comprised 38 members from many of the special fields of medicine and from allied fields. Selected medical members of this committee were appointd as a special subcomittee on rheumatic fever.

Advisory committees such as the above serve three purposes. They contribute important technical information to the administrative agency, they serve as a test for proposed administrative policies and they function as an educational medium. The agency using such committees is always in some danger that the dividing line between advice and policy formation will be violated, with the committee usurping authority in the latter area. To prevent such an occurrence the Bureau has emphasized the advisory nature of its committees and has resisted the tendency of committees to assume that a vote on a matter of policy is anything more than a guide. While members of advisory committees theoretically represent only themselves, when they are appointed by or are members of an organization, there is a possibility that they may serve as spokesmen for their organization policies. And a particular policy may not be one that takes into consideration the interests of all groups—professional, economic, geographic and other.

The intimate nature of medical care has been mentioned. The evidence in the committee hearings refutes any impression that in this field of administration those in positions of authority can become arbitrary and dictatorial. The members of Congress not only discussed and questioned administrative policies but they interpreted the policies in terms of specific cases among their constituents. In this process there is a lesson for the future. Regardless of whether a particular plan for medical service is governmental or voluntary, easy means and an easy process of expression for individuals or groups must be a strong part of political and of administrative policy.

The Line of Administration

In the Children's Bureau general administrative authority is centered in the offices of the Chief and the Associate Chief. Under the general supervision of the Chief and Associate Chief is the Director of the Division of Health Services, who is responsible for the administration of the health grants-in-aid to the states. The

Division includes professional consultation services in obstetric, pediatric, etc., as well as nursing, nutrition and medical-social units. It was to the Division of Health Services that the organization and the administration of EMIC were assigned.

In accordance with the policy of many governmental agencies the Bureau emphasizes the decentralization of administrative functions. The states and territories have been divided into regional areas and each area has its office with a regional consultant staff. Thus, the strength or weakness of the Bureau in its relations with the states depends largely upon the strength or weakness of the regional offices. As far as the health programs are concerned the chief burden rests upon the eight Regional Medical Directors. In the programs for maternal and child health and for crippled children it is the Medical Director who is expected to interpret to the states the policies and the recommendations made by the Bureau. And, in theory at least, the same interpretive role for EMIC was assigned to the Medical Directors.

The Bureau has no direct authority within the states; indirectly, its policies and recommendations derive their strength from financial support and education. The Bureau's policy in the administration of Federal funds for maternal and child health and crippled children shows evidence of great flexibility. In some of the states the programs are well organized, in others they have lagged in organization and in services for a variety of reasons. Yet, over a decade has passed since the adoption of the Social Security Act. The variable progress in the states is mentioned because among so many state health officials the Bureau is credited with being "tough" and uncompromising.

It is within the states that the greatest variety of health administrative policies and mechanisms are found, to say nothing of variable political policies. If these factors introduce complicating elements in long-range programs their effects are multiplied many times when intensive short-range activities are proposed. At one extreme in the range of administration there is the central type of state administration built around and dominated by a single personality. At the other extreme is the decentralized administration with the chief strength in the local areas—cities and counties. Within the states each health department has an advisory committee from the medical profession to consult on maternal and child health services. In some of the states the advisory committees assume a dominant role, in others the committee is rarely called into session. Thus, whatever feature of administration is considered, the complexities are increased by the political and administrative policies within the different states.

The Experience of EMIC

It was into the established channels of the Bureau's administration and, through the Bureau, into the variable channels of state health administration that the functions of EMIC flowed. Had EMIC been a long-range project with relatively slow movement it is likely that the pattern of development would have been comparable to that of the crippled children's program.

Since no one could predict the duration of the war, the numbers in the armed forces or the proportion of those with wives, no precise estimate of the total number of maternity cases and infants that might receive the EMIC services could be made. Even so, the immediate needs and demands for services were greatly underestimated; in the light of what happened, the first appropriation made by Congress was pitiably small. The underestimate is the probable explanation of two features of EMIC that were prominent in the evolution of the program. One was the assumption that EMIC could be fitted into the existing framework of administration, national and state, without any great disruption of the current activities. When, as in 1943, EMIC was conceived and planned only in terms of a six million dollar emergency program[3] such an assumption is understandable and valid.

The second feature relates to the cost of administering EMIC. Again it is the relatively small early estimate of services and costs that established the pattern. Once the estimates and the testimony showed that EMIC could be absorbed by central, regional and state administrations without adding to the overhead costs[4] there developed a resistance in Congress to any appropriations for administration. It was not until EMIC grew to huge proportions that Congress allowed 2½ percent of its over forty million dollar appropriation for the fiscal year ending in 1945 to be expended for state administration. Meanwhile the state administrations had been overwhelmed by the magnitude of the program and in many instances the entire staff of the divisions of maternal and child health could not keep abreast of the rising demands for services.

The urgency of the services made it certain that long-established habits and customs of negotiation, conference and education would be broken. The most common criticism of EMIC that was ex-

[3]Part I, Chapter III, p. 28

[4]Part I, Chapter III, p. 28.

pressed by state health officials dealt with the subject of pressure tactics that surrounded the initiation of the services. While national agencies, such as the Children's Bureau and the American Red Cross, underestimated the demand for services, many state health departments questioned both the demand and the need. As stated by one state health commissioner in an EMIC conference, "We have deferred accepting any of the funds . . . which had been offered to and accepted by a number of the states . . . on the basis that our inquiries indicated that there was no special need for them. . . . They (patients) were either taken care of through welfare or through the activities of the Red Cross or the Army Emergency Relief." The same opinion was expressed in many other states and it influenced the attitude toward the whole program. The pre-EMIC use of the B Fund for the maternity care of the wives of servicemen was regarded as limited to needy cases; EMIC was something that called for an abrupt reversal of medical policy and a new role for the state health departments in their relations with practicing physicians.

The dilemma of the Bureau in getting EMIC started is apparent. As a governmental administrative agency it was in no position to say to state health departments, "Congress is considering an emergency appropriation. We think the appropriation will be approved and, therefore, we suggest that you get ready for the administrative job. Arrange conferences with hospital officials and physicians, etc., etc." This cannot be done with regard to any health appropriation or legislation that is before Congress and it is only following favorable Congressional action that the arrangements to provide services can be made.

Whether the Bureau was wise in the steps taken to achieve speed in the organization of EMIC services can be debated endlessly. To those who argue that more time should have been allowed the answer might be given that the period of gestation does not increase to suit a schedule of conferences and a program of education. And this answer will draw the reply that for other health conditions of a pressing nature, such as venereal disease control, time was taken despite the knowledge that new cases were occurring daily.

As stated, the most prevalent criticism that was expressed by state health officials involved the pressure that was exerted to initiate EMIC. As soon as Congress appropriated funds wide publicity was given to this action. And those entitled to the services were urged to apply to state health departments for the necessary forms and directions. Before the departments had time to adjust to the idea of EMIC, let alone time to prepare forms and procedures, the deluge began. And regardless of whether the pressure consisted of the flood of applications or arose from the American Legion, the Red Cross or other agencies the resentment at being forced into action was directed toward the Children's Bureau.

The evidence is clear that widespread publicity concerning available benefits preceded anything like adequate preparation to administer EMIC and adequate information to health departments, physicians and hospitals. Even so, in some of the states the resistance was great enough to delay the program for months. Whether as little time as a month of preparation and education would have made any noteworthy difference in the attitude is now an academic consideration. From the results of the field study it is felt that even such a short period would have produced a more wholesome response. It is true, also, that without pressure some of the states would still have been deliberating over EMIC on V-J Day.

With the necessity for speed a good deal of confusion was generated inside and outside the Bureau. While the heads of the Bureau insisted that EMIC was only the expansion of an existing service, with the usual formalities of Federal-states relations, lesser officials took the position that the program was Federal. There was much to support the latter opinion in the changed atmosphere that typified the central administration of EMIC.

As EMIC expanded and the problems multiplied, more and more decisions were made in the central office and transmitted to the states. And the early administrative latitude allowed to the states became more narrow for a number of reasons. As will be shown, in some instances the states transmitted requests and proposals that were not in accord with the adopted policies of the Bureau. In a number of cases the proposals arose as a result of medical pressure upon the state health departments and it was easier for a department to put the burden on the Bureau than to take the responsibility of rejection. With each such action a precedent was established by the Bureau and with the increase in precedents the authority of the state diminished. At the same time the state administrators showed a growing disinclination to handle "exceptional cases" on their own responsibility. Many feared that their judgments would not be supported and rather than take chances the cases were referred to the Bureau for decision. This added to the concentration of administrative authority in the central office.

Contributing to the confusion in the minds of state health officials were the changes in required, recommended or suggested policies. Certain inconsistencies needed clarification, certain rulings were made retroactive and policies were changed as they were tested in practice and as experience accumulated. The fact that administration was being learned by a process of trial and error and that in many of its aspects there were inadequate guides, was given little weight by the states as a reason for the changes. And other than going through certain of the routine processes of regional administration the Regional Medical Directors, trained primarily in obstetrics or pediatrics, were overwhelmed. They were faced with the physical tasks of covering large areas, interpreting Bureau policies to the states and serving as channels of communication from the states to the Bureau. For the small number of regional Directors the task was an impossible one.

Considering the above factors and adding to them the national shortage of physicians and the high occupancy rates of the hospitals the most striking feature of EMIC is that the job was done. Through pressure and through centralization, despite much opposition and a lack of enthusiasm in the states, maternity and infant care were provided.

Certain lessons from EMIC are obvious. First, despite much writing on the subject of a national health plan not nearly enough attention has been given to the details of administration. This was demonstrated time after time in the relatively restricted services included under EMIC and will be shown more specifically in succeeding chapters. Neither the Children's Bureau nor any other Federal agency was prepared for an adequate administration of EMIC; the same situation prevailed among state agencies.

The second lesson stresses the value of time and its use prior to any widespread distribution of medical, hospital and other health services. With the most effective use of time a period of from one to two years would not be too long for reasonably adequate preparation. It would be a period when administrative experience would be reviewed and administrative policies prepared and subjected to critical analysis by all groups concerned. At the same time, the period would be used to correct the major administrative defect, the lack of training facilities and of administrative personnel. As a part of the problems of training and personnel much more attention should be given to the question of the agency for state administration in any governmental program. Field interviews elicited the opinion from certain state health officials that some agency other than the health department should have administered EMIC. Whether the same officials still hold this opinion or whether it is widely prevalent is not known.

The third lesson relates to local administration and its role in education and regulation. Effective local administration offers the greatest hope for a program that will be understood by the medical profession, hospital administrators and the beneficiaries of services. Where administrative authority was centralized in a state and was remote from physicians and patients, the difficulties were great. Where the administration was decentralized the attitude was different; as a practicing physician summarized it, "One thing we like about this program is that we can phone our health officer and find out what we are supposed to do." In this connection, if there is any place in the scheme of organization for a regulatory type of board it is at the local level. Such a board, representative of those who provide and those who receive services, is close enough to those who are affected by its regulations to be receptive to public or professional responses. And it offers the medium of communication through which a "grass-roots" reaction to national or state policies may express itself.

A fourth lesson from EMIC is that many of the states contain a cross-section of the problems of the nation. A very common comment from a variety of sources was to the effect that "every state is different and once the funds are granted the state should handle its own problems according to its needs." The statement is not a profound one in terms of the responsibilities that attend the granting of funds but the implication is that state problems can be handled in a simple fashion. An analysis of the kinds of problems that developed and that are discussed later is the best proof that the comment indicates a lack of knowledge of administrative processes and issues. Many who have experienced the problems also endorse grants-in-aid and state responsibility with enthusiasm but it is for reasons other than any assumption that administrative policies will be greatly simplified and administrative complexities will disappear.

Chapter VII

THE BENEFICIARIES OF SERVICES

The phenomenon of change and compromise in a social movement is comparable to the experience of two men who start walking from a given point, one going east and the other west. One man has an imperceptible tendency to pull to the right, the other to the left. Not until they meet face to face is there any realization that they have been moving toward a common destination.

So it is with many of the issues in the broad social movement that involves the health services. Before there can be any productive discussion of the beneficiaries in a health plan or of the experience of EMIC in this area of controversy, it is necessary to review certain issues and the changes in positions and actions during the past 15 years. Much that has occurred shows that apparently conflicting groups have arrived at or are moving toward a common destination. And much that has occurred serves to clarify and classify the current problems in some order of relative importance.

In the United States almost exclusive attention is being given to the financing of medical and hospital care. Nothing is to be gained by deploring what the public and the professional groups conceive to be the primary problem. And less is to be gained by confusing this issue with political philosophies, charges of bad faith or of personal aggrandizement. The use of the draft statistics to prove something and the use of the same statistics to disprove something confuses rather than automatically cancels each claim. The confusions mask the real movement toward satisfactory compromise.

Basic to the existing payment plans is the acceptance and the application of the principle of health insurance or, for those who might quibble over this phrase, sickness insurance. It is but a few years since the principle was a matter of vigorous medical debate. No matter how it might be applied the principle was described as a dangerous innovation, an "entering wedge." The issue was settled in 1934 when the principle received professional endorsement and, as evidence of public approval, resulted in the rapid growth of prepayment under hospital or medical society auspices. Thus, health insurance, per se, is no longer an issue; its value as a dignified way to strengthen the security of the individual and family is accepted.

The existing health insurance plans, particularly those open to the general public provide limited protection. While the limitations in the plans sponsored by hospitals have decreased greatly, the prevailing services in the medical society plans include obstetrical care, usually limited to delivery, and surgery for hospitalized patients. The significant feature, however, is the general agreement that comprehensive services are desirable and should be introduced as soon as proper financing and administrative methods can be developed. Thus, those who continue to insist upon limiting the protection, now and in the future, to what are called "catastrophic illnesses" are opposing the tide of opinion and agreement. There can be no acceptable definition of "medical catastrophe" that does not take into account the economic level of the person or family concerned.

The phrase "national health plan" has served as a powerful semantic stimulant. Its very mention arouses a good or bad response according to the individual's interpretation of its meaning. But, here too, an evolution, an approach toward a common ground, is observable.

When prepayment received official professional endorsement it was emphasized that its application should be localized. Experience in Michigan and California pointed to the desirability of state programs and professional approval followed the demonstrations. Some time later, in 1946, after it became evident that state bounderies were artificial barriers to the future success of the health insurance schemes professional support was given to a national health plan. As stated previously, to further this development a central office was established in Chicago under the auspices of the Associated Medical Care Plans, Inc., to integrate the activities of state and local plans and to evolve a national medical program. As a precedent to this step, the American Hospital Association had created an agency to integrate the work of the Blue Cross hospital plans.

These, then, are matters that at one time or another were critical issues; today they are approaching or are within the area of general accord.

Probably the most debated current subject in the whole field of medical care is compulsory versus voluntary health insurance. The impression is given that here is a choice as sharply defined as black or white; there is no possibility of blend, no common ground, no compromise. Surrounding the whole subject is an extraordinary flow of rhetoric and emotion. The issue is often described as the keystone of an arch; if it is moved by so much as a millimeter the existing structure of medicine will collapse. What calls for critical analysis is the implication that it has not moved, that this issue, unlike others, shows no evolutionary changes.

When the hospital plans were first organized the promotional and sales activities were directed wholly at employed groups. In some instances any employer contribution, other than moral support, was opposed as a violation of the principle of voluntary acceptance or rejection of hospital prepayment by employees. The change from this policy is impressive. Both the hospital and the medical plans have recognized and have stated frankly that employer contributions are a vital element if the plans are to grow on a sound basis. In accordance with this policy the percentage of employer contributors has been increasing from year to year.

It may be said that this is no deviation from any previous stand, that it means only that employers voluntarily participate in a plan. But what about the contracts resulting from the bargaining between management and labor that specify that the employer shall pay all or a part of a health insurance cost? Whatever title may be given to this type of pressure the element of compulsion is there. Most significant, when a group of employees has obtained concessions in the form of medical or hospital services, or both, by the legal process of collective bargaining the voluntary plans regard such a group as an attractive addition to their lists of beneficiaries.

As stated recently by a medical leader, in reference to the Health and Welfare Fund of the United Mine Workers, "The American Medical Association has offered to cooperate in working out a plan which would be satisfactory to all concerned. . . . Health funds will probably be a factor in future collective bargaining."[1] The conclusions that may be drawn are that compulsory payment, per se, has become less of an issue or, at the least, that it should be classified as of two types of compulsion, good and bad or acceptable and non-acceptable. There is no logical alternative to the accumulation of evidence that while the theory of compulsion is resisted with vigor the applications of compulsion are being accepted.

Adding weight to the above choice of conclusions is the professional support given to Senate Bill 545 introduced by Senators Taft, Smith, Ball and Donnell. Among other features the bill provides for Federal grants-in-aid to the states for medical, hospital and other services to people unable to pay the costs of their needs. Senator Taft estimates a population of 28 to 35 million, about 20

[1]Bauer, Louis H., *Private Enterprise or Government in Medicine.* Charles C. Thomas, Springfield, Ill. p. 130, 131.

to 25 percent of the total, in this unfortunate position.[2] From other sources the estimates are higher but the important feature of the bill and especially of its endorsement is that tax funds are involved as a subsidy from the Federal Government to states to organize and distribute medical, hospital and other services. With the above population estimates it cannot be assumed that the medical profession interprets the bill as providing care only for those on welfare rolls. Nor can it be assumed that anyone would call Federal tax funds "voluntary."

Those engrossed in controversy and conflict are inattentive to or have missed the most striking feature of the past decade. The earlier picture of opposing groups separated by "Grand Canyons" of differing opinions has changed. One by one many of the important differences have been resolved or narrowed. Today the "key log" in the medical economic jam is not the one of compulsion versus volition; it is the one called the "means test." In a dozen ways and forms the means test presented itself as a problem in the administration of EMIC.

The Means Test

The means test, as an issue in medical care, represents both a measurement and an economic philosophy or tradition. As a measurement, and in its most common historical application in the United States, the means test is a formula whereby social agencies, public or private, accept or reject applicants for aid. Whatever the aid—food, clothing, medical care—the evidence of inadequate "means" to obtain what is regarded as a need is basic to any "relief" that may be provided. The test of means comprises both the evidence and its evaluation and there are different tests for various needs. The help a person or family receives is provided on a basis of what may be called a "sliding scale," that is, the relief given is the difference between the person's or family's available resources and the costs.

As a welfare device the use of the means test, as a preliminary step to the granting of relief, is somethig that the average person regards as a social penalty for failure, whatever may be the cause of the failure. There is a psychological resistance to any form of means test because of its association with failure and with charity. This is especially so whenever a group to which a means test is applied is set aside as a minority.

2Research Council for Economic Security. *The National Health and S. 545.* p. 8.

What does all this have to do with the medical and hospital care of people who are not receiving any of the usual kinds of public assistance, who are employed, who regard themselves and are regarded as self-supporting members of their communities? Particularly, what relation has it to the desire for future protection against the costs of medical and hospital care when an employed person or a member of his family becomes ill? The answers may be found in certain customs and traditions that are associated with the practice of medicine.

The statement that necessary medical care should be available to all people regardless of their ability to pay, or their means, expresses the traditional position of the medical profession. To make the principle work, physicians are expected to adjust their fees to fit the means of the patient. The method was a fairly effective device when, as in the earlier scope of medical care, the costs were limited, largely, to those for the services of physicians. The sliding scale of fees was informal and private; it depended upon the physician's impressions and judgment; under earlier conditions it was regarded as a solution of the major medical economic problem.

The conditions have changed; the tradition remains. Industrialization has brought dramatic social and economic changes in urban and rural living and no less dramatic have been the changes and the growing complexity of personnel and institutions providing medical care. And throughout the growth and the attempts to cope with the problems of distributing services, the means test and the sliding scale of fees have persisted as confusing elements. The following appear to be the realities with regard to these elements:

1. To make the sliding scale a workable instrument it would be necessary for each practicing physician to include among his clientele a cross-section of all income groups, from the lowest to the highest. Further, there would need to be enough patients from the high income groups whose high fees would balance the low fees or the free service to the low income groups.

No detailed statistical study is needed to show that neither of these situations is descriptive of a cross-section of modern medical practice. The data on population income during past periods of prosperity refute any assumption that there are enough people of high income to counterbalance the great number of those with lower incomes. As to the future, there is little evidence to change this view. In a recent publication it is pointed out that a $2,500 income in 1950 may be expected to have the purchasing power of a $2,000 income in 1941.[3] Those "consumer units" with annual incomes above $5,000 will also pay the bulk of the income taxes. For families with two or more persons the estimates of the percentages in the various income groups in 1950, assuming "high levels of activity," are as follows:[4]

Income Class	Percent of Families
Under $ 500	7
500 - 1000	12
1000 - 1500	13
1500 - 2000	13
2000 - 3000	24
3000 - 5000	21
Over 5000	10

Thus, in the future as well as in the past no more than one-tenth of the families would be in the highest income group.

2. Probably the most important and, at the same time, the least publicized and least considered element in the theory of the sliding scale is the attraction by a relatively small percentage of physicians of those families or single persons in the higher income groups. The phenomenon results in the limitation of the practices of the great majority of physicians to those families or persons with annual incomes below $5,000 and, for many physicians, to the income groups below $3,000. This situation, more than any other, is responsible for the lack of solid progress toward an acceptable compromise of the differences with regards to means tests. And the regrettable fact is that there are so few tangible data about it.

For example, Physician A practices in a given community and the *majority* of his patients come from the "over $5,000" income group. Physician B, in the same field of medical practice, and in the same community, derives his patients from the self-supporting groups with annual incomes below $3,000. There is a very prevalent and, it is suspected, an erroneous assumption that the *average* fees of the two men for a specified service would show an extremely large difference. While, information on the subject is very limited it points to the fact that the averages of the two physicians for a service, such as maternity care, are not extremely different. It is not unusual to hear an obstetrician say, with some amazement, that when his income is divided by all of his cases—free, part-pay and full-pay—the result is an average income per case that is about or

3Dewhurst, J. Frederic and Associates. *America's Needs and Resources.* Twentieth Century Fund, New York, 1947. p. 66.

4Ibid. p. 67.

below the fee suggested by the county medical society. Thus, while an average for Physician A, with a majority but by no means all of his patients coming from the high-income group, might be $60 for a specified service, that of Physician B would amount to $40. The confusing element is that neither physician thinks in terms of averages. Physician A, considering his position with respect to a prepayment plan, is unwilling to relinquish the privilege of charging $300 to a few cases or $500 in an extremely rare instance. And Physician B, looking toward the future with hope, questions a proposal that may limit his economic opportunity. As will be shown later the resistance has little to do with who makes the proposal for prepayment, i. e., whether it is made by a government agency or a voluntary prepayment plan.

As the situation now stands those who oppose any application of a means test take the position that prepayment should offer full protection for all income groups, from the lowest to the highest. Against this position is the one that prepayment should offer full protection to low-income groups and only partial protection to those with higher incomes. Reduced to its bare elements, the issue is where to draw the line, if any, in the scale of incomes.

Governmental Services and the Means Test

For certain health or medical services provided by or through governmental agencies relatively little or no attention is paid to the means test. Examples are the services for tuberculosis and mental illness. In more recent years the services for crippled children have expanded through the use of Federal grants to states and here, too, the chief consideration, within the limits of the combined Federal and state funds, is medical need rather than economic status.

Probably the most widespread as well as the most comprehensive current medical program that excludes any means test is that of the Veterans' Administration. For service-connected illness the veteran's medical need is the primary concern. This is true whether the services are obtained in a veteran's hospital or, under a new plan, in "home town" private offices or institutions. Veterans, however, make up a special group as far as the usual obligations and operation of a governmental medical program are concerned.

The fact must be recognized and accepted that, as a rule, there is a certain odium attached to public medical service and, especially, to the public clinic. Whether the latter is supported by private or public funds the tendency to think of it as a place for the treatment of the poor is prevalent. Even when there is no attention paid to a means test this tendency serves as a deterrent to the use of the facilities. Thus, toward anything that has or is interpreted as having about it an atmosphere of charity the means test is self-applied. Its automatic effects in curtailing the use of the clinic by self-supporting groups is the same as if the test were official. Nor does this reaction express itself only toward the public clinic. It is exhibited, though perhaps less vigorously, toward charity services that may be rendered privately. Regardless of how or where services are obtained any system whereby the individual needing care must present proof of inability to pay is looked upon as a last resort.

In EMIC, why were the early estimates of the number of deliveries so much lower than the experience? To be sure, they were based upon the number of cases that had applied for aid to the Red Cross, to health departments or other organizations. However, these were largely cases that had no other recourse than an appeal for aid. Nothing in EMIC was to give even an impression of charity, yet the estimates were far too low. No dogmatic answer to the question can be given but the early calculations took it for granted that 25 percent of those entitled to the services would ask for them.[5] Later the estimate was raised to between 75 and 85 percent with the probability mentioned that it might be higher. In effect, even those who planned EMIC were conditioned by past experience with the public tendency to self-apply the means test.

What happened is seen in the story of the appropriations. Here was a different public response to publicly financed medical services, a reversal of previous experience. As one physician in New York stated, he was "surprised at the people who accepted the services of EMIC." He was referring to those patients in his community who had never even thought of accepting "charity."

The interpretation of why so many patients sought the services of EMIC will never be unanimous. Some will hold that it is a sign of deteriorating moral fibre, an example of an urge to get something for nothing. Others, looking for distinct differences between this program and the usual expenditures for public medical services, will note a combination of two new factors. First, there was no means test for those included in the scheme and the medical care was regarded as "purchased" by reason of service in the armed forces. Second, and equally important, it was a majority group that was entitled to care, not a minority. The people entitled to care constituted an estimated 75 percent of the Navy and 87 percent of the Army

[5]Part I, Chapter III, p. 32.

personnel.[6] Neither of the factors that make up the significant compound has about it any tinge of social failure.

Non-Governmental Services and the Means Test

It was said that the means test is a blocking issue regardless of the source of any proposal to eliminate it or to arrive at some compromise. That the test and the sliding scale of fees are parts of the voluntary health insurance plans of medical societies is self-evident. The usual policy is to establish an income limit for the beneficiaries of the services included in a medical society plan. A fee schedule is adopted, setting forth the amounts that the plan will pay to participating physicians for specified services. The physicians agree to render the services in the plan without any added charge if the beneficiary has an income below the established limit. If the beneficiary has an income above the limit, the physician receives from the plan the fee that is specified in the schedule and is also permitted to charge the patient an additional fee. The size of the additional fee is a matter of private arrangement between the physician and his patient. Thus, the means test and the sliding scale are important elements in the great majority of the present voluntary medical plans.

The general pattern of the annual family income limits adopted by the plans shows the level to be at $2,500 to $3,000. They may be as low as $2,000 or as high as $4,000. Since the method of arriving at a family income is usually difficult the plans tend to leave the judgment as to whether a particular family is above or below the limit to the physician. The arrangement is a loose one and causes some bewilderment and criticism. In the same family one physician may render service without any added charge, another physician may make such a charge. There is nothing to show that the first physician was right and the second physician made on overcharge, but there is much to show that such errors of judgment will occur when an arbitrary income level has millions of families close to both sides of the line of division. Family income and individual or family ability to pay are complex matters that cannot be analyzed by a few simple questions or determined by snap judgment.

The commercial insurance companies are affected, also, by the means test and the sliding scale. As a rule the company sells to beneficiaries a contract that provides for a certain amount of cash for a specified service. How much may be charged for the service depends upon the physician that the patient chooses. And not until a need arises does a beneficiary know the extent of the protection

6EMIC Conference, Washington, November 18, 1944.

that he has purchased. In at least one instance, as an attempt to correct this defect, the commercial companies requested a state medical society to accept a standard fee schedule for single persons with incomes below $3,000, husbands and wives, below $4,000 and families (husbands, wives and dependents under 18) below $5,000. The proposal was rejected after a poll of physicians' opinions.

With the voluntary hospital plans the issue of the means test is not prominent. Though many hospitals provide charity services of one type or another, for full-pay patients there is no general tradition of a variable or sliding scale of charges for the same service. A hospital may charge a lower rate for the use of the operating room by a ward patient, many hospitals charge lower rates to government welfare agencies but under the pressure of meeting the costs of operation these customs are being replaced by a more realistic and business-like policy. Primarily, the variable charges in a hospital are based upon the choice of accommodations—private or semi-private rooms or ward beds.

In connection with the choice of a particular income limit by a voluntary medical plan the phrase "ability to pay" appears often. Its use and application to describe the purpose of a plan have never been defined clearly. Ability of subscribers to pay for what? Does it mean the ability to pay for protection against medical need? Or does it mean ability to pay added fees if and when the contingency arises? Presumably, those regarded as able to pay added fees would be in a position, also, to purchase more than partial protection. It may be held that a limit of $2,500 or $3,000 permits the adoption of lower rates to subscribers but, with the emphasis upon employer contributions and government subsidies to the low-income groups, it can be argued that a higher and more protective income level would permit a higher scale of fees to physicians. Pervading the whole subject is the impression of something inherently bad in the purchase of full protection and something innately good in added fees to be paid when illness occurs.

EMIC and the Means Test

The opposition of the Children's Bureau to the means test is part of a long-standing policy. An increasing number of mothers and children have been aided through the service and educational programs of the Bureau and the state and local health departments. The most successful elimination of the means test is seen in the services for crippled children, in a number of the states, but as already stated, only a small part of the population and a small percentage of physicians are involved.

In the earlier hearings on appropriations before the Congressional committees there was some tendency by committee members to associate EMIC with a form of public relief. Among the reasons for rejecting the first request of the Bureau for $1,200,000 is the statement by the Committee on Appropriations that "There is no requirement of lack of financial ability as prerequisite to the benefits."[7] When, later, the request for $4,800,000 was being considered one committee member expressed a strong conviction that "the regulations should limit these expenditures to those who are actually in need of this assistance. . . ."[8] After it was decided that EMIC was "an expression of gratitude" there were no further references by the members of Congress to a means test, as such. But indirectly there were many issues raised in and out of Congress that are related to this subject.

In the states it was difficult for the health departments to make a quick adjustment to the new policy. Prior to EMIC the funds from the Children's Bureau for the obstetrical care of the wives of servicemen had been expended for the needy cases; with the initiation of EMIC the underlying basis or qualification for maternity and infant care changed. In some of the earlier plans submitted to the Bureau by the states and in some of the application forms there were statements or implications that EMIC was intended for the low-income group of cases. The directives from the Bureau were clear but custom confused the interpretations.

The responses of the medical profession were variable. In general, EMIC was endorsed as a wartime effort by the American Medical Association and by the state societies but there were reservations concerning the administrative policies and methods. While the means test and the sliding scale were prominent issues they were not clearly and sharply defined—just as they are not clearly and sharply defined in the voluntary plans. In the Congressional hearings, at the meetings of the advisory committees of the Children's Bureau and in the field interviews the subject of paying a cash allotment to an expectant mother and having her make her own arrangements for hospital and medical services was discussed time after time. This was the recommendation by the American Medical Association and it was offered by state medical societies in formal resolutions. The suggestion was opposed by the American Legion, the National Congress of Parents and Teachers, the YWCA and various labor organizations. Those who spoke for the medical profession in favor of cash allotments to expectant mothers were resentful of any im-

7U. S. Congress. House of Representatives. Report of Committee on Appropriations, February 24, 1943. p. 6.

8Hearings on Appropriation Bill for 1944. H. R. 2935, April 17, 1943. p. 250.

plication that the issue was the schedule of fees to be paid for services. Dr. W. W. Bauer speaking for the American Medical Association stated that the resolution recommending cash allotments had nothing to do with the amounts allotted. "The problem in the mind of the medical profession is the problem of Federal control and the feeling that there is not sufficient opportunity for the program to be controlled in the states where it serves and where the needs of the locality are best known."[9] On the other hand, the resolution from the Minnesota State Medical Association recommended a cash allotment of $100 for the physician's services in a maternity case or double the amount being paid.[10]

Some of the state plans submitted for Bureau approval included proposals for cash allotments and others would have permitted patients to pay supplementary fees to physicians and hospitals. Based upon the interpretations of the purpose of the appropriations by Congress and supported by the opinion from the Solicitor's Office all such proposals were rejected. Why the states prepared plans containing policies contrary to the established rules is clear in certain cases. Rejection was anticipated but it was easier to put the burden on the Bureau rather than refuse what a state medical advisory committee had suggested.

Although the means test appears throughout EMIC as a controversial element it is a mistake to describe the program as completely lacking any such device. The exclusion of the first three pay grades constitutes an automatic means test. For the Army this meant that the line was drawn to include about 87 percent of the "population" and exclude 13 percent on the basis of income. With such a great majority included in EMIC, the program did not experience the usual public reaction toward publicly supported or "free" medical service.

In subsequent chapters it will be noted that the means test and the sliding scale of fees appear as underlying factors in issues that arose and in decisions that were made. Despite the tendency to postpone facing these problems there is a certain inexorability in the way they continue to obtrude themselves and to occupy the center of the medical economic stage. The proposal by Senator Taft and his colleagues (S. 545), if adopted, will call for decisions in the states. Meanwhile the voluntary medical plans face the same problems; how they settle them in terms of solutions that are satisfactory to the medical profession and are in accord with the realities of public income and public need will serve as a positive test of professional statesmanship.

9Testimony on H. R. 4899, April 27, 1944. p. 508.
10Ibid., p. 519.

Chapter VIII

PAYMENT FOR PHYSICIANS' SERVICES—POLICIES, METHODS AND PROBLEMS

The problems of payment for services are not new; the fact that they could not be pushed into the background and had to be faced in terms of decisive action is what gives EMIC its value as a laboratory of experience. It is in the payment of physicians that the greatest difficulties arise because of the number of elements that must be considered. In presenting the subject of payment to physicians four major factors will be discussed. These are (1) the source of payment, (2) the route of payment, (3) the form of payment and (4) the amount of payment. Payment to hospitals will be considered later.

Payment to Physicians: The Source of Payment

Payment for medical services may come from one of two sources or from both. The patient may pay from his own resources which may include his savings or those of the family, through loans or by installment payments over a period of time from earnings. Or, payment may be made by an agency designed to meet the problem. The agency may be non-governmental or governmental, such as a welfare organization or as in EMIC, the state health department. In the non-governmental group would be included all of the private philanthropic agencies for services to the relief and low-income families and the many prepayment plans devised by industry, medical groups, hospitals, medical societies, insurance companies and others. As discussed in the preceding chapter, payment may come from a combination of the sources with an agency paying a portion of the bill and the patient paying the remainder. The combination would include, also, those instances where a patient makes a "partial payment" to a physician and the physician contributes according to his concept of or ability to apply the sliding scale of fees.

On the surface the facts regarding the source of payment do not appear to suggest complex problems; actually they are responsible for many complications. Since the trend is toward payment by an agency the discussion will deal in the main with this source.

As soon as the source of payment shifts from the patient to an agency the many loose and informal arrangements that have existed must be formalized as written policies, rules and regulations. The policies, rules and regulations may be broad and flexible or they may be rigid and cover or try to cover every situation that may arise. However, the general process of preparing policies and rules is the inevitable accompaniment of any form of organized payment whether it be through a government agency, a commercial insurance company or a medical society plan.

Another complicating factor is the attitude of the average physician toward the paying agency. If the agency is a prepayment plan organized by the medical society he is much less critical of administrative policies and procedures than in the case of a government agency. Nominally, at least, he is one of a group that sponsors a medical society plan and any criticism of the way it works is a matter for society consideration rather than public expression. In the final analysis he regards it as "his" plan and subject to his control. And especially on many of the most crucial issues of payment his society plan offers an automatic solution in the proviso that supplementary fees may be charged to patients with incomes above a specified limit.

When the source of payment is a government agency the profession is inclined to view policies and rules with suspicion. All actions are under close scrutiny and all proposals are analyzed critically. There is a fear of domination, particularly Federal domination, and of the encroachment of government upon the rights and privileges of private practice. The resulting atmosphere that surrounds the conferences to clarify issues and reach compromises is heavily charged with suspicion that begets friction. And the final result is an emphasis upon what is wrong with rather than what may be right about the program.

EMIC offers an interesting example of the shift from informal private-practice arrangements for payment to formal written policies. At the same time the example demonstrates the manner in which a program expands rapidly, as in the case of EMIC, or more slowly, as in the medical society plans.

When a physician accepts a maternity patient in private practice for antepartum services, delivery and postpartum care at an agreed-upon fee he knows that certain situations may arise. The great majority of patients will need the usual or "normal" services but a certain number will develop complications of pregnancy that necessitate a greater amount of or more difficult treatment. The physician may or may not increase the fee for the more complex case. But other conditions, unrelated to the pregnancy, may occur and call for surgical, radiological or other services at an added expense to the patient.

When the B funds were being used prior to EMIC little thought was given to added payment for complicated cases or to unrelated conditions that might arise during the period of gestation or the six weeks period following delivery. In a memorandum issued May, 1942 to the state health agencies the Children's Bureau stated, "Thirty-five dollars ($35) might be agreed upon as the state rate for payment to the attending physician for complete medical service during the prenatal period, including at least five prenatal examinations, and also for labor, for the puerperium (including the care of the newborn infant) and for postpartum examinations." While the directive stated that the fee should cover "complete medical care" it did not explain whether complications of pregnancy were to be included and it made no mention of the treatment of illness unrelated to pregnancy. As a demonstration that nothing can be taken for granted when policies are being written, not even what are assumed to be established customs, the expressed policy resulted in a good deal of confusion. Questions were raised by physicians as to whether the policy permitted added government compensation for complicated cases or gave them the privilege of charging the patient for extra care. The omission of any reference to unrelated illnesses made it clear that they should be excluded from the organized payment for services.

On the subject of complications the Bureau clarified the issue in a pre-EMIC memorandum dated January 1, 1943 with the statement that "Payment should be made on a case basis. . . . Inclusive rates for complete medical service during the prenatal period, labor, and the puerperium, including at least five prenatal examinations, for complications or operations, for care of the newborn infant and postpartum examinations should be established by each state health agency." Thus, it was made apparent that payment for complications of pregnancy was to be covered by the inclusive fee for the case. The policy was issued over three months prior to the creation of EMIC and at a time when limited funds made it necessary to select cases on a basis of need. During the course of EMIC and with only minor revisions the policy remained in force.

No official action was taken on conditions unrelated to pregnancy or, as they were called later, "intercurrent non-obstetric conditions." But the pre-EMIC period had demonstrated that among the cases authorized for maternity care there arose frequently a need of service for such conditions. When the need occurred the economic burden fell upon the patient, or, if the patient had no means, upon the physician who provided the service or upon a relief agency. If a relief agency were brought into the case it meant that two sources of funds had to be used. In March, 1943, after the first appropriation for EMIC, *Information Circular No. 13* gave some recognition to the problem.

The circular stated that, "As the need arises fee schedules for non-obstetric surgery and specialized consultant service should be considered by the State health agency in conference with a technical advisory committee selected and appointed by the State health agency." While this instruction left the door open for payment for non-obstetric intercurrent conditions it did not constitute a clear cut directive to do so, and some confusion remained regarding this problem. It was not until the issuance of EMIC *Information Circular No. 1* in December, 1943 that the policy of the Bureau was stated as follows: "Complete maternity care: For 'complete maternity care,' that is all services rendered by the attending physician (1) to the mother during pregnancy, labor, and the postpartum period from the effective date of the authorization until 6 weeks after termination of pregnancy, *including office treatment of intercurrent conditions whether attributable to pregnancy or not,* and (2) to the infant during the first 2 weeks of life: the rate of payment as established by the State health agency, but not to exceed $50. . . . Additional payments may be authorized by the state or local agency to attending physicians who qualify as consultants in a surgical specialty, for major, non-obstetric surgical operations needed during pregnancy and 6 weeks postpartum for *conditions not attributable to pregnancy:* At a rate established by the State health agency but not to exceed a total of $50 for pre-operative, operative, and post-operative care. . . . Additional payments for the attending physicians' services may be authorized by the state or local health agency during pregnancy and 6 weeks postpartum for the home or hospital treatment of *intercurrent conditions not attributable to pregnancy, which do not require major surgery.*"

With this statement of policy it became clear that the EMIC program was to pay for *all* health services required by those eligible for care under the program during the period of pregnancy. Thus, the patient was assured of the right to receive, without cost to herself or her family, all medical and hospital care needed from the time of the authorization of maternity care until six weeks after delivery, and the care of her infant during the first year of life. With this clarification of policy there no longer remained any problem as to the responsibility for payment; it rested entirely with the program.

The same trend toward expansion as exhibited by EMIC is discernible in the voluntary medical and hospital plans and constitutes a very significant evolutionary process. Certain of the medical plans that limited maternity services to the delivery and post-delivery care in a hospital have included prenatal care; the surgical limitation to hospitalized patients has expanded to include surgery in the physician's office. Particularly among the hospital plans, many of the earlier limitations have been deleted from the contracts for services. Apparently one of the most consistent characteristics of any organized program of payment is the tendency to include more and more services.

One other aspect of the source of payment is assuming greater and greater importance. Suggestions have been made that tax funds for medical and hospital care be expended through existing agencies such as the voluntary health insurance plans. The issue arose in EMIC when the Michigan State Medical Society proposed that Michigan Medical Service, a prepayment plan sponsored by the society, be designated as the agency of the government to pay individual physicians for EMIC cases. According to the proposal, physicians would bill the Michigan Medical Service which, in turn, would bill the State Health Department periodically for the care of EMIC patients. The plan was urged upon the Bureau by the medical society with the nominal support of the Division of Maternal and Child Health of the Michigan State Department of Health. The proposal was rejected when the Solicitor of the Department of Labor ruled that it was illegal for a non-governmental agency to disburse Federal grants-in-aid. The medical society protested but the ruling was not reversed.

Apparently there are differences of legal opinion on the subject of a non-governmental agency disbursing tax funds. The Veterans' Administration in its program of "home town care" by local physicians and hospitals uses the various medical and hospital plans as disbursing agencies. And the previously mentioned Senate Bill 545 provides that such plans may be utilized as administrative mechanisms by the states. According to the statements of many medical leaders there is much enthusiasm behind the proposals to use medical and hospital plans as agencies to administer Federal and state funds for medical care. How much of the enthusiasm is based upon realistic projections into the future is not known but it would seem that a measure of caution is indicated.

Assuming that their use is legal there are two ways in which the existing voluntary plans may function. One is to receive and pay bills for services on a "cost-plus" basis. The procedure may be a dangerous one both for the government agency that is responsible for expenditures and the voluntary plan that serves as the intermediary. Cost-plus is usually under suspicion as an uneconomic way of expending funds; it provides little inherent incentive for careful administration and a consistent and rigid review of bills rendered. Ultimately the government agency must show that its spending methods are not loose and, therefore, what may start as a cost-plus arrangement undergoes changes. The government agency may adopt and apply control methods, or what amounts to the same thing, insist that the disbursing plan perform these functions.

The other way that an existing plan may be used would require an agreement between the plan and the government whereby the plan, for a specified sum per beneficiary, would guarantee that necessary services would be rendered. Such a contract could not have been written on a state or local basis for EMIC or for veterans because in neither instance is there adequate knowledge of the number of potential beneficiaries for a specific period of time. But this lack does not obtain, as examples, for the recipients of old-age assistance and other relief categories or for a defined low-income group.

A contract to guarantee services at a specified annual payment per person would require a readjustment of the great majority of voluntary plans. For a relief population it would be necessary for a plan with limited services such as surgical and obstetrical care in hospitals, to provide comprehensive services. And, above all, the subject of adequate controls* would need much more serious attention. These are some of the reasons for the statement about "realistic projections into the future."

Route of Payment

Major changes have taken place in the route of payment. Where, formerly, the patient made a direct payment to the physician the introduction of paying agencies, such as the prepayment plans and the EMIC program, has brought its own series of issues. Among these the chief one involves payment by an agency to the patient, who, in turn, is expected to pay the physician or payment by the agency directly to the physician.

To the public the controversy over the route of payment is something of a mystery. As the layman sees it, the important thing is that the physician be paid and when heated arguments about the

*Discussed in Chapter X.

route of payment are given a prominent position it is interpreted as "arguing over technicalities." Yet, to the physician, both the source and the route of payment are matters of deep concern. Some are inclined toward the view that the concern is comparable to a child's fear of darkness—and try to counter it with soothing expressions and vague assurances.

When the average practicing physician is asked why he objects to a shift of payment from the patient to an agency the usual response is difficult to analyze. His fears and his opposition are expressed in such terms as "regimintation of the profession" and the bad effects on the "physician-patient relationship." In discussing the EMIC program an official of a medical society in one of the states included in the study stressed the importance of the direct financial relation between physicians and patients. He said, "Should this link be removed, the feeling of responsibility and the sense of understanding between physician and patient would disappear. The patient would lose confidence in the physician and the physician would lose interest in the patient." While many would disagree with this opinion it is a very prevalent one. Interviews with many physicians support their opinion that a direct financial tie is an essential element in the physician-patient relationship.

Interesting enough, the above comment was made by an official in a state where a medical society plan is in operation. For services to patients with incomes below the limit established by the plan a direct payment is made to physicians, bypassing the patient. But the official was talking about EMIC, not the state society plan, and his comments and those of many others indicate the degree to which the source of payment affects the professional viewpoint in those states where the medical societies operate the service type of prepayment plans.

The "service type" of plan has been mentioned. It was described in Chapter VII in the discussion of the means test and consists of a guarantee of services to beneficiaries below a specified income. Above the income the physician may charge a supplementary fee. As against the more common service plans, there is the "cash indemnity" plan where all patients, regardless of income, are assured cash for specified services. The patient makes his own financial arrangements for services and the cash from the plan may be paid to the patient or the latter may assign the cash amount to the physician who renders the service. Thus, the route of payment in the existing plans presents a confusion of policies.

Administratively it makes a vast difference whether the agency makes a payment to the patient or directly to the physician. When cash is paid to the patient the agency is limited to the performance of certain fiscal functions. All it can do is determine eligibility to receive service, verify the fact that the service has been received and issue payment according to its contract. The physician comes into the transaction only to verify that service was rendered. He is not bound by any fee schedule and the agency has no adequate way to control the quality or quantity of services. To be sure, the administration of cash payment to patients is less complex than the administration of services to patients. As will be discussed in Chapter X, service administration requires attention to standards relative to quantity and quality of services, techniques to assure that the patient receives what has been purchased and methods to assure reasonably adequate payment to physicians and institutions.

Basically the confusion regarding the route of payment may be attributed to the "normal" process of change. It is never a simple matter to discard or change a tradition and those who are interested in administrative methods recognize and adjust to the fact that the process takes time. The EMIC policy concerning the route of payment brought out and settled, temporarily and arbitrarily, a primary issue that has been growing more acute within the medical profession—the issue of the means test and the sliding scale. For the patients in EMIC there was to be no means test, the sliding scale was eliminated and the route of payment was from the agency to the physician.

Some medical societies refused to participate in the EMIC program. As an example, the society in Sacramento County, California, was so vigorously opposed that it adopted a resolution stating its antagonism to the source of funds and, further, that maternity and pediatric care to the wives and infants of servicemen would be given without charge by the members of the society. Subsequent experience showed that making the resolution work was another matter. As the load of what would have been EMIC cases increased, the burden of the free care concentrated upon a very small minority of the practicing physicians. Unable to devise ways to assure a reasonable diffusion of the burden on a basis of free service, the society abandoned its earlier position.

Form of Payment

Three forms of payment to individual physicians are found in the various systems of medical care. They are (1) fees-for-services, (2) capitation payments and (3) salaries. While variations may be in use each is attached to one of the above forms.

In the United States the prevailing form of payment is the fee-for-service. It is the most firmly established form and through it the physician receives compensation according to each service that is rendered. The fee-for-service is the basis of private practice; it is the form of payment used by the great majority of voluntary plans; it is the form that is chosen and demanded by an overwhelming majority of physicians.

A common variation of the fee-for-service, and the one used in EMIC, is the fee-per-case or the case-payment. In this form the physician agrees to combine certain different types of services for a single payment. In maternity care the services include prenatal examinations, delivery and postpartum care. The method is no great departure from the one that prevails in private practice where no agency is involved in the payment. Nor is it unusual to find it applied to other than maternity cases. The voluntary plans use it in paying for surgical cases even though a specific type of case, such as an appendectomy, may require a greater or lesser number of services.

The second form of compensating individual physicians, the capitation payment, has had little application in the United States.* It is a method of paying for general practitioners' services. Those who are in a scheme of payment choose their physicians and the physician is paid at a flat monthly, quarterly or annual rate for each person on his list. Regardless of how little or how much service a person receives the payment to the physician does not vary. Because it is such a departure from the customary form of payment any mention of the capitation fee excites a strong adverse response from the medical profession.

Under the conditions of practice in this country it is unlikely that, aside from professional antagonism, the capitation fee could be applied as a workable method of paying for general practitioners' services. The measure of success that it has had in England is attributable, in large part, to the single fact that *only general practitioners' services* are included in the British scheme of health insurance.

In the United States three features of medical practice operate against the use of capitation payment. The first is the difficulty of a precise definition of "general practice," the second is the unlikelihood of all general practitioners providing all of the services that would be included in such a definition and the third one is the fact

*In certain areas the capitation form of payment is used to compensate *groups* of physicians for relatively comprehensive medical services. In the above discussion the emphasis is upon payment to *individual* physicians.

that in so many instances the same physician would provide both general and special services. Thus the same physician would be compensated on a capitation basis for some services and on a fee basis for others. And in so many cases it would be his own diagnosis that would determine whether his service would be covered by the flat payment or by added fees for "special" service. When, unlike the British scheme, an agency must pay for both types of services, the problems of control appear even greater than the administrative complexities that accompany a system of fees for all types of services that are included.

The third form of payment is the part-time or full-time salary for the physician. It is used only for a minor portion of the services that are distributed in the United States. As a variant of the salary, payment "per clinic" or "per clinic hour" is the method used for certain services. As a rule the full-time salary form of payment, exclusive of medical administrative personnel, is found in institutions such as those for tuberculosis and mental cases, in industrial medical service plans, in the combined group practice and group payment organizations and in cooperative medical services. As with the capitation payment, medical resistance to proposals for salary payment is great.

The conclusion is inevitable that, whatever may be the form of payment in some distant future, the problems of the present and for any forseeable period are those that attend the fee-for-service payment. To say that this method is the choice of the medical profession is to put it mildly. Yet the administration of a fee-for-service system in a manner that is equitable both to physicians and beneficiaries has been given little critical attention. Too much energy has been expended in debates on the form of payment; too little objective study has been given to how this choice of payment may be applied successfully.

Amount of Payment

It is the fourth aspect of payment, the amount, that affects each physician in a way that is specific and tangible. Even on this subject, as was indicated in the discussion of the means test and sliding scale, the measurement of the adequacy of a particular fee is anything but precise. Within his own practice it is unusual for a physician to work out an average fee for a particular service, such as maternity care. Since any agency that pays on a basis of fees-for-services must adopt a schedule of fees, the physician with little knowledge of his own averages cannot make direct comparisons. He may make a comparison of the proposed schedule with one adopted as a general guide by the county medical society. But the guide is not nearly as specific as the proposed schedule; many of the items suggest what should be basic fees and may carry the phrase "and up." Hence, when a schedule is proposed there is a tendency to compare its items with the highest fees that are remembered rather than the average fees received.

It is in the preparation of a fee schedule for a state or for the nation that there arise the many perplexing problems that are inherent in current medical practices. As it is now, the following situations affect the amount of payment; they are presented as an indication of the variations and complexities that must be faced in any preparation of a fee schedule.

1. Georgraphic differences.

The chief difference is found between customary fees that are charged in urban and rural medical practice. Since the average cash income of the farm population is lower than that of urban groups a fee schedule that attempts to strike an average benefits the rural physician and is resisted by urban practitioners. Unfortunately there is inadequate information on the costs of rural versus urban practice and too little data on the actual average fees received by the two types.

The fact cannot be overemphasized that the problem of geographic differences is not one that involves only large divisions of the whole country, such as the North and the South. It is not less simple in any of the populous states where physicians' practices show the whole range of geographic differences from metropolitan to remotely rural.

2. Medical differences.

Within the medical profession there is a range of fees for services rendered by general practitioners or by specialists. Since the great majority of specialists are found in cities the result is a range of fees for the same service in urban communities. The subject is one that has aroused much discussion in medical circles and has been a cause of many decades of conflict between general practitioners and specialists. The realities of the matter are that there has been an increasing and, to the medical profession itself, a disturbing trend toward specialization and, further, that the public expects to compensate specialists at higher rates than non-specialists. Regardless of the merits of any argument against specialization the preparation of a fee schedule necessitates attention to the realities of existing customs.

3. Economic differences.

Whatever the customary fees may be and regardless of rural or urban residence the concept of the sliding scale prevails. Some people have greater, others, lesser, ability to pay for services. Thus, there is a third factor, another range of fees, that calls for consideration.

Adding confusion to the complexities that are an inherent part of fee agreements is the dual role or position of the practicing physician. As a member of the profession he is the exponent of the tradition that the interests of the patient or the public must be the first consideration of medicine. At the same time, the physician is operating a business from which he must derive his livelihood and his economic security. The mixture of the two roles increases the difficulty of any forthright discussion of or attack upon the problem of fees.

In the profession's relations with the public the first role predominates; to speak of fee schedules as influencing the physician's economic position is regarded as descending to mercenary levels and as lowering professional prestige. The approach, therefore, becomes oblique; the subject of fees is interwoven with professional tradition and when recommendations are made they are identified primarily with the public interest. It is the phenomenon of the dual role that makes it difficult to determine which sentiment is uppermost when any issue of payment arises. The phenomenon is not a carefully studied and planned strategy to confuse issues but it does prevent the refinement of problems that might lead to more satisfactory solutions.

Here and there, medical societies are beginning to take a more direct and, to the public, a more understandable position with regard to fees as they affect the physician's economic position—regardless of the source or the route of payment. And in the field study of EMIC the individual practitioner, speaking for himself rather than stating any public policy, was very frank in his discussion of EMIC fees as they affected his practice and his income.

The Experience of EMIC

The objectives of EMIC, maternity and infant care, were sharply defined; to achieve the objectives EMIC plunged into the currents and crosscurrents of medical payment. The pressure of time required a direct crossing. Congress had decided that the Federal Government was to be the source of funds and the state health departments the paying agencies; the Children's Bureau was committed to the policy that payment must be from the agency to the physician; the method of payment was to follow the pattern of the traditional fee-for-service which might cover a case, as in maternity care, or a period of time, as in well-baby services. It was in connection with the amount of payment that major problems arose and resulted in changes of policy as well as in administrative details.

From what has been said, an ideal rate of payment for a medical service would be one that would cover all of the existing variable conditions in the country. Such a rate would be adjustable to the broad geographic differences in fees, the differences between urban and rural fees in a state and the differences between general practitioners' and specialists' fees in a community. And, in addition, the ideal rate would be a fair one to the public. With the above factors to consider it becomes evident that any rate—national, state or local—must be a composite of compromises.

The most apparent feature of the problem of fixing a rate of payment to physicians is the lack of any scientific approach to a solution. The rates and their variations are based upon little that can be assigned tangible and measurable values. Without such values there is no means of determining, objectively, what a rate should be. The alternative to objective determination is the arbitrary adoption of a middle course, a rate that is average. By its very nature the average figure falls somewhere near the middle of a range of rates and it results, automatically, in paying one group of physicians more and another group less than their usual rates. Thus, the position of any agency that bears the responsibility of adopting rates is never an enviable one.

In establishing rates the use of an advisory committee is an important preliminary step. The committee must be representative in order to contribute information and communicate professional opinion as well as serve as a liaison with various professional groups. To these ends the Bureau utilized the regular advisory committees and invited other members of the medical profession to present their views. In the transcripts of the committee meetings many pages are devoted to the subject of rates and the opinions expressed provide a cross section of medical opinion. To the criticism that was expressed in the states, that the Bureau did not take the advice of its advisory committee, the question might be asked, "Which advice?"

Any impression that the Bureau adopted an arbitrary rate for the country as a whole is in error. In an information circular issued in March, 1943 it was stated that the care rendered by general practitioners for maternity cases "averaged $35 per case in the various states or if prenatal care was provided in a prenatal clinic an average of $25 is usually paid for medical care during labor (at home or in an approved hospital) and postpartum care and examination approximately 6 weeks after delivery."[1] It would have been difficult for the Bureau to support its statement of the average fee with adequate data; it would have been equally difficult to refute the statement because of the lack of satisfactory information to prove it wrong.

EMIC started with a statement of the average payment to general practitioners as a guide to the states. Although only Federal funds were being used the policy permitted the states to recommend their own rates of payment. It was assumed that the subject would be discussed with the state medical advisory committees and a satisfactory decision would result. But, by April, four-fifths of the states had adopted the $35 rate and only two asked for rates above this "average." Unaware of the action taken by most of the states, some located in the southern "low-fee" area of the country recommended rates that they regarded as usual and that were below $35.

It was not long before the states paying less than the $35 rate learned what was being paid in the other states. The demand was made and granted that they, too, be permitted to pay the average rate. Thus, what was conceived as an average became the standard. Subsequent demands were made in the "higher-fee" states that the $35 rate be increased to $50. Almost immediately after permission was given to increase the rate the rest of the states demanded like treatment. The end result was that the Bureau established the rate of $50 not as an average but as a maximum and with all states paying at this rate no further increase was granted. The maximum became the standard EMIC fee for maternity care throughout the country. What had started as an attempt to vary a fee according to existing geographic differences became a single national rate. What EMIC demonstrated in a period of months was a predictable event.

In private practice, with the fees paid by patients from savings or current income, the adjustment of fees to the variable regional economic differences is an automatic process. Each physician has the privilege of remaining in such an area or leaving it; these are the only alternatives since there is no effective way to fix the responsibility for low fees and demand more equitable payment according to the fees charged elsewhere. The physicians, for example, in certain locations in Georgia, Nebraska or Mississippi have no satisfactory way of achieving the average level of fees in New York or California.

[1] *MCH Information Circular No. 13.*

With the introduction of any form of centralized payment the means of reducing the geographic differences become tangible. Instead of individual patients there is an agency against which pressure by the medical profession to correct what are interpreted as inequities may be exerted. And the speed with which pressures were exerted in EMIC offers some measurement of the medical dissatisfaction over the existing regional differences.

It is probable that regional and state differences in the rate of payment might have continued if EMIC had been a program that was financed by Federal and state funds.[2] Had there been a "formula" whereby Federal funds were contributed on a variable basis it is likely that the states would show variable fees. Thus, if the Federal allotment to Georgia amounted to $25 per maternity case it is probable that with the state contributions, the total fee might have been set at $35. In wealthier California a Federal allotment of $15 per case, plus the state contribution, might have resulted in a fee of $50 or $60 or more. But the leveling effect of a single national fund, as a source or agency of payment, is almost certain as far as regional variations are concerned. It may be somewhat delayed, as in the variable state fee schedules of the Veterans' Administration. Nonetheless, the experienc of EMIC is significant regardless of whether a national governmental or a voluntary payment plan is envisioned.

EMIC's experience with the second problem of variable fees, that within the states and relating to urban and rural differences, only duplicates what has happened many times. "Low-fee" areas have been mentioned in terms of states. Within the low-fee states there are lower fee rural areas and higher fee urban areas; in the high-fee states there are the same variations. In short, the national problem is duplicated in the states and when a payment agency is organized in a state it faces the same problem of customary variations in fees.

One of the striking facts about EMIC is that no state recommended a variation of fees within the state, according to urban and rural services. California might ask, as an example, why the rate in that state was not higher than in Nebraska but there was no suggestion that in California the $50 rate be reduced in some counties to $35 and increased to $60 in San Francisco and Los Angeles. Many physicians expressed the view that there should be urban and rural

[2]In July, 1946, Amendment No. 8 to *EMIC Information Circular No. 1* authorized that "State-appropriated funds may be used to supplement federal funds for the purpose of increasing the maximum rates to be paid by the state health department." Coming so late in the program, the policy resulted in no changes in state payments.

differences but when asked for supporting reasons spoke only in such general terms as "cost of living" and "cost of practice."

The problem of urban-rural variable rates either is an artificial one to be solved by establishing a single rate or it is real and no practical solution has been offered. Despite some criticism of EMIC over the single rate, no range of rates based upon urban and rural service has been established by any voluntary medical service plan. Nor is there any available record of any urban-rural range in a fee schedule adopted by a state medical society for services under the Veterans' Administration. For a state medical society to assign different values for services, according to physicians' locations, would draw fire from many county societies.

The events of the past decade show a distinct trend toward a greater comparability of physicians' fees throughout the country. Apparently the elimination of low points and high points is an inherent part of prepayment whether the sources of payment are governmental or voluntary. Influencing the trend is the more widespread public interest in and knowledge of rates and fee schedules. As long as a fee is a private informal arrangement between a physician and a patient its amount is a matter of conjecture to other physicians and patients. The conjecture is eliminated when there is a formal arrangement and it appears in print. As a formal arrangement it may go beyond establishing rates for those immediately involved and influence the fees for those outside the scheme of payment.

Thus far the discussion has been based upon the concept of "same service, same fee," i.e., the same service in Massachusetts, Michigan or California calls for the same rate of payment by EMIC. As stated previously, there is a third type of variability of rates; it obtains in the fees charged by specialists as against those of general practitioners. The concept here is "different service, different fee." What may be the difference in service or its degree are matters of disagreement between general practitioners and specialists. But that the public attaches a higher value to specialists' services and that specialists' rates are higher than those of general practitioners cannot be argued. In this aspect of payment EMIC tried to conform to custom.

Nothing so arouses the antagonism of the profession as the implication that an administrator or an administrative agency intends to judge the competency of physicians. For example, Section 211 in Senate Bill 1320[3] states that: "Any such individual who is found

[3]S. 1320. To provide a national health insurance and public health program. Introduced by Senators Murray, Wagner, Pepper, Chavez, Taylor, McGrath. May 20, 1947.

to possess skill and experience of a degree and kind sufficient to meet standards established for a class of specialist services shall be deemed qualified to receive compensation for specialist services of such class as benefits under this title. . . . In establishing such standards and in determining whether individuals qualify thereunder, standards and certifications developed by professional agencies shall be utilized as far as is consistent with the purposes of this title. . . ." Despite the reference to standards developed by professional agencies it did little to allay the antagonism or concern of the profession. In essence, it was contended that the designation of specialists is a responsibility that should remain within the profession.

Attempting to conform to the facts that there are specialists and that, in general, their services are regarded as being of more value and their rates are higher than those of general practitioners, the Children's Bureau issued the following statement of policy:

"Rates of payment for medical services rendered by obstetricians who are certified by the American Board of Obstetrics and Gynecology or assistant consultants who have had 1 or more years of graduate training in obstetrics in an approved residency may be approximately one-fourth to one-third higher than the rates of payment for services rendered by physicians who have not had such additional graduate training and experience."[4] The statement of policy brought into the immediate foreground the whole subject of designating specialists. The state health departments were to consult with their medical advisory committees concerning standards and the actual process of selection. In effect the profession was placed in the position of determining standards of competency and suggesting the ways in which they might be applied. What had been discussed and debated as a broad principle, professional responsibility for judging competence, faced the test of administrative application.

The standards suggested for EMIC seem quite simple and clear. There is an American Board of Obstetrics and Gynecology and an American Board of Pediatrics. Both of these boards and many others have been created within the medical profession and each board has its rules whereby a physician may be approved as one who has special qualifications. Approval is based, primarily, upon the fulfillment of requirements of graduate training and experience in the specialty. In recognition that certain physicians are "en route" to board approval EMIC permitted the higher rates of payment for those who had completed a minimum of formal graduate training

4*EMIC Information Circular No. 1,* Section 9 (a), p. 7. Later, in March, 1945, the policy was revised to permit rates of payment 50 percent higher.

in obstetrics or pediatrics. Apparently the suggested standards lend themselves to virtually automatic application—until some of the features of medical specialization are examined.

Unlike the practice of medicine, specialization within medicine in the United States is not surrounded by legal requirements and protections. A physician before being granted a license to practice must present evidence of his qualifications. There is the requirement in virtually all of the states that he must be a graduate of an approved medical school, must have completed a year of hospital internship, etc. A number of the states require an examination in "basic sciences;" many states will grant licenses to physicians already licensed in states with equal standards. Whatever may be the licensing procedure, it is a part of state law that is intended to assure by formal examinations and other means the general competency of all physicians who are granted licenses.

Once a physician is granted a license to practice medicine there are no further legal requirements that must be met if he chooses to specialize. The routes toward specialization are varied; the most formal one is that established by an American Board, including rigid educational and experience requirements. The most informal route is taken by the physician who gradually acquires experience in a specialty and, accordingly, begins to limit his practice. Hence, the pattern of specialization in the United States shows a wide range from the formal approval by an American Board to the informal approval of a small or large number of practicing physicians in a local area. Even though a local physician may not have fulfilled the board requirements his colleagues, practicing in the same community, may regard him as specially qualified and express their regard for his special ability by referring cases to him.

In the light of the existing pattern the designation of specialists —in obstetrics, pediatrics, surgery or other fields—loses its simplicity. If approval by an American Board were the only criterion the problem would be solved automatically. The same is true for those physicians who have not been approved yet, but are definitely in the channel leading to such approval. But outside of both of these groups are the many who regard themselves as specially qualified and whose protest against exclusion from any official lists of specialists would be certain.

Under the circumstances the state medical advisory committees were faced with an almost hopeless task. Any series of standards in obstetrics or pediatrics comparable to those of the American Boards would have resulted in a quick and adverse response from many members of the profession. Anything short of the board requirements would have led to the charge that the standards of quality were being lowered. The third alternative, no choice, was generally followed; the basic fee of $50 that might have been increased by 50 percent remained as the single fee for all physicians with one exception among the states studied, Nebraska.[5]

In Nebraska, according to physicians interviewed, the EMIC rate for maternity care was about equal to the usual rate in private practice outside of Omaha and Lincoln. In some of the rural areas of Nebraska, as with those of Georgia and Mississippi, the rate exceeded the average. With few exceptions, the small number of physicians who qualify as specialists are located in Omaha and Lincoln. Under circumstances where the great majority of physicians are general practitioners and, an item of some importance, the average general practitioner knew little about the provision for a higher rate to specialists, such a differential was established. How it might work in a different type of state where many physicians partially specialize is unknown. The delicacy with which differential rates between general practitioners and specialists must be handled is shown by the comments of a young physician practicing in a small community in Nebraska. He stated that he could qualify as a specialist according to the EMIC requirements. However, he felt that if he were classified as a specialist the other physicians in the area would resent his being given such a preferred status.

The significance of the EMIC experience with the three major aspects of variations in rates throughout the country cannot be overemphasized. It is doubtful that any national health plan, centrally financed, can establish variable rates on a geographic basis. A plan financed by a combination of central governmental or voluntary funds and state funds might lend itself to variable rates. Whether such a plan would be endorsed by the profession in the "low income states" is questionable.

[5]Connecticut proposed the following qualifications for consultants where the ratio of certified physicans to population is less than 1 to 10,000 within a radius which can be traveled in 30 minutes:

Type a. (1) At least one year's rotating internship including at least two months of the specialty. (2) One year's hospital training in the specialty, plus (3) Five years of practice including the specialty, plus (4) Member of hospital staff for the specialty.

Type b. (1) Two year's hospital training in the specialty. (2) Five years of practice including specialty. (3) Member of hospital staff for the specialty.

Type c. (1) One year's rotating internship. (2) Graduate work in specialty six to twelve months. (3) Head of local hospital staff for the specialty for at least ten years.

Type d. (1) At least two years' hospital training one of which was in the specialty, plus (2) Practice limited to the specialty for three years.

"Public Health Committee Discusses Emergency Maternity and Infant Care Program," *Connecticut State Medical Journal* 8:625 September, 1944.

The experience of EMIC with variations in urban and rural rates within the states supports the abundant experience of the voluntary medical plans. The concept of "same service, same rate" is expressed in a most tangible form in the fee schedules that have been adopted by statewide medical society plans. The same is true of the schedules for services under the Veterans' Administration.

EMIC contributed little to the solution of the third problem of variable rates—higher fees for specialists' services. But the experience was extremely valuable in the sharp attention that was focused upon the nature of the problem and its complexities. No matter what wide acceptance a principle may receive it cannot be applied without specific administrative policies. And, in this case, the policies must be based upon the development by the profession of a more controlled process of specialization.

The importance of the rate of payment for services is usually given a secondary place in public discussions by members of the medical profession. However, it is apparent that the attitude of the practicing physician toward services of a charitable or semi-charitable nature has changed. As a rule, the limited funds for public medical programs have resulted in extremely low rates of payment to physicians. Many agencies have found it easier to persuade physicians to give services at low costs than to obtain added funds from public bodies. Though physicians have continued to provide services, their resentment at being asked and expected to shoulder these burdens has grown. The social agencies have been slow in their own adjustments to this condition but they recognize that the resentment is justified and that the rates of payment must be increased. The Children's Bureau, especially in its program for crippled children has tried to follow a policy of reasonable payment. And in EMIC an attempt was made to follow the same policy.

The attitudes of physicians in the states included in the survey, toward the EMIC rate of payment offer some interesting commentaries on the problems of payment. Those interviewed included local medical practitioners as well as representatives of state and national medical leadership. Their comments, taken from the notes of the field staffs, show that there is a direct relation between the professional attitude toward EMIC and the rate of payment, i.e., where, as in maternity cases, the $50 was approximately the going rate or exceeded the usual rate the reaction was favorable. And where, as was the situation in the larger cities, the EMIC rate was lower the reaction was unfavorable. One national medical leader residing in California stated, relative to the attitude of physicians in small cities, "After all, you have to consider the fact that to many of them $50 represents a good fee."

In a subsequent chapter dealing with economic controls other administrative factors that are a part of payment for physicians' services will be considered.

Chapter IX

PAYMENT FOR HOSPITAL SERVICES—POLICIES, METHODS AND PROBLEMS

Only by comparison with the problems of payment to physicians do those of payment to hospitals offer fewer complexities. For physicians at least four major factors are involved—source, route, form and amount. For hospitals, the source and route of payment may be regarded as secondary; the form and amount of payment are primary. This is said despite the fact that some hospital administrators oppose government, and particularly Federal Government, as a source of payment and as a growing influence in hospital planning and construction.

During the past few years significant changes have taken place in the public concept of the general hospital. The former acceptance of the hospital as a nonprofit institution precariously perched on the edge of insolvency is being replaced by the view that it is a valuable community utility providing services that must be maintained. As a community utility, the place of the hospital, its organization, its administration and its potential contributions are undergoing widespread analyses and evaluations. As the knowledge of community needs expands, the importance of adequate financial support for hospitals increases.

Rates of payment to hospitals may be determined more objectively than those to physicians, since hospital rates are related to the tangible costs of rendering services. In theory, at least, hospital rates are equal to the costs of providing specific services plus a margin to take care of the depreciation and replacement of equipment and buildings. In practice, the determination of equitable rates has presented certain difficulties. Some of the problems are inherent, others originate in the differing policies of hospital administration and financing.

What the public sees in the usual day-to-day operation of a hospital are the services rendered to the sick. The patients may occupy single rooms with one bed (private), rooms containing two to four beds (semi-private) or larger rooms with five or more beds (ward). Depending upon the extent of available services, the hospital may provide personnel and the space and equipment for X-ray, physiotherapy, various laboratories, operating and delivery rooms, pharmacy, etc. Patients must be nursed, they must be fed, there must be medical and business records, the building must be heated and laundry and other housekeeping services must be maintained. These are the services provided for "in-patients" and the facilities may be used as well for those patients that do not occupy beds ("out-patients") but come to the institution for particular services.

In addition to the above there are other roles that many hospitals have accepted and though these are less prominent in terms of public awareness, they are vital elements in the consideration of payment. The hospital is a service institution but many are, also, educational institutions. As educational institutions they provide the training facilities and the teaching personnel to qualify young women for the career of nursing. And while in the majority of schools student nurses are expected to contribute a certain portion of the training time to the hospital services, as a part of the learning process, the contribution falls short of balancing the total cost of the training. Therefore, somehow and from some source the deficit must be made up.

The second educational activity is found in those hospitals that are approved for and participate in the training of physicians. "Hospital internship," as a prerequisite to practice, means that the great majority of medical graduates must receive one year of training in an acceptable hospital. If the physician intends to specialize his training in a hospital may extend to four years. Here again—though there is a good deal of vagueness regarding the financial burden placed upon the hospital—the institution plays a desirable educational role and it may be a costly one.

Added to the two sectors of hospital operation—service and education—is a third one. The hospital is looked upon as a center of charity, a place where no person who needs service is turned away. Just how the hospital is to ensure this socially comforting state of affairs is somewhat obscure.

The chief source of hospital income is from the services to the sick. The money may come directly from the patient or from a governmental or non-governmental agency. This means that the service function of the hospital is expected to carry itself plus all or a part of the costs of education and charity. It is true that there may be gifts and organized "drives" of one sort or another to aid hospitals. But these endeavors cannot assure the stability and continuity of program that are so necessary if the hospital is to fulfill all of its obligations. The alternative is to establish rates for services that will cover all costs.

Much of the controversy concerning hospital rates would not exist if standard procedures of record-keeping and cost accounting had been adopted. The American Hospital Association has urged all hospitals to introduce standard methods but prior to the past five years the progress in this direction was slow. Thus, rates have been established with too little knowledge of actual costs and once established there was and is the usual aversion to change. As a result hospital charges vary extremely for comparable services such as laboratory, X-ray, etc. In a particular hospital one service may be provided at cost or below cost; in another, at two or three times the cost. No one can question the need of a well-administered institution to show annual balance sheets that balance; the conflicts that arise are concerned with matters of policy and the general inconsistency of the pattern of distributing costs.

The classification of hospital patients into "full-pay," "part-pay" and "free" represents the attempt of a hospital to meet the economic problems of different income groups. When the chief source of income is from services it is obvious that "full-pay" is more than that; it is "full-pay-plus" in terms of actual costs. And "part-pay" may be actual cost or a varying percentage thereof. Under such circumstances there arises a question of policy that should concern the community more than the hospital. Is it an equitable arrangement to expect self-supporting people who experience the misfortune of hospitalization to bear their own burden of costs and at the same time be compelled to contribute to charity and to education?

One other confusing and unjustifiable factor has added to the problem of hospital financing. It is the long-established custom whereby public or private welfare agencies pay hospital rates that are much below the costs of operation. It is in connection with services to patients receiving aid that the community may contribute its just portion of hospital costs. Instead of following such a forthright and fair policy low hospital rates to many of the agencies have been the rule, with other sources of funds expected to make up the difference in costs. As will be shown later, such governmental agencies as the Children's Bureau and the Veterans' Administration are doing much to change the custom.

The basis of hospital payment presents two important variations. Customarily, hospitals charge private patients according to the specific services rendered. Itemized statements are prepared with charges listed for each service such as bed and board at a fixed rate for the type of accomodation and for other services utilized such as laboratory, X-ray, operating room, drugs, etc. As a departure from the itemized type of charge some hospitals use what is known as the "inclusive rate." Under this system hospital operating costs are computed over a period of time and the average total cost per patient day is determined. It is the average cost that is used as a fixed rate per day for all but the unusual services that are received by the patient.

As might be expected there is a good deal of controversy regarding the basis of payment when hospital bills are paid through an agency rather than by individual patients. In the relations between hospitals and voluntary prepayment plans, such as Blue Cross, the conflict has reached an acute stage with certain hospitals withdrawing or threatening to withdraw from the hospital plans. The hospitals that charge according to specific services rendered criticize the Blue Cross when payment from the agency according to a fixed schedule does not equal the amount that might have been received if the Blue Cross subscriber-patient had paid for all the services at the going rates. Against this criticism the Blue Cross contends that it cannot pay charges that differ by as much as 1,000 percent on certain items among hospitals in the same community. As stated by one Blue Cross director, "Until hospitals have a standard system of pricing, which is related to a standard system of determining costs, it is suicide for a Blue Cross plan to get caught in such a payment policy. . . . Until hospitals agree to standard charges for items of service or a uniform cost formula, no other device than a fixed schedule is practical."[1]

The Experience of EMIC

The most successful feature of EMIC was the system of payment to hospitals. And nothing demonstrates so clearly the value of administrative experience that may be gained from existing "laborratories" of medical administration. Long before EMIC was introduced the Children's Bureau had dealt with hospitals on a smaller scale. Out of the experience with maternal and child care and, especially, with the program for crippled children certain policies had emerged with respect to hospitals. Thus the Bureau was in position to initiate hospital payment for EMIC patients with a certain background of "know how." This does not mean that no mistakes were made; it does mean that hospital payment produced the least friction or criticism of EMIC.

By the time EMIC began to function the Children's Bureau had

[1]E. A. vanSteenwyk, "Blue Cross is Raising Payments," *Modern Hospital* 70:66 January, 1948.

adopted a policy of hospital payment that, with its later widespread application through the EMIC program, has had an enormous influence upon the general pattern of payment throughout the country. Contrary to the usual policy of public or semi-public agencies, as well as to the earlier systems of payment by voluntary hospital plans, the Bureau had held that hospitals should be paid upon some reasonable basis of cost. In view of the existing "hit-or-miss" bases of payment the policy was an abrupt departure from current general practice. Thus, preceding EMIC was the work and the experience that led to the suggested formula of hospital payment.

The formula suggested by the Bureau as a basis of hospital payment for EMIC cases is shown in Appendix xvii. Although the Bureau did not insist that all states follow a uniform procedure there have been few variations in the essential information obtained. There is nothing startling about the formula—except its simplicity and underlying logic. The hospital is recognized as an indispensable community utility with annual costs of operation that must be met by annual income. The formula consists of the means of arriving at the total costs of operation by presenting the expenses for each of 16 services such as administration, dietary, medical and surgical service, housekeeping, nursing, X-ray, laboratory, etc. Some hospitals may provide all of the services, others less than the 16. For more detailed instructions concerning each service the hospital is referred to the manual *Hospital Accounting and Statistics* published by the American Hospital Association.

The total annual operating costs serve as the basis for computing the cost per patient day and the "reimbursable cost" per patient day. The cost per patient day is determined by dividing the annual operating costs by the total days spent by patients in the hospitals.* To this figure 10 percent is added for depreciation of buildings and equipment, rent, interest, etc.**

The reimbursable cost, which is the day-rate to be paid to the hospital, is intended for the care of patients in rooms with two or more beds. An earlier memorandum issued by the Bureau (Sept. 1, 1943) specified ward services but this was changed on April 15, 1944 to services "ordinarily in rooms with two or more beds." Since the over-all costs of operation include the costs for all hospital patients—private and others—the reimbursable cost for EMIC patients is placed at 85 percent of the total cost per patient day for those

*Exclusive of newborn-infant days during the time when the infants' mothers are patients in the hospital.

**Revised as described on p. 147.

hospitals that report that 30 percent or more of their patients occupied private rooms.*

The hospital is not required to use the formula; if for some reason it cannot or does not wish to provide the data it may accept what was established as a flat rate of $4.25 per EMIC patient per day. Permissible exceptions to the use of the formula are allowed for those hospitals with less than 25 beds and receiving less than $500 annually from EMIC, Crippled Children's or Maternal and Child Health funds and for hospitals that are publicly supported and where the rates are established by laws that apply to the purchase of care under the maternal and child health and crippled children's programs. An excepted hospital may, if it wishes, submit a statement and be paid according to the formula; otherwise it is paid at a rate established by the state health department. A publicly supported hospital with a rate established by law is paid the rate without question. Neither exception has caused any administrative difficulty although in one of the states surveyed, Mississippi, it created an unusual situation.

A statute in Mississippi required that no hospital may be paid from public funds more than a maximum determined by the state hospital commission, a body that has insisted upon low hospital rates. At the beginning of the EMIC program the rates were set at the low figure of $2.50 per day for adults and $1 for children. Later, the rate for adults was increased to $3 per day. The EMIC director in Mississippi asked the Children's Bureau whether the state might pay the maximum allowed by law and the patient or family be permitted to supplement the payment to the hospital. The Bureau suggested that, since the funds used by the state health department to pay for EMIC patients were entirely Federal, the state law be revised or re-interpreted to permit payment on the basis of the reimbursable cost of hospital operation. A ruling by the state attorney made it permissible for the state to pay more than the maximum rate to hospitals when state funds were not involved. Despite the ruling most of the hospitals remained on the minimum flat rate allowed by the state hospital commission. Here was an instance where a state law and state custom prevented the application of the reimbursable cost formula.

Certain features of the basis of hospital payment are prominent. In the first place the formula draws a sharp line between items of hospital cost that may be included and items that must be excluded.

*Later changed to 100 percent of the cost.

Excluded are the costs of research and education. While both activities are vitally important, funds to pay all or a part of their costs are not considered as fair charges to be borne by the relatively small annual percentage of the total population (about 10 percent) that utilizes the facilities of the hospital. Since the principle of reimbursable cost appears to be spreading its application on the above basis should serve to direct public attention to the need of a more stable and a more general support of hospital research and education.

Other aspects of the formula concern the details of its application. Though the principle has received widespread support from hospital administrators many suggestions to improve the formula and some criticism deserve attention. One criticism is that the payment of hospital costs in accordance with the procedure that has developed does not place any premium upon the efficiency of hospital management, i.e., if cost statements are accepted without any question regarding the efficiency of hospital operation there is no economic incentive to good management.

It is true that a cost formula covering hundreds or thousands of hospitals cannot ensure efficient administration. At the same time the limitations of this or any other basis of payment must be recognized. The formula does require an orderly method of cost accounting which, per se, is a first step toward more efficient administration. Future refinements of the method may focus attention upon the need of more precise standards of efficiency but such standards should be regarded as a joint responsibility of hospital organizations and agencies designed to pay hospital costs. Meanwhile, all that can be said is that a formula of reimbursable costs is not a panacea; it is a more orderly and equitable method of payment for hospital services.

The fact that a hospital might show an excessive cost was recognized in one of the policies adopted for EMIC, effective July 1, 1944.[2] The Children's Bureau advised the executive offices administering EMIC in the states as follows:

"If the statement received from any hospital appears to establish an excessive cost per patient day as compared with costs per patient day for services of comparable quality in other hospitals in the State, the State agency should establish a maximum rate under these programs (EMIC, Crippled Children, etc.), a rate that shall be reasonable in view of the average per diem costs in hospitals throughout the State." The purpose of the directive was clear; its achievement doubtful in the terms expressed. "Comparable quality" and "reasonable," as related to average costs, have no meanings that are pre-

2Memorandum on revised policies for the purchase of hospital care, issued April 15, 1944, p.4.

cise. All that could be done was to establish an arbitrary upper limit beyond which a hospital would not be compensated.

The strict application of the principle of reimbursable costs drew criticism from those institutions, Catholic and Protestant, where a portion of the hospital services are donated. In calculating its costs a hospital is directed to show the total amount of its expense as well as the expenses of the series of items that must be deducted from the total. Among the items is the "estimated value of donated or voluntary services."* Since "maintenance . . . of members of religious orders" may be included as operating expense the issue is whether or not a hospital should be permitted to charge the equivalent salaries if the same services were purhased rather than donated. It was the policy of the Bureau to exclude equivalent salaries, limiting its reimbursement to actual costs.

Although the problem is relatively small, in terms of the total funds expended for hospital care, it raises questions that are of immediate as well as long-range importance. As to the immediate aspects, it is easy to become involved in controversy—specious and pointless—about how an individual spends his or her money. The question here is not whether hospital funds are used to strengthen the finances of religious orders; the issue is whether the services rendered are generally accepted as a part of hospital operation regardless of the auspices under which a hospital functions. If this principle is accepted the function of the agency administering the funds is to define the hospital services. It should neither be given nor accept the responsibility of assigning money-values to the services; to attempt such a procedure would mean, in effect, that the agency would establish wage or salary patterns. The responsibility of establishing money-values falls upon the organization under which the hospitals operate. Here, too, a formula is required that gives consideration to what are customary values in the nation, the state or a local area. It will not be an easy task to develop such a formula but until it is developed the issue will continue to be a constant source of friction. And the fact that EMIC comes to an end does not change the problem for other governmental as well as voluntary payment programs.

The payment for donated services in the hospital goes beyond the contributions that are religious expressions. In many institutions it is customary for physicians to contribute their services to ward patients. And, in turn, the custom has its origin in the tradition that ward patients are "wards," in the sense that they are able

*See revision described on p. 148.

to pay only a part or none of the expense of their needs. The hospital service may be free or the rate to a public or private welfare agency may be less than hospital costs; physicians' services may include those of interns, residents, salaried physicians and others who, though they engage in private practice in the community, contribute a portion of their time to the care of ward patients.

The change in the above custom and tradition appears to follow an unmistakable trend. Prepayment plans have created new methods of hospital financing and these exert their effects upon the contributions of services to ward patients by physicians who have no salary-connection with the hospital. The first prepayment plans were for hospital care, only, and the subscribers were given the opportunity to purchase care in a ward or semi-private room. Obviously, those who purchased the protection were regarded as self-supporting persons. When they occupied ward beds there seemed to be little justification for the rule that non-salaried physicans' services were to be free.

In several instances physicians rendering services to patients in free clinics of hospitals have raised the question as to why they should not be paid for services to EMIC patients. Many of the hospitals have opposed such payment on the ground that it would violate the tradition of their clinic service and set a precedent that might lead to future difficulties. As far as the salaried medical personnel were concerned (interns, residents and other) EMIC permitted the hospital to include salaries and maintenance as a part of the reimbursable cost formula. But the whole problem is far from solution; practicing physicians who hold the view that medical care is a broad social responsibility are critical of those means of meeting the responsibility that place an undue burden of free service upon the physician.

The most frequent criticism by hospital administrators was that the formula did not provide a fair payment for "short stay" cases. Due to crowded conditions what was regarded as a normal hospitalization for maternity cases, ten days, was reduced in many hospitals to three or four days. For the average maternity case the greatest use of hospital services and, therefore, the largest costs including those for the delivery room, anaesthesia and nursing occur within the first two or three days. As stated by the administrators, if there is a normal stay of ten days the heavy earlier costs are spread over the entire period but if the case remains only three or four days the average per diem rate would fall short. This was the basis of the criticism and there was strenuous objection from the administrators who felt that they were being penalized because of the pressure on their facilities.

At the beginning of the EMIC program the situation was aggravated by the fact that the Children's Bureau insisted that for cases remaining over 14 days the reimbursable per diem rate be reduced by 25 percent after the 14th day. The reaction of the hospitals was that if the per diem rate should be reduced for long-stay cases, it should be increased for short-stay cases. The protests brought a revision in Bureau policy. With the issuance of the revised policies in December, 1943 (*EMIC Information Circular No. 1*) no mention was made of reduced rates but no change was made for the short-stay cases. Actually, the revision of the policy on long-stay cases meant little in a period when crowding in hospitals made such cases relatively rare.

There are two issues that underlie the criticism about short-stay cases. One involves the problem of economic control which is discussed in the next chapter. The other is concerned with the payment by any agency for a particular class or type of hospital case. The reimbursable cost formula was based upon the annual cost of all cases hospitalized and the principle is a fair method of arriving at an average per diem cost. Some types of cases cost more, others less, and the difficulty arises when the average for all is used to pay for selected cases that are served at higher costs. The problem is largely one of adequate accounting; certainly no paying agency should propose or expect to pay less than costs.

Relative to the above problem of higher-cost cases the Children's Bureau pointed out that certain of the costs would be counterbalanced by non-obstetrical patients hospitalized under EMIC. These were the patients treated for non-obstetric intercurrent illnesses and, more particularly, the pediatric cases. Whereas the usual hospital rate for the pediatric ward is lower than the rates for adults, the Bureau in accordance with the policy of paying one per diem rate does not differentiate between pediatric and other cases.

The issue of short-stay or long-stay cases where an agency pays for all types of hospitalized cases is an artificial one. It results from the confusion of the average per diem reimbursable cost with the custom of charging each patient according to an itemized account. The reimbursable cost is inclusive; as an average its application means that some patients pay more and others less than they would have paid if each account were itemized. Anyone may oppose the principle of charging on the basis of an average cost but if it is accepted as the form of payment there is little consistency in variable charges for long-stay or short-stay cases. Obviously, the annual costs of the hospital divided by the total patient-days includes short- and long-stay cases.

As stated earlier, the principle of the single reimbursable cost formula cannot be regarded as a panacea. As it is applied and as experience accumulates rules may be adopted to cover unusual situations and cases. For example, the hospital payment by EMIC for a maternity case followed the usual hospital custom of including the infant in the per diem payment for the mother for a two-weeks period. Should the infant require continued hospitalization it becomes a pediatric case and payment is made at the regular per diem rate. However, an exception to the above rule occurs when an infant is exposed to unsterile conditions at birth and cannot be placed in the nursery. One hospital reported a case where the maternity patient did not arrive at the hospital in time and an infant was born before the delivery room was reached. It was necessary to place the infant in the pediatric ward for which there could be no added charge despite the increased expense to the hospital. The case was extremely unusual and the amount of money involved was minor, yet the administrator gave the exception enough weight to stress it.

While hospitals have criticised certain of the details of EMIC payment the general attitude toward the basis of payment is highly favorable. An editorial in *Hospital Management* summarizes the attitude as follows: "The astonishing rule of the EMIC organization in paying very nearly full actual cost for its patients may freely be credited with having advanced enormously the cause of collecting adequately from the responsible authorities for their wards when cared for in the non-governmental non-profit hospitals. This rule was so reasonable, and yet so entirely unusual, that it struck hospital people everywhere as one of those wonderful things which somebody should have thought of much earlier; and it naturally resulted in a general demand, everywhere, that all governments do the same thing."[3]

That other important Federal Government agencies are doing the same thing is shown by the joint action of the Children's Bureau, the Veterans' Administration and the Office of Vocational Rehabilitation. Early in 1947 the three agencies agreed to pay hospitals according to a revised reimbursable cost formula. The changes eliminated the 15 percent differential for ward services, permitted hospitals to calculate their costs at intervals of six months rather than annually, and allowed, within specified limits and as an oper-

[3]Editorial, "Payments by Government." *Hospital Management* 63:49 May, 1947.

ating cost, the actual amount of depreciation carried on books. Also allowed to Catholic hospitals was a limit of $75 per month paid to Mother Houses for each Sister on duty in the hospital.

In a number of instances hospital administrators mentioned the effects of the EMIC program upon the payment policies of city and county governments. There appears to be developing a more realistic approach to the problems of hospital payment and the EMIC basis is becoming something of a yardstick. What is happening cannot and should not be interpreted as a trend that marks the end of charity *in* hospitals. It does mean, however, that there is approaching an end to the concept of charity *by* hospitals, especially those forms of charity that depend for their economic support upon the hospital surplus derived from providing services to patients at rates above costs.

CHAPTER X

ADMINISTRATIVE CONTROLS—ECONOMIC

In Chapter VII the means test was described as the chief issue facing those who are responsible for the political policy governing organized payment for medical services. Once this issue is resolved in an equitable manner the successful operation of a scheme of payment depends upon the administrative policies that are adopted and the way they are applied.

Among all of the problems of administration one predominates —administrative controls. And it is a paradox of administration that the subject of controls, upon which the success of a plan of payment depends, has been given the least attention in the literature of administration. It is administrative control that affects the quality of the services received by beneficiaries; it is administrative control that is the chief protection against insolvency. As will be noted in the EMIC program the two functions often overlap to a point where it is impossible to designate a particular control as intended, solely, to improve services or to protect funds. The divisions that appear in this report are arbitrary in certain cases and, therefore, those who view a particular control as intended only to improve services may take exception to its classification, also, as an economic control.

Economic control is the necessary accompaniment of sound administration when the charges for services received by patients are borne by a financing agency such as a government bureau or a voluntary medical or hospital plan. No plan, especially where payment is in the form of fees or other stated amounts for specific services, has been organized without controls to prevent insolvency. It is the fear of insolvency, the "inability to pay one's debts as they fall due," that is responsible for the numberless devices to protect funds and assure the continuation of services.

The lack of sufficient funds to pay the bills for services may be due to an underestimate of the medical or hospital needs of the people for whom the scheme of payment was devised. In this case the insolvency is attributable to actuarial miscalculation. The second cause may be due to a utilization of services that is in excess of the real needs. And a third factor, mentioned because it is especially prominent during any period of inflation, and has reached an acute stage in the administration of voluntary plans, is the tendency of persons or institutions providing services to demand increases in compensation without allowing the paying agency sufficient time to adjust its rates to the beneficiaries. It is apparent, then, that whenever solvency is endangered the action that is taken must be related to one or more of the major causes.

The fact that the causes may occur in combination is the best evidence that no actuary can estimate a demand for services without giving close attention to the proposed administrative procedures. When he deals with the "contingency" of medical or hospital care he must link his calculations to an administrative process that is relatively solid. If administrative policies are violated or are applied ineptly the actuarial foundations crumble and insolvency follows.

It has been stated that no existing plan of payment is devoid of controls. What is called "adverse selection of risks" is a danger against which every plan establishes certain rules. When the actuary makes his estimates he considers the medical and hospital needs of a cross-section of the potential beneficiaries. The administrator, therefore, must conform within reasonable limits to the pattern established by the actuary for such factors as the age and sex of beneficiaries. In addition and to prevent the concentration of "bad risks," i.e., beneficiaries with conditions that will require the use of the services, a fairly high percent of any group that desires protection must join the plan. If, as examples, those who promote the plan are consistently inattentive to the percentage, accepting 20 percent when the actuaries have established the lowest limit at 50 percent; if a disproportionate number of females are included or if the groups comprise too great a number of people at ages where the use of service is high, the costs and the income fail to balance. When this happens it may be said that the actuarial estimates were too low, but in each of the examples cited the actuary had based his estimates upon one population and administrative policies have changed the basis.

Of the two major causes of insolvency, actuarial underestimate and use of service in excess of need, the latter is the most feared. It is feared because any attempt at control is assumed to arouse antagonism and disturb "public relations" or "professional relations." The fears themselves indicate what might be the causes of excessive demands. They may be due to patients demanding more than necessary services; they may be due to physicians or hospitals providing services that exceed the needs of patients. And neither cause can be counteracted by general exhortations that "This is *your* plan and whatever happens to it happens to *you*."

The control devices to prevent economic collapse may be classified, in general, as follows:

1. Proration of payment.

In the great majority of voluntary medical and hospital plans and in a number of the tax-supported plans the physicians and hospitals that provide the services underwrite or guarantee the contracts between the paying agency and the beneficiaries. If for any reason the agency cannot meet all of its obligations the physicians in a medical plan and the hospitals in a hospital plan assure the services for the life of the contract. For the services they render, the physicians and hospitals are paid according to the means that are available. The agency may be able to pay only 75 percent of the obligations and, accordingly, each bill is reduced by 25 percent. Thus, the burden of inadequate funds is shared equally in terms of a percentage reduction of payment. Underlying this method of protecting the beneficiary, whereby the physicians and hospitals underwrite the risk, are the implications that actuarial estimates may be too low and that the next contract with the beneficiaries will correct the mistake.

Proration of payment, so widely accepted in principle, arouses an understandable though ill-defined resentment whenever it must be used. Administrators are placed in a defensive position; their promotional efforts, their business methods and other details are scrutinized critically. Though vague statements about actuarial underestimates, inadequately supported by factual evidence, are given the little weight they deserve, not nearly enough attention is paid to economic controls or their lack.

The failure of proration lies in its very essence, the generality of its application. When it is used in a medical plan every physician is penalized an equal percentage of his bills for services. Yet the majority of the physicians know that the causes of the difficulty, be it due to excessive demands of patients or excessive services by physicians, are not equally distributed. Thus the majority recognize that a penalty is being exacted for an occurrence that involves a minority and they know, too, that action which is limited to an increase in the rate to subscribers is only a temporary expedient.

2. Limitations on services.

Those who justify present limitations or exclusions of services on the ground that protection now and in the future is necessary only against "economic catastrophies" give little attention to the differing nature of such catastrophies according to the differing incomes of families. A catastrophic illness is usually defined as one that necessitates hospitalization for adequate treatment. But for many families the medical services that lead to hospitalization may be classified as economic catastrophes to be postponed as long as possible. Those who are interested in preventive medicine, aside from specific services such as antepartum and well-baby care, stress the importance of early diagnosis and early treatment as vital steps in the prevention of prolonged illnesses or deaths.

It is to the credit of the voluntary plans that the majority are expanding their services and that the objective is to provide comprehensive care ultimately. One of the major reasons for present limitations or exclusions is the inability or the fear of the inability to control the utilization of services in excess of needs. Examples of the usual exclusions or limitations are general practitioners' services in homes and offices, X-ray services inside and outside the hospital, and the restriction of medical services to obstetrical and surgical cases that are hospitalized.

3. Barrier payments.

The barrier payment as an economic control is a device that is used widely in health insurance. Its most outstanding example is seen in those schemes open to the general public that have attempted to include home and office medical services. Patients utilizing the services are required to pay for the first or the first and second office or home calls and the remainder or a specified number of subsequent calls are charged to the prepayment plan. Or the principle of payment for first services may be reversed, as in the utilization of X-ray, and the patient is required to pay the charges that exceed a specified limit, such as $15 or $25. The same procedure is followed where obstetrical patients pay charges above a flat amount such as $50. The method is intended to erect an economic barrier against excessive use of services; where used to control home and office calls it is regarded as a measure that reduces the so-called "nuisance cases." What effect the barrier payment has upon the advice given to the public to seek medical attention early or how much economic control actually results from its use are subjects that call for much more study.

Another suggested application of the barrier payment is intended to control hospitalization under the special conditions that accompany the expansion of medical and hospital plans. The special conditions arise from the trend toward the inclusion of all hospital services and all physicians' services for hospitalized patients. When this occurs and, at the same time, services outside the hospital are excluded it is logical to assume that the demand for hospital care will increase. It will not take long for the subscribers of the plans to learn that many services ordinarily provided outside the hospital will be obtainable without added cost if they become hospital in-patients. As it is now the limitation of physicians' services to hospitalized surgical and obstetrical patients has functioned as a fairly effective automatic control. The incentive to enter a hospital and pay the physician for non-surgical or non-obstetrical services as well as undergo the added expense for the utilization of diagnostic facilities above certain specified values is not a strong one. As a sidelight on this aspect of control it is significant that even the above limitation with respect to surgical service in hospitals is undergoing changes in some of the plans. Rather than have patients enter hospitals for minor surgical procedures some of the plans have revised their rules and now pay for surgery performed in physicians' offices.

In order to control excessive utilization of hospitals when all of the services of physicians for hospital in-patients are included in a prepayment plan, a type of barrier payment has been proposed. It would require the payment by patients who are not hospitalized for surgical or obstetrical care, i. e., medical patients, of the average per diem costs of hospitalization for the first one, two or more days. More important than the particular device is the problem it poses regarding the expansion of prepayment plans. The question involves the sequence of steps in a scheme of prepayment that expects to expand services until a comprehensive program of care is offered. Before moving to the provision of full hospital and physicians' services for patients that are hospitalized should there be an intervening step to include certain services, such as diagnostic and home and office care? The question calls for intensive medical and administrative consideration.

4. Other methods.

Many other methods of economic control are found in almost all prepayment plans. These include authorization of services, administrative review of services and accounts, and the requirement in some instances that the patient must attest to the fact that the services have been received. Additional variations in methods will be presented in the experience with the EMIC program.

The number and variety of economic controls indicate the importance of the subject. It is true that the amount of payment for services is a weighty factor in the professional response to a payment plan. But not less important is the professional reaction to methods of control. When the average physician describes an experience that he interprets as "regimentation" or speaks of a "third party" intervening in his relations with the patient or criticizes "red tape" he has in mind, usually, some form or instance of what may be interpreted as an attempt upon the part of an administrative agency to apply economic controls.

Realism forces the conclusion that economic controls are a vital part of any plan of organized payment. They indicate sound business practices and rules from which no institution or profession can or should expect exemption. It takes a certain amount of time to develop adequate specific controls but whatever method is used it should conform to one criterion that is basic. This is the assumption that the great majority of physicians and hospitals do not contribute to and are not responsible for excessive services, that willful deviations from the pattern of reasonable needs involve relatively small minorities. No substantial evidence has been produced showing that the assumption is wrong; it follows, therefore, that foremost among the criteria of control is the principle that the majority must not be penalized for the acts of a minority.

To any statement that the principle is obvious and is accepted by everyone the answer is: it is accepted in theory and violated widely. The violations occur in prorated payment, in many of the limitations of service, in barrier payments and other devices. Though the reason for the control and the center of administrative attention is the minority, the burden of the usual control method is borne by the majority and their ultimate reactions, irritation and antagonism, are certain.

The Experience of EMIC Hospital Controls

The two direct economic controls of hospitals were eliminated early in the EMIC program. One was the rule that after the 14th day of maternity care the payment to the hospital would be three-fourths of the reimbursable per diem cost. The purpose of the rule was obvious; it was intended to prevent hospitals from deriving the economic benefits of keeping patients longer than necessary. The device was a "carry over" from a period antedating EMIC when the pressure on hospitals to provide beds was not great and when a few institutions might have resorted to such a questionable practice. It was a time when a relatively small number of hospitals were included in the program.

The expansion of EMIC to include many hospitals and the rule of payment beyond 14 days brought to a sharp issue the problem of short-stay cases. The intention of the rule to curb a minority aroused the antagonism of the majority. Hospitals where any economic violation was extremely remote could not understand why there should be any penalty for the case that developed complications and required hospitalization longer than 14 days. And it contributed little to satisfaction to be told that exceptions to the rule might be reported and if justified would be allowed. The rule was rescinded and none more specific was adopted because, as it developed, a much more acute problem was to obtain enough hospitalization for maternity patients rather than to prevent services beyond the needs.

The other direct hospital control serves as a perfect demonstration of how an apparently minor requirement, one that is a common practice in business, may produce some explosive results. Early in EMIC the Bureau suggested the requirement that the financial report of a hospital should be examined and certified by a public accountant. Since the report was the source of what was established as the reimbursable cost the provision was regarded as ordinary and sound business procedure. The protests from hospital administrators were vigorous to the point of threatened withdrawal from the program.

Undoubtedly some of the hospital administrators felt that their systems of accounting would not stand the scrutiny of a certified accountant because their systems did not follow the recommended standards of accounting and record-keeping. Other administrators stated that they regarded the rule as a costly procedure and a reflection upon their integrity. Whether or not there is any relationship between this response and the use of a standard or non-standard accounting system is unknown. At any rate the requirement was changed to permit a responsible hospital official to sign the statement.

It is apparent that no administrative agency using the method of paying reimbursable costs can fulfill its responsibilities without some assurance that financial statements are reasonably accurate. The method planned by the Bureau, though it was not carried out, called for a sampling and checking of hospital statements at irregular intervals by Bureau auditors. Except for the provision that a state health department might adopt an arbitrary limit for reimbursable hospital costs, the hospitals were subjected to virtually no economic controls when EMIC reached full-scale operation. It is doubtful that any paying agency would be able to function in normal times on such a basis.

Physician Controls

The economic controls applied to physicians' services in EMIC cover almost the whole range of existing devices. A control may be more than a method; often it expresses administrative fears of what might happen, with no indication of its possibilities or probabilities. It should be emphasized here that insolvency, as a problem of the average voluntary plan, was not a threat to the continuation of EMIC. After Congress had acted to finance the program it could be assumed that reasonably adequate funds would be available for the necessary services. But, aside from the possibilities of Congressional reviews or investigations of expenditures, no administrator can be mentally comfortable if he feels that funds are being spent without returning fair values. In EMIC, therefore, the effect produced was a comparability of administrative problems with those in any agency where a specific amount of money must pay for the utilization of the services that are included in a contract.

EMIC added some new features to the concept of control. Whereas, the majority of payment agencies use economic controls to protect their funds against an excessive use of services, rarely does one find any consistant emphasis upon a program that urges beneficiaries to make full use of necessary services. The Bureau, using national, state and local educational media, urged those entitled to EMIC benefits to seek them. At the same time other methods were used to provide or assure economic protection to EMIC patients.

The "case" method of payment has been described as a variation of the fee-for-service. Where the control makes itself felt is in the definition or the specification of what constitutes a case. In this instance the maternity case had a specified content of five prenatal visits, the delivery and the postpartum examination. If less than the requisite services were provided the physician received less than the total case payment. And the same policy prevailed with respect to "time payments" i.e., it was specified that for a period of time a certain number of services would be rendered. If the number were less the payment was reduced accordingly.

The wisdom of the case (or time) method of payment with a required minimum of service as against the fee method with an allowed maximum is questionable. In the one instance services are required; in the other, services are allowed. As a choice of methods and despite what may be said about the burden of record-keeping an "allowed service" policy would have produced the same end with much less friction. A number of physicians expressed irritation because when a patient postponed her first visit until the last month of pregnancy the prenatal care could not include five visits and therefore the fee was reduced. On the other hand, when a patient appeared early in the pregnancy and was a case that required more than the minimum number of prenatal visits no increase in the payment was permitted. Any argument that in the long run the cases would "average" could only be futile—pshychologically, as well as arithmetically, for the physicians who served only a few patients.

During the course of EMIC California requested permission to pay on a case basis without holding the physician to the rigid minimum prenatal and postnatal services in each case. The State Department of Health, through some oversight of the Children's Bureau had been paying physicians on that basis for about six months. To support the contention that the method was both simple and fair an analysis of the maternity cases showed that in a high percentage (over 90) the number of prenatal and postnatal services received had equalled or exceeded the requirements. Following this demonstration the California request was approved in accordance with a new general rule. The rule specified that the same principle of payment would be approved in any state where in at least 80 percent of the cases the services equalled or exceeded the minimum. Many states could not meet this minimum and in these the rules regarding prenatal and postpartum payments were not changed.

The most significant admixture of economic controls and efforts to improve the quality of care* is found in the Bureau suggestions covering conditions that might call for additional fees to physicians. Relative to intercurrent non-obstetric conditions the attending physician was not allowed extra fees if the condition was treated in his office.** If the condition required home or hospital care exclusive of surgery additional fees were allowed in accordance with an established fee schedule. For non-obstetric surgery, added fees were allowed only to the attending physicians who were qualified in a surgical specialty. For obstetrical surgery fees were allowed only to qualified consultants. Thus, if an attending physician performed a Caesarian section no fee in addition to the regular case payment was allowed but if the patient was referred to a qualified consultant the latter was paid according to the schedule of fees for this major surgical service. Circumcision if performed during the first two

*Discussed in Chapter XI.

**This rule was revised in *EMIC Information Circular No. 1*, March, 1945, (Item IV E, p. 18) to permit additional fees in cases requiring an exceptional amount of care.

weeks after infants were delivered did not carry an added fee for the attending physician; if the operation was performed later a fee was allowed.

In the above examples two purposes are apparent. The primary one was to assure surgery by those qualified and to curb unnecessary surgery; the protection of funds was a secondary consideration. Yet each example is one where the attempt to curb was based upon the application of an economic control. Whether the measures achieved the objectives is not known but the subject calls for further analysis and study. The controls used throw a spotlight on problems discussed previously, i.e., the designation of medical specialists and the payment of variable fees.

Dual Controls

Some of the control methods were applied both to physicans and hospitals. The outstanding examples in EMIC were the rule with regard to supplementary fees and what is discussed later as the "all or none" requirement. Both of these controls were intended to protect the beneficiaries of the services.

One of the most rigid policies concerned supplementary fees. As stated in *EMIC Information Circular No. 13*, "Authorization for medical or hospital care should be made by the State health agency under agreement with the attending physician or the hospital that no payments will be accepted from the patient or family." And, further, "Payments should be made to the hospital upon receipt of invoices . . . and a statement that the hospital had not charged nor received payment from the patient or family for any of the services rendered."

The rules controlling supplementary fees created problems that were not solved satisfactorily. Virtually all existing hospital prepayment plans, as well as legislative proposals that include hospital insurance, offer the protection of care in a ward or semi-private room but permit beneficiaries to purchase out of their own funds hospital accommodations that are more costly. The medical needs of the patient are regarded as cared for by the system of organized payment; those who want "luxury service" have the privilege of spending their own money for it. In EMIC the sole consideration was the need of the patient; hospitals were not permitted to "sell" private rooms and the regulation on this subject required hospitals to "provide whatever accommodations are indicated by the patient's medical condition at the per diem rate paid by the State health agency."*

**EMIC Information Circular No. 1* (Revised March, 1945) II 8, p. 3.

The policy behind this feature of the administration of EMIC, as stated by different Bureau officials, showed certain confusion. As one official expressed it, "If she (the expectant mother) wishes to purchase luxury care over and above what the State agency has made arrangements for furnishing in the hospital, she wouldn't be eligible for care under the program." Thus, EMIC is interpreted as a form of public relief.

Another view was that the wives of the members of the armed forces neither requested nor wanted anything but the same equitable treatment that their husbands were experiencing. But, from the administrative standpoint, the most logical reason was that to have permitted patients to purchase more costly accommodations in hospitals would have made it impossible to enforce the rule prohibiting physicians from charging supplementary fees to patients regarded as "able to pay." Under the circumstances it was necessary to apply the principle of no supplementary payment regardless of prevailing custom. If it contributed nothing else to this subject, EMIC demonstrated that policies regarding services in hospitals and services by physicians are interdependent. If, for example, the income level of the beneficiaries of a voluntary medical plan is raised the issue of supplementary physicians' fees for patients who of their own volition purchase private room accommodations in a hospital cannot be dodged.

The "all or none" principle which is related to the rules against supplementary fees, provided that the patient must receive all of the services—medical and hospital—without the payment of any added fees or costs. Even though the patient might be willing, EMIC would not approve payment from the Federal funds to a hospital, leaving the medical services to be purchased by the patient. Nor would a physician be paid by EMIC if the patient paid for hospital services. Only in those cases where one service was contributed was payment permitted for the other and, at first view, the rule looks like an example of administrative rigidity and domination.

The main purposes of the all-or-none principle were the economic protection of the patient and, as discussed in the next chapter, the improvement of services. The adherence to the principle created a number of difficult problems but it is hard to see how EMIC could have worked without it and still have achieved its objectives. A physician who felt that the patient could pay for the medical service, especially if there were no hospital bill, could make a direct charge according to his judgment of the patient's means. And in communities where, for one reason or another, hospitals could not or would not participate in the program the chances of patients paying for hospital care if physicians' services were provided through EMIC would be increased. To have relaxed the rule would have violated the interpreted directive of Congress to the Children's Bureau—that the wives and infants of servicemen receive necessary maternity and infant care without cost. Though there were criticisms of the rule, the great majority of physicians and hospital administrators interviewed felt that it did function to curb practices by a minority of institutions and physicians that would have been harmful to the economic welfare of patients.

That the all-or none principle served as a method of bringing pressure on hospitals and physicians to participate in the program is apparent. Thus, if some physicians in a community wanted to provide care for EMIC patients and the hospitals were opposed, medical pressure would be exerted to change the hospital policy. Also, the reverse of this situation would occur as it did in a county in New York where at the beginning of the program both the hospitals and the obstetricians decided not to participate. Since non-participation in what was regarded as a war effort carried the responsibility of assuring that necessary services would be rendered, the hospitals began to feel the economic disadvantages of the policy. The hospitals urged the obstetricians on their staffs to participate and began to admit EMIC patients from other physicans. As the program expanded the earlier policy was abandoned and the obstetricians became participants.

In many of the interviews with hospital administrators and practicing physicians the most common suggestion was that the rule should provide for exceptional cases. At times it was impossible for state health departments to enforce the all-or-none principle. The program showed that hospitals render their bills more promptly, as a rule, than do physicians. When, after the hospital bill had been paid, it was learned that the physician had changed his mind about participating in EMIC and rendered a bill to the patient a strict application of the rule would have required the department to obtain a refund from the hospital. To demand a refund from a hospital that had rendered the services in good faith, telling the hospital to collect from the patient, would have been an administrative absurdity. Fortunately, the type of case described was rare.

Throughout the study the same suggestion for rules that could be relaxed to cover exceptional cases in all phases of EMIC was repeated. The suggestion is sound but unlimited administrative flexibility is not without its dangers. The chief danger is that the exception, if not controlled, will grow until it becomes the rule.

An example of this process will be presented in the discussion concerning the quality of services.

EMIC was a demonstration of economic controls for the protection of the beneficiaries of services. Unlike other schemes of payment where a specific income must provide services for a definite period of time the EMIC controls were not formulated with the main idea of protecting the central fund. As happened, when more money was needed the Children's Bureau turned to Congress. Thus, none of the usual economic controls was a part of EMIC—neither proration, nor the usual limits on services nor barrier payments. The chief emphasis was placed upon obtaining adequate services for each patient under rules that prohibited supplementary payments.

There is little evidence of any consistent attempts in the states to enforce the rules. Each state that submitted a descriptive plan to administer EMIC was asked to outline its process of action in the event of violations of rules. The penalties usually recorded included the withholding of future authorizations from those who refused to conform and forcing reimbursements from physicians or hospitals that charged supplementary fees. But to write such penalties is one thing; to enforce them is not only different but also rare.

The problem of economic controls before EMIC, as well as the problem before all types of payment plans, can be stated in a word —enforcement. When physicans submitted requests for EMIC authorizations the requests contained the provision "I agree not to accept payment from the patient or family for the services authorized." For the great majority of physicans there was never any question about fulfilling the terms of the agreement. Many might have been opposed to the whole program, many might have felt that the fees were too low, or that certain administrative policies were unfair, but regardless of these sentiments, they fulfilled their committments.

Neither can it be questioned that a minority violated either the letter or the spirit of the agreement. Only rarely is it possible to write a rule that is "air-tight"; the purpose of the rule may be clear but a way to dodge the purpose may also be apparent. For example, one way to conform to the written rule regarding supplementary fees and yet obtain supplementary fees was mentioned a number of times during the field survey. The request for the authorization of physican's services contained two descriptions of the maternity services. One was for "complete medical services, including care during the prenatal period"; the other was for medical services beginning with labor and it provided for a lesser fee. A way was open to charge the patient directly for prenatal services by delaying the

EMIC request so that it would cover the period beginning with labor. Though the combined fees from the patient for prenatal care and from EMIC might be appreciably larger than the $50 for complete services, the great majority of physicians, shown this "opportunity," would have only one response, "Not interested."

Under what conditions may economic controls function successfully? The answer seems clear in accordance with the criterion described as basic—that no penalty should be exacted from the majority for the acts of a minority. Successful controls in any system that pays fees for services should be a joint undertaking with clear responsibilities accepted by the profession and the paying agency. When there is an adequate routine analysis of accumulated records the minority group stands out; it is self-selected because of its deviation from a reasonable pattern of services established by the entire group. And once the process of self-selection is completed the profession faces its responsibility to act. Nothing is gained by the profession from any policy of a "united front" against a voluntary or government paying agency; the majority needs no such front, the minority thrives upon it.

EMIC did not last long nor were the emergency circumstances of its operation conducive to anything but short-range planning. But it lasted long enough to show the importance of economic controls, long enough to show the danger of minority violations, long enough to demonstrate the need of more attention to controls as the most crucial administrative problem that attends fee payments.

CHAPTER XI

ADMINISTRATIVE CONTROLS— QUALITY OF SERVICES

An enormous amount of confusing controversy surrounds the subject of the quality of medical care in the United States. Scientific facts are invested with political meaning, political opinions are given the weight of scientific facts and statistics comprise the heaviest ammunition of debate. Speeches are made, books are written and campaigns are planned to prove that, medically speaking,

1. The United States leads the world.
2. The United States lags.

Why the country leads or lags, according to the tables, charts and graphs that are presented, seems to depend upon what is being proposed or opposed. Out of it all the one solid grain of truth that emerges is that, in the present state of knowledge and method, the science of measuring or weighing the factors that comprise national health is in an extremely elementary stage of development.

With the exception of maternity services few studies of the quality of medical care have been made. The maternity studies have concentrated upon the causes of maternity deaths and have produced valuable information to support the emphasis upon the need of postgraduate medical education. But often the quality of medical care is judged by quantitative measurements and in many instances quantitative regulations are adopted to improve quality. Too seldom is there any sharp differentiation between the availability and use of medical services and the quality of what is received.

The methods of improving quality may be classified as educational or regulatory. The educational activities are subdivided, further, into professional and public programs. The professional programs are intended to acquaint professional groups, such as physicians, with new methods and other improvements in the health services. The public programs are concerned largely with creating the urge in people to do certain things and abstain from others. The public is advised to see physicians early during the course of an illness, immunizations are recommended, maternity cases are urged to obtain prenatal care, etc. All these programs of public education have an indirect connection with the quality of care in the sense that attention is directed to certain desirable types of service.

Though there is much talk about the relationship between the quality of medical care and the type of payment plan—voluntary or government—few of the plans of either type stress administrative policies aimed toward the improvement of quality. In general, the policy is to provide the services that are available in the community. If it were for no other reason than this one, the efforts in EMIC to improve quality would deserve special attention. While the history of the Children's Bureau shows an almost exclusive emphasis upon the educational approach, EMIC presents an almost equally exclusive approach through the use of regulatory measures.

In general the medical profession feels that all matters that pertain to the quality of physicians' services should be left to medical organizations. Proposals to control quality are interpreted as attempts to dictate to the physician how he shall practice medicine. Strong medical opposition to any form of "external control" is understandable since no feature of private practice is guarded more zealously than the right of the physician to make his own decisions concerning the care of his patients. At the same time it is recognized by medical leaders that quality varies extremely. A small percentage of physicians in practice are graduates of unapproved schools, others have not kept abreast of the advances in medicine and others may be careless. In many instances an educational program alone cannot produce the desired results; administrative controls or regulatory procedures must serve as a complement to education.

The Experience of EMIC

The experience of EMIC with administrative controls to improve quality is presented under two headings. One set of controls was aimed at the improvement of physicians' services; the other, at the improvement of hospital care.

Physicians' Services

The first element of quality-control and one that has been used too little, is the information that each physician submits when he presents his account for services rendered to a patient. Reasonable administrative simplicity requires that the amount of detail must be kept to a minimum. Yet, in a system where fees are paid for services, patients' names must be reported along with the number and dates of visits, laboratory services for which charges are made, the use and the purpose of X-ray services and other information.

In the EMIC program the reports included services considered routine in maternity and infant care as well as the diagnosis, services and other information on the illnesses of mothers and infants. Such reports of physicians' services are the rule in all voluntary payment plans; they are the first element of administrative control and a routine analysis of their contents should provide the basis for a program of postgraduate professional education.

It was with some hesitation that permission was given by the Children's Bureau to the states to pay for maternity care at a single rate even though some of the cases did not receive the specified number of antepartum or postpartum services. To be sure the single-rate payment resulted in a simplification of records and reports but the Bureau stipulated that it would be allowed only where there was proof that 80 percent of the cases had received the minimum prenatal and postpartum care. The minimum requirements serve as examples of administrative controls to improve the quality of service. More than that, they are examples of an attempt to improve quality by requiring a certain type and quantity of service.

The various professional responses to the standard of five prenatal services are of interest. With the exception of the previously-mentioned complaints because certain patients delayed their requests for medical attention, the great majority of physicians accepted the five or more services as a procedure that they followed routinely. But in other instances during the field survey questions were raised or antagonism was expressed. As reported in a southern state, "Not a few physicians practicing in the area have asked what the prenatal visits are for and what they are supposed to do at such visits. They have practiced for years without giving any thought to prenatal care." In another state a graduate of an unapproved medical school said, "I don't see the necessity of requiring all these prenatal visits. I think it represents a political attempt by the state health department and some influential physicians to put some of us out of business." And in a third state the director of the maternal and child health program said "One of the big problems in EMIC is the fact that many physicians, especially the older men in the rural areas, had no concept of the importance of prenatal care to pregnant women. Such things as pelvic measurements, routine blood tests, etc., are entirely new to them." Many patients received care while living in other places than their home communities. That they will expect the same quality of care from their home-town physicians in connection with future pregnancies is shown by the number of better qualified physicians who quoted their patients as saying "I never got care like this; next time I'll ask for it."

These are but a few of the statements made during the course of the study. They cannot be interpreted as any measurement of the quality of services throughout the country but they do show the importance of administrative controls for a minority of physicians. And they demonstrate further that such controls, unless they are complemented by a program of professional education, will produce less than the desired results.

Another major administrative control, mentioned previously, was intended to prevent unnecessary surgery. This was the rule that no addition to the maternity fee would be allowed for surgery, such as delivery by Caesarean section, when performed by the attending physician. If the surgery were necessary the physician could perform it without an added fee or could refer the case to a consultant who would be paid a fee. Later, a rule was adopted to permit the payment of a non-obstetrical surgical fee to an attending physician who was qualified in a surgical specialty. Obviously, the rules were intended to reduce unnecessary surgery by removing any economic incentive and, at the same time, assure that indicated surgery would be approved or performed by qualified surgeons. The efficacy of the general rules cannot be judged but it may be assumed that the physician who would be influenced by the fee in his decision to perform surgery is the same physician who would devise ways to by-pass the rule through such arrangements as fee-splitting or other violations of ethics.

Adequate records have been mentioned as the first element of administrative control to improve quality. These are the records that tell the story of each physician's practice; they are the medium through which the minority of physicians that require control select themselves. The burden of the routine analysis of the records is a responsibility of the administrative agency; once the process of self-selection indicates the need of action the responsibility should shift from the agency to the organized medical profession. It is this sequence of responsibility, culminating in professional action, that assures a resonable protection of the public and, likewise, affords reasonable protection to the majority of the profession.

One other experience of EMIC in the area of quality-control repeated what has happened in virtually all of the broad-scale Federal programs to provide physicians' services. This experience refers to maternity care and not to pediatric services. In the latter, as well as in the crippled children's program, no question has been raised concerning the limitation of services to those that are provided by Doctors of Medicine. But for maternity care other groups of practitioners, licensed by the states, are permitted to provide services.

For the Bureau to limit maternity services to Doctors of Medicine would have been regarded as a violation of States' rights. Since it is the state that determines who shall practice medicine, only the state has the privilege of limiting services to specified practitioners. As an example, in Wisconsin the State Health Department took the position that payments for EMIC maternity care would be made only to Doctors of Medicine. But, considering the traditional Federal-state relationships, it is hopeless to expect any Federal agency to correct what the medical profession regards as defects in the laws governing practice in the states. This was the experience of EMIC in its program of maternity care; it is the growing experience of the Veterans' Administration in the development of "home town" services for veterans.

What, then, were the results of the attempts in EMIC to improve the quality of professional practice? It is obvious that the rules that have been described cannot be applied successfully without integrated programs of professional and public education. Rules that assure certain services on a quantitative basis—such as the number of prenatal services—cannot be interpreted as assuring, also, an adequate content. Nor does a general rule intended to improve quality through the use of economic curbs achieve satisfactory results. Such rules only serve to irritate where they are not needed; they invite counter-measures and violations where most needed. In short, EMIC demonstrated that improvement of quality is fundamentally important to any plan for medical care and that control measures, to be effective, must be accepted as the dual responsibility of the administrative agency and the organized medical profession.

The over-all impression of the EMIC controls intended to improve the quality of physicians' services is that of an administrative agency entering a new and unsurveyed area. Under such conditions each rule becomes a process of trial and error; each step toward the goal is accompanied by a seeking for secure footing. And the impression is heightened when one turns from an examination of medical controls to an analysis of hospital controls. The latter presents progress over a more solid administrative terrain marked by the guideposts of experience established through the trials and errors of the past.

Hospital Services

Efforts to improve the quality of hospital services in the United States began in 1918 when the American College of Surgeons formulated the "Minimum Standards for Hospitals." Of the 692 hospitals surveyed by the College in 1918, approximately 13 percent were approved; in 1941 a total of 3,688 hospitals were inspected and 2,995 or almost 78 percent were fully or provisionally approved. Although the number approved by the College represented only 30 percent of the hospitals in the country the number of beds in these institutions comprised about three-fourths of the total.[1] Great, indeed, have been the contributions of the College in raising the standards of hospital services.

In 1927 and 1928 the Council on Medical Education and Hospitals of the American Medical Association adopted two sets of minimum standards for hospitals offering internships and residencies in the medical specialties. Thus, prior to the activities of the Children's Bureau to improve hospital services two strong national professional organizations had established standards. However, none of the standards has a legal status; a hospital may not apply for approval nor does a rejection by the College or the Association mean that the institution is prohibited from further operation.

The EMIC funds were not the first to be administered by the Bureau to make available hospital and medical care. Prior to EMIC the Social Security Act, adopted in 1935, included an appropriation of $2,850,000 for grants to the states to improve and extend the services for crippled children. The Bureau was designated as the administrative agency and policies were adopted to raise the standards of services. The standards that were formulated with the help of advisory committees served as guides for the designation of physicians and other personnel qualified to render services and for the approval of hospitals and convalescent and foster homes to which children might be sent for care.

In general and as a starting point approval was given to institutions judged satisfactory by the College and the Association. In addition, it was suggested that state agencies, in establishing their hospital standards, consider the special requirements for the care of crippled children as presented in the recommendations of the Bureau's advisory committee. It was recommended that an approved hospital include on its staff a certified orthopedic surgeon and provide accredited physiotherapists and nurses as well as the physical facilities necessary for adequate treatment. By 1939 a total of 561 hospitals had been approved for the program.

As an interesting sidelight, and because it has a bearing upon the experience in EMIC, the hospital standards of the College and the Association were found to be inadequate to cover the special

[1] "Twenty-Fourth Annual Hospital Standards," *Bulletin of American College of Surgeons* October, 1941. p. 298.

needs of crippled children and this situation led to the development of additional hospital requirements. The influence of this earlier experience as a guide to EMIC policies may be noted in the statement made in 1943 by Dr. Martha Eliot, speaking at a conference with the state and territorial health officers. She said, "The inclusion of sub-standard hospitals in the crippled children's program at the beginning of our experience shows how difficult it is to take a later stand that involves dropping a hospital that does not meet state standards. Once a hospital has been approved it is almost impossible to exclude it and I think that this should be borne in mind as you begin to go forward with a new program which will involve hospital care."

Other experiences of the Bureau also played a role in the selection of EMIC policies relative to hospitals. Following the adoption of the Social Security Act the attention of the Bureau was directed toward the improvement of maternity and infant services in hospitals. Very little was being done by the states to supervise hospitals and, therefore, the Bureau prepared a list of suggestions for the states to consider if legislation to control the standards of hospitals were being prepared. And accompanying the suggestions the Bureau urged that the states take action. By 1940 the Bureau was able to report to its General Advisory Committee on Maternal and Child Welfare Services that "five states have recently adopted rules and regulations for the conduct of hospitals and homes accepting maternity patients and several states have strengthened the existing rules and regulations on this subject. The health departments of 17 states and Hawaii now have the responsibility of licensing and regulating hospitals or homes accepting maternity patients." In the majority of the states this was the only hospital legislation that existed and a broad administrative experience had accumulated by the time that the problem of hospital control arose in EMIC. For example, it was from a background of experience that the Director of Maternal and Child Health in Oregon stated at a conference on EMIC, "In 1939 we passed a law requiring all maternity hospitals to be licensed and, at that time, we ran into the same difficulties that many of the states are having now. Some of the hospitals were opposed; some had to be closed. But after a few years the value of licensing hospitals and maternity homes became apparent in the reduction of the maternal death rate."

With the added impetus given by EMIC to the improvement of hospital services, by March, 1944, the health departments in 38 states had legal authority to inspect, approve and license hospital maternity services and maternity homes. In the remaining states the departments assumed authority on a tentative basis since the acceptance of EMIC funds required the acceptance, also, of the Bureau's basic requirements with respect to hospitals. However, the assumed authority had its limitations in that the State officials would inspect only those hospitals that expressed a desire to participate in the EMIC program.

Georgia serves as an example of the sequence of events following the introduction of EMIC. The health department, lacking legal authority to adopt and enforce hospital standards, took the position that "Only those hospitals in Georgia with minimum requirements as established by the Children's Bureau shall be eligible for participation in the program. Such inspections will be made prior to participation by professional staff members of the division of Maternal and Child Health or of the division of Public Health Nursing or other competent persons designated by the division of Maternal and Child Health. Should it be necessary in the interest of the program to utilize hospitals approved by the American College of Surgeons, the department may elect to use this (approval) as a basis for establishing such hospitals as eligible for participation."

Describing the hospital conditions in Georgia at a meeting of the Fifth District Medical Society, the state Director of Maternal and Child Health said, "It is an unpleasant truth that our inspection of hospitals, both teaching and non-teaching, reveals that many hospitals in Georgia cannot measure up to the very minimum requirements established for hospital facilities under the program. Though some of the deficiencies are due to war conditions, many are in no way related to the war. This is the situation that the medical profession must face realistically."

The support given by the medical profession to the work of the health department is shown in a committee report from the state medical society to the department. The report stated that "The committee upheld the Georgia Department of Public Health with regard to the basis for approval of hospitals in this program. The committee insisted that the highest possible standards be maintained when conditions permitted, but that certain minimum requirements not be relaxed for any reason. The committee recommended the continued disapproval of hospitals that do not meet minimum requirements and advised the Georgia Department of Public Health to enforce strictly such standards as it deemed wise after considering the situation in each locality."

Individual physicians interviewed on this subject expressed the same type of approval. A prominent obstetrician who, incidentally, was not at all sympathetic to EMIC said, "There should be a state provision for the inspection and licensing of hospitals; it is something badly needed in Georgia. In the absence of state authority the health department has been doing a good job of inspecting and of enforcing standards for the EMIC program and probably many small hospitals will make improvements." The prediction was correct; while some of the hospitals resisted and were antagonistic to the idea of being told "how to run their affairs" the general attitude was one of cooperation and many hospitals undertook the alterations necessary to meet the standards. The situation in Georgia is not described as an exception; it is presented as an example of comparable occurrences in many states.

Despite its background of experience in the administrative control and improvement of hospitals the Children's Bureau faced new and acute problems in EMIC. Here was a program that involved virtually every community in the country; many states lacked comprehensive legislation to improve hospital standards; many sub-standard hospitals existed; hospital facilities were already overcrowded. There existed, also, the standards of the College of Surgeons and the American Medical Association and it was assumed widely that any institution that met one or the other of these standards was equally satisfactory for the provision of the special services that are a part of maternity care. For many institutions the assumption was in error.

It should be emphasized that the Bureau suggestions for the approval of hospitals constituted minimum *requirements* — not minimum or adequate *standards* for the care of maternity cases and infants. The requirements are shown in Appendix xi and they demonstrate both the flexibility of the program in certain respects and the rigidity in others. As expressed by Bureau officials there was some hesitation in publishing minimum requirements that were embarrassingly low and the states were urged to develop their own requirements "as high as are practicable under existing conditions." In the states that had legal authority and had been working for a number of years to improve hospitals the requirements, being lower in a number of respects than the states' standards, created a special problem.

At the other extreme were the states in which hospital control was new and in which even the minimum requirements introduced new concepts of adequate maternity facilities. Among the most prevalent reasons for rejecting a hospital were the following:

1. The use of an operating room as a delivery room. The requirements stated that where this condition was found patients

"shall be delivered in their own rooms, except in cases of Caesarean section." The purpose of the rule was to prevent delivery under conditions that might lead to infection.

2. The failure to provide facilities that permitted the separation of maternity patients from other types of patients. Here, too, the purpose of the requirement was to prevent the transmission of infection from appendicitis, pneumonia or other cases to maternity patients and infants.

3. Inadequate graduate nursing care.

4. Inadequate nursery facilities.

In any administrative process there always arises the problem of permitting exceptions to a general rule. As would be expected there were many situations in EMIC that called for special consideration and decision. For example, in one state a physician applied for payment after his patient was delivered in a non-participating hospital. The health department accepted the statement that the delivery was on an emergency basis and approved payment to the physician. The patient was permitted to pay the hospital. The case was an emergency exception to the "all or none" principle and in comparable situations might have set an acceptable administrative pattern. However, the results following this action were unfavorable; the approval of the exception was followed by a series of applications from the same and from other physicians, all requesting approval of EMIC care in the same hospital on an emergency basis. To have granted the requests would have established an administrative policy that would have made the minimum requirements so much meaningless print. The administrative problem in this instance has nothing to do with the question of the adequacy or the inadequacy of the facilities in the non-participating hospital. If the hospital actually possessed adequate facilities but refused to participate or to request approval, the refusal itself would open the way to deliveries in other institutions with inadequate facilities. The latter could bypass inspection and rejection under the guise of non-participation, i.e., merely by stating that it did not care to participate in the program.

There was, also the problem of hospitals with closed staffs. Some physicians were willing to accept EMIC patients but found that the hospitals open to them were not participating. Though another hospital in the community accepted EMIC cases the particular physicians could not use it because they were not members of the hospital staff. Under such conditions none of the alternatives open to a physician was satisfactory. The patient could be delivered in her home or the patient could be released to another physician who was a member of the participating hospital's staff or the EMIC program could be forgotten, with the patient paying both the hospital and the physician. Despite the unsatisfactory alternatives the EMIC administrator could not permit his whole program of hospital control to be blocked by the problem of open or closed hospital staffs. To have permitted exceptions in such cases would have meant the adoption of a policy permitting the delivery of a maternity patient in any hospital to which a physician had access.

In reviewing hospital control as a part of EMIC it is easy to become submerged in the complexities of the exceptional cases that comprise a very small percentage of the total. In the main, however, the results of and the general reaction to the program of hospital approval and participation were very favorable. The state health departments undertook and carried out an enormous task, many of them engaging in hospital inspection as a completely new activity. Another example of the favorable medical attitude toward hospital improvement was expressed in Mississippi, editorially, as follows: "As a consequence, this work of the Maternal and Child Health Division has been of great value in protecting the health of many mothers other than those who applied to the EMIC program. It has resulted in many changes in the physical lay-out of maternity wards and nursing, as well as in the addition of necessary equipment such as incubators for the premature infants. In view of the considerable increase in hospital deliveries this function of the division is all the more important."[2]

The comments from physicians and hospital administrators in other states support the value of hospital control in EMIC. The superintendent of a hospital in Massachusetts said, "Unquestionably, the EMIC program contributed greatly in raising the quality of care offered in many hospitals throughout the country." And the same opinions were expressed in the other states that were visited.

The Children's Bureau is neither the first nor the only Federal agency given responsibility for expending funds for hospital care. But, more than any other agency, the Bureau has given impetus to the improvement of the quality of hospital services. In an earlier chapter it was stated that many of the policies of the Bureau, with respect to the administration of EMIC funds, were based upon the immediate and the emergency character of EMIC. At the same time other policies and actions were tied to considerations beyond the

[2]Editorial, *The Mississippi Doctor* July, 1944.

emergency. No aspect of EMIC demonstrates the dual purposes of the policies more than the minimum requirements for the improvement of hospital care and the methods of their administration.

CHAPTER XII

SUMMARY AND CONCLUSIONS

When the United States became a nation at war normal production at normal speed for normal purposes shifted abruptly to abnormal production at abnormal speed for abnormal purposes. Many of the efforts were undertaken without reasonably adequate preparation and most of them lacked guiding precedents. The lack of preparation and precedent contributed to many mistakes that were condoned by the American public because it was recognized that in lieu of experience the alternative is the process of trial and error. The only assurance demanded by the public was that there be no evidence of venality attached to any action or failure to act.

EMIC developed as an accompaniment of war and, yet, with regard to precedent, EMIC was different. The first appropriation by Congress was made upon the assumption, as shown by the testimony, that EMIC was an expansion of an existing program, not a new one. Thus, from the outset, there arose the confusion of interpretations as to which realm of EMIC was Hygeia's and which was Mars'. Assigned to a peacetime agency rather than to a new one created by the war, EMIC absorbed automatically a long series of precedents. And the precedents, in terms of the origin of the Bureau, its purposes and policies, its administration of the Sheppard-Towner Act, its functions and programs under the Social Security Act and its conflicts, serve as a backdrop against which any current activity, such as EMIC, must be viewed. The very existence and association of EMIC with this peacetime agency raised the question in the minds of many, "After the war, what?"

That the Children's Bureau has many enthusiastic friends is a fact that has been demonstrated throughout its existence. Powerful organizations and individuals were responsible for its creation in 1912 and these and others have rallied to its support when any issue threatened its existence. The protagonists will assign little weight to the controversy that was a part of EMIC or to criticism of the organization and administration of the program. They will look upon the whole effort as a job that needed to be done and was done to the extent of providing services to over 1,200,000 maternity cases and care to over 230,000 infants.

On the other side is the fact that the Bureau during its growth and the expansion of its programs has developed antagonists that cannot be classified as minor ones. In the testimony regarding the future of EMIC, the Bureau stated without qualification that it viewed the program as a war activity with a limited duration, i. e., EMIC was not being projected into the future. At the same time, the Bureau has been utterly frank in its statements of objectives—the organization of an adequate system of health services for the mothers and children of the country. The agency becomes, therefore, an exposed target for those who fear the growth of anything interpreted as "socialized medicine" and especially, any form of Federal activity in the field of medical care.

Thus, the friends of EMIC tend to center their attention upon the accomplishments; the critics concentrate upon the complexities of rules and regulations, the evidence of domination by government and the apparent confusion in planning. These are the types of selective factual evidence that strengthen dogmatic opinions and provide little else than food for controversy. One side is preoccupied with ends and the other, with means.

To many of the officials and members of the medical profession, EMIC was a form of distasteful war medicine. EMIC was launched in a period of vigorous debate on the subject of a national health plan. In a short time it became apparent that while EMIC was an emergency program it was, also, a national health plan. Yet, to oppose the program vigorously and publicly was to be accused of a lack of patriotism, an unsympathetic attitude toward those who were doing the fighting. How to express the fear of and the animosity toward EMIC without drawing the fire of public opinion was regarded as a crucial question of policy by certain local medical societies. Behind these considerations lies the dual character of EMIC as an effort of the war and at the same time as a threat to future peacetime policies.

It is not improbable that the attitude of the medical profession influenced many of the adverse responses of state health departments. Among health administrators there is wide disagreement concerning the future role of health departments as agencies to administer various types of public medical services. By the great majority of departments EMIC was interpreted as a new and greatly expanded venture in medical care. The fact that services for crippled children had been administered for many years had little bearing on the attitude. EMIC brought acute problems of professional relations and there were additional features that disturbed health departments.

The particular issues of the past are of secondary importance in this study but it is important to the interpretation of episodes to know that at the time EMIC was started there were old antagonisms, submerged and smoldering. The war and the emergency nature of EMIC combined to introduce a period of armed cooperation. Under EMIC the antagonistic forces were cancelled by the urge to contribute to the war efforts, even though many individuals might have doubted that the contributions were necessary or real.

It has been said that EMIC, by its assignment to the Children's Bureau, inherited the precedents of the Bureau. With such an urgent need for an accelerated administrative tempo, one of the first casualties among precedents was the established formula of Federal-states relations. This is a formula where the diplomatic amenities are of crucial importance. Time must be expended lavishly—time for lengthy conferences, time for education, time for the extended personal and postal negotiations leading to agreements. One of the most rigid rules in the book of Federal-state etiquette is that neither by act nor expression should the representative of a Federal agency dominate or seem to dominate a state agency.

In the atmosphere of war the concept of getting the job done, regardless of costs and feelings, usually prevails. Getting the job done in EMIC was the chief purpose and no matter how great might be the verbal emphasis upon States' rights the need of speed forced the central administrative agency into a position where the program became Federal rather than Federal-state, in the usual sense. Had anything like EMIC been started as a peacetime program it would have taken three months to complete preparations for preliminary discussions with the states. Within the same period, the plans of 38 states for the actual administration of EMIC had been approved by the Bureau. To assume that this could have been done without a detailed blueprint that served as a master plan for the states to follow is to forget the usual pattern of Federal-state action.

The need of speed brought its predictable results. Regulations were adopted to govern many of the details of administration and new experiences resulted in changes in regulations. Those affected by the changes felt harassed but this, in itself, did not differ greatly from the reaction to other war efforts by state and local health departments. Where the response to EMIC differed was in the tendency of those concerned with state health administration to view the program with an eye to the immediate tasks and an eye upon possible future policy. What state health departments saw and interpreted as a possible foundation for future Federal domination was disturbing to them.

The interesting feature of this attitude, concern over the future, is that it is observable, also, in the actions of the Children's Bureau. Getting the job done was the primary task but getting it done regardless of costs, as an example, was another matter. As a cost of war, the absorption of a fee of $50 or $150 for maternity care is relatively unimportant. But if the fee is regarded as setting a possible pattern of postwar costs of maternity care it becomes extremely important. It was the peacetime outlook, rather than the wartime psychology that appeared to govern many of the Bureau's decisions on important questions of costs and other aspects of EMIC.

EMIC serves as a striking demonstration of joint effort and of administrative resiliency. It would be hard to find another wartime program that grew to such comparatively huge proportions and still remained within the framework of an existing national, state and local peacetime administration. The accomplishments in meeting the problems, disregarding the antagonisms, conflicts and fears, are a monument to the combined contributions of medicine, public health and the hospitals. Maternity and infant care were the goals; maternity and infant care are the achievements.

The hearings before Congressional committees stand as a tribute both to the committee members and to the public servants who offered testimony. Health services, such as maternity and infant care, play an important and intimate part in the lives of the people. The regrettable concept, held too generally, of insulated officials who are not susceptible to the will or need of ordinary citizens is refuted by the hearings and testimony. And the penetrating and, at times, the discomforting questions and observations of the members of Congress are reassuring evidences of the vitality of the democratic process. It is, also, a matter of note that the response of the elected representatives to the objectives of the Bureau is highly favorable and that there is an underlying admiration of the frankness and even of the militancy of the Bureau officials in their activities to provide services for mothers and children. But the fear of "socialized medicine" is likewise apparent.

The guiding principles of public organization and public administration have a direct application to any widespread health plan, be it for a state or the nation; be it voluntary or compulsory. To permit a plan to function successfully there must be an agency with the strength to adopt political policy and the authority to make it effective. This appears to be one of the chief issues that faces the voluntary medical and hospital plans today in their movement toward greater centralization in the states and toward the consolidation of state plans into a national scheme. Autonomy is a precious quality but, like a strong condiment, it must be used with discretion.

The authority to adopt political policy carries with it the responsibility to control the administrative agency that applies the policy. In the case of the Children's Bureau there were the general controls of Congressional hearings and investigations, the financial controls exerted by the President and the Budget Bureau and the legal controls of the Solicitor. In turn, the Children's Bureau exercised authority over the states through regulations governing the grants of funds.

As an example of the comparability of problems and to some extent, at least, the comparability of solutions, the recent action by voluntary plans is significant. A number of the plans, attempting to cover employes in interstate industries have centralized their activities with respect to financing the services.[1] Though the plans in the different areas have different rates, these are averaged to arrive at the single rate to be charged. From the average single rate each plan will receive what has been its regular rate—some will receive more, others less than the average. But, if it is assumed that the differences in area rates are justifiable, what the pooling process means is that a central authority utilizes the principle of variable grants-in-aid.

In the line of administration the most important center of two-way communication between the Children's Bureau and the states is the regional office. That the Bureau has recognized administration as a technical vocation is shown by the appointment, late in the EMIC program, of non-medical administrative assistants to the Regional Medical Directors. It was at the point where the states were allowed the greatest flexibility—record systems, reporting, incumbrance of funds, payment for services—that they needed and would have welcomed much more help from the day the program began. And, probably as a next step, there should be a greater coordination of Federal health activities through the consolidation of the regional offices of the two major agencies, the Children's Bureau and the United States Public Health Service.

The assumption that the administrative costs of EMIC could be absorbed by state health departments was an error that affected the whole program. It was responsible for much of the criticism that came from overworked staffs and for other complaints caused by the slow movement of authorizations and delayed payments for

[1]Virginia Liebeler, "News of Hospital Plans," *Hospital Management* 48:45 May, 1948.

services. Coupled with the lack of administrative funds, as a cause of complaint, was the pressure of the Bureau and the public to get EMIC started and, once started, the changes in administrative policies and details.

Viewing the rapid evolution of the program, one of the chief lessons from EMIC is the importance of the period of time that precedes the initiation of any widespread medical plan. Public medical programs and many of the existing voluntary plans have paid heavily for the lack of attention to existing administrative experience and the values of administrative research. EMIC also demonstrated the future importance of training facilities and trained medical administrative personnel. These matters have been a concern, also, of the voluntary prepayment plans in the country.

That health insurance is assuming the proportions of a broad social movement in the United States is apparent to anyone who reviews the action over the past 15 years. Impressive also, is the degree to which the attitude of compromise is replacing the "unalterable" positions that have been taken by various groups in the past. One of the chief issues that is now being brought into the area of compromise is the income level of the population that should be included in a prepayment plan. Complicating the decision is the tendency to confuse prepayment with the concept of the sliding scale of fees. But in many of the voluntary medical plans the income level below which recipients of services are not expected to pay added fees is being raised—in some cases to a $4,000 or $5,000 annual family income.

In the Congressional hearings, in the relations with the medical profession and in the details of administration EMIC demonstrated the importance of this issue. It arose in the discussion of payment and it was one of the impulses behind the almost endless debate on he subject of cash allotments to recipients of services. It was the elimination of the means test and the traditions connected with payment for medical services, primarily the sliding scale of fees, that caused the major conflicts in the administration of EMIC.

EMIC payment for services was a composite of compromises. To observe the problems that arose, the policies adopted and the complementary issues that developed is to see, at an accelerated pace, the evolution of payment through the voluntary plans. The problems that arose in EMIC had to be answered by the adoption of new policies or the revision of old ones. The refuge of waiting for an "educational program" to bring a solution could not be used in an emergency situation.

No phase of EMIC shows quite so clearly the importance of a background of administrative experience as the method of payment to hospitals. After a brief and relatively minor preliminary flurry of disagreements, payments to hospitals became the least troublesome feature of the program. Though the EMIC program has ended it has left a lasting impression upon the policies governing hospital payments by public agencies and by voluntary prepayment plans. No less important has been the influence upon the improvement ot hospitial facilities.

While the means test is described as the most important issue involving the beneficiaries of prepayment programs, the economic control of services is the most important issue in the relations between governmental or voluntary prepayment plans and professional groups and hospitals. No prepayment plan can make any claim to social soundness if its solvency is in danger. Administrative controls constitute safety measures in which the great majority of the members of the medical profession and the hospitals have a vital stake. Yet, in this area of administration there has been the least research and critical analysis of existing experience. And EMIC served as a sharp reminder that the protection of economic controls must extend beyond those who provide services and include the recipients.

The most discussed and debated subjects in health economics are the quality of existing services and the influences of prepayment plans upon future quality. The subjects need objective review and clarification. Health is a composite of many factors and hardly a beginning has been made in the science of measuring or weighing these factors. Going to one extreme or the other, it is easy to choose either the best or the worst examples of services in the United States and base arguments and proposals upon the selection. But the improvement of services via the method of debate is wasted effort. EMIC served to show something of the tangibilities of the problem and the size of the organized and continuing program needed if substandard services, wherever they are found, are to become good services, good services are to become better services and better services become the best. These are not problems to be solved by any one group or any one agency.

EMIC was a huge undertaking. Congress decided that maternity and infant care were problems of the war to be solved by organized action. How they were solved, regardless of differences that arose, is a tribute to the professions, the institutions and the agencies that participated.

APPENDIX

Number of Maternity and Infant Cases Authorized in the United States from Beginning of Program through November, 1946.[a]

Month		Maternity	Infant
	Total	1,163,571[b]	189,740[b]
April, 1943 through February 29, 1944		229,960[c]	3,897
1944	March	37,204	3,897
	April	35,868	4,332
	May	41,768	4,418
	June	42,547	4,197
	July	37,095	3,690
	August	41,578	4,422
	September	38,668	4,393
	October	36,774	4,831
	November	35,229	5,604
	December	27,235	4,798
1945	January	34,217	6,053
	February	29,678	5,902
	March	34,179	7,070
	April	34,031	6,541
	May	37,257	6,805
	June	32,567	5,737
	July	31,544	5,542
	August	30,994	5,153
	September	30,402	5,363
	October	32,340	6,297
	November	28,007	5,452
	December	23,639	4,866
1946	January	26,538	5,598
	February	24,583	5,011

[a] Includes the 48 states, the District of Columbia, Alaska, Hawaii, and Puerto Rico.

[b] These figures differ from the sums of the individual items because of changes in the cumulative totals submitted by some state agencies without corresponding changes in the monthly figures.

[c] Includes infant cases, which represent only a small proportion of the total.

March	26,502	6,056
April	24,230	5,843
May	21,716	5,771
June	18,321	5,177
July	15,780	5,140
August	14,158	4,941
September	11,320	4,720
October	10,443	5,185
November	7,888	4,716

Form M. (March 29, 1943)

State Health Agency
Division of Maternal and Child Health

Emergency Maternity and Infant Care Program

Application for Maternity Care

Patient's name____________________Date of birth________
(Last) (First) (Middle)

Present address______________________________
(Street) (City)

________________________Tel. No.__________
(County) (State)

Name of husband______________________________
(Last) (First) (Middle)

Branch of service______________________________
(Army, Navy, Marine Corps, Coast Guard)

Rank or rating__________Husband's serial No.__________

Husband's service mailing address____________________

On the basis of the above facts, I am requesting maternity care under the Emergency Maternity and Infant Care Program of the State health agency.

Signature of patient____________________Date signed________

Note: Any woman is eligible for care, irrespective of legal residence or financial status, whose husband is an enlisted man in the armed forces of the United States (Army, Navy, Marine Corps, or Coast Guard) of the fourth, fifth, sixth, or seventh grades. (This excludes families of commissioned officers; master, major, first technical, staff, and platoon sergeants; chief, first, and second-class petty officers.)

Only maternity care rendered by physicians or hospitals meeting the qualifications or standards established by the State health agency can be authorized.

Request for Authorization for Medical or Hospital Service for Maternity Cases

(To be filled out by private or clinic physician)

Month of pregnancy________Expected date of confinement________.

Date patient given first physical examination by me during this pregnancy________________________

Delivery is recommended: At home__________In hospital__________.

Name of hospital recommended______________________________

I request authorization for payment for the following services to be provided this patient and the newborn infant in accordance with rates for payments, conditions and standards established by the State health agency. I agree not to accept payment from the patient or her family for services authorized.

Indicate below the services for which you request authorization:

Complete medical services including care during the prenatal period, labor, and the puerperium, as well as care of complications, obstetric operations if needed, postpartum care, care of the newborn infant, and a postpartum examination six weeks after delivery, routine blood test for syphilis, hemoglobin determinations, and urinalyses.________________________( )

Medical services during labor and the puerperium including care of complications, obstetric operations if needed, postpartum care, care of newborn infant, and postpartum examination six weeks after delivery______________________________( )

Hospital care for a period of not to exceed two weeks at a rate agreed upon between the hospital and the (State Health Agency).______________________________( )

Other, describe (see note below)________________________

____

____

I have ascertained from the patient's allowance card or other data in her possession that the serial number is correct: Yes______No______.

Signature of attending physician____________________Date________

Note: If necessary, authorization, if accompanied by supporting data, may also be requested for the following services for this patient: consultation by specialists, bedside nursing care, ambulance, unusually expensive drugs or diagnostic procedures or for hospital care of longer than two weeks duration. When such authorization is requested, state the person, agency, or firm recommended to provide this service.

Authorization will not cover services rendered prior to the date of application except for emergencies.

This form should be sent by the attending physician or clinic to the Director, Division of Maternal and Child Health, State Health Agency.

Form M-1 (March 29, 1943)

State Health Agency
Division of Maternal and Child Health

Emergency Maternity and Infant Care Program

APPLICATION FOR MEDICAL OR HOSPITAL CARE FOR INFANT

Child's name________________________Date of birth________
(Last) (First) (Middle)

Name of child's mother________________________
(Last) (First) (Middle)

Mother's present address________________________
(Street) (City)

________________________Tel. No.________
(County) (State)

Name of child's father________________________
(Last) (First) (Middle)

Branch of service________________________
(Army, Navy, Marine Corps, Coast Guard)

Rank or rating____________Father's serial No.____________

Father's service mailing address________________________

____

On the basis of the above facts, I am requesting care for this child from the Emergency Maternity and Infant Care Program of the State health agency.

Signature________________________Date signed____________

(Relationship to child________________________)

NOTE: Any infant under one year of age is eligible for care, irrespective of legal residence or financial status, whose father is an enlisted man in the armed forces of the United States (Army, Navy, Marine Corps, or Coast Guard) of the fourth, fifth, sixth, or seventh grades. (This excludes families of commissioned officers; master, major, first, technical, staff, and platoon sergeants; chief, first, and second-class petty officers.)

Only care rendered by physicians or hospitals meeting the qualifications or standards established by the State health agency can be authorized.

Request for Authorization for Medical or Hospital Care for Infant

(To be filled out by private or clinic physician)

Physician's statement briefly describing child's illness________________

____

____

____

Date child first observed by me during this illness________________

I request authorization of payment for the professional services to be provided by me to the above-named child in accordance with rates for payments, conditions and standards established by the State health agency. I agree not to accept payment from the child's parent or family for services authorized.

I also request authorization for the following additional services—hospitalization, consultation, bedside nursing, unusually expensive drugs or diagnostic procedures—(specify name of individual or agency you wish to give such services or care):

Consultation by____________________M.D., Specialist in__________

Name of hospital recommended________________________

Other______________________________________

I have ascertained from the allowance card or other data in the parent's possession that the serial number is correct: Yes____ No____.
Signature of attending physician____________________Date__________

Note: Authorization can only be given for care of sick children requiring three or more home, office or hospital visits per week of illness. Initial authorization is not issued for a period of more than three weeks.

If necessary, authorization, if accompanied by supporting data, may also be requested for the following services for this patient: consultation by specialists, bedside nursing care, ambulance, unusually expensive drugs or diagnostic procedures or for hospital care of longer than two weeks duration. When such authorization is requested state the person, agency, or firm recommended to provide this service.

Authorization will not cover services rendered prior to the date of application except for emergencies.

This form should be sent by the attending physician or clinic to the Director, Division of Maternal and Child Health, State Health Agency.

Form M-2 (March 29, 1943)

State Health Agency
Division of Maternal and Child Health

Authorization No.________________

Case No.________________

Emergency Maternity and Infant Care Program

AUTHORIZATION FOR SERVICES AND CARE

Date________________

To:________________________ ________________________
(Person, agency, or firm) (Patient's name)

________________________ ________________________
(Address) (Patient's address)

________________________ ________________________
(Name of attending physician)

This is to certify that the (State health agency) will assume responsibility for payment for the following services to be provided the above-named patient:

(This space to be used for specifying the services authorized, period of time covered by the authorization, and rate to be paid by the State health agency.)

The patient (or parent) has been notified that this authorization has been made effective as of____________________.
(Date)

Signature________________________
(Name and title of authorizing agent)

NOTE: Invoices for physicians' services, when submitted to (Official's title) together with attending physician's final medical report, constitutes the basis for payment of services.

(Copy of all authorizations should be sent to attending physician)

Emergency Maternity and Infant Care Program
Estimates and Appropriations

1. Fiscal Year 1943

Dec. 21, 1942	Children's Bureau expressed need for	$ 1,817,200
Feb. 1, 1943	Approved and sent to Congress	1,200,000
Feb. 24, 1943	House bill reported excluding item	——
Feb. 26, 1943	Keefe offered amendment on floor; lost on point of order	1,200,000
Mar. 9, 1943	Senate Committee offered amendment providing	1,200,000
Mar. 12, 1943	Senate passed amendment	1,200,000
Mar. 15, 1943	House agreed to Senate amendment	1,200,000
Mar. 18, 1943	Act approved	1,200,000

2. Fiscal Year 1944

Mar. 24, 1943	Children's Bureau expressed need for	6,000,000
Apr. 13, 1943	Approved and sent to Congress	4,800,000
June 14, 1943	House bill reported	4,000,000
June 24, 1943	Senate Committee recommended	4,800,000
June 29, 1943	Senate passed	4,800,000
June 30, 1943	Conferees approved	4,400,000
July 12, 1943	Act approved	4,400,000

3. Supplemental Appropriation Fiscal Year 1944

Aug. 25, 1943	Children's Bureau expressed need for (Includes 3% or $622,799 for State adm.)	20,076,235
Sept. 16, 1943	Approved and sent to Congress (Nothing for State administration)	18,600,000
Sept. 22, 1943	House J. Res. 159 reported	18,600,000
Sept. 22, 1943	House passed	18,600,000
Sept. 24, 1943	Senate Committee recommended	18,600,000
Sept. 28, 1943	Senate passed	18,600,000
Oct. 1, 1943	Act approved	18,600,000

4. Supplemenal Appropriation Fiscal Year 1944

Apr. 17, 1944	Children's Bureau expressed need for	6,763,600
Apr. 29, 1944	Approved and sent to Congress	6,700,000
May 3, 1944	House J. Res. 271 reported	6,700,000
May 5, 1944	House passed	6,700,000
May 9, 1944	Senate passed	6,700,000
May 12, 1944	Act approved	6,700,000

5. Fiscal Year 1945

Oct. 5, 1943	Children's Bureau expressed need for	24,100,000
Jan. 10, 1944	Approved and sent to Congress (H. Doc. 561)	20,000,000

Mar. 31, 1944	— President sent to Congress amended language to include army aviation cadets, not more than 4% for State administration, and appropriation to be immediately available	——
Apr. 20, 1944	— Supplemental request for 1945 by Children's Bureau for (Not more than 4% or $1,620,000 for State administration)	22,810,400
Apr. 29, 1944	— Approved and sent to Congress	22,800,000
May 27, 1944	— House bill reported (2% for State administration; excluded army aviation cadets)	42,800,000
June 1, 1944	— House passed (2% for State administration; excluded army aviation cadets)	42,800,000
June 13, 1944	— Senate Committee reported (3% for State administration; included army aviation cadets)	42,800,000
June 15, 1944	— Senate passed (3% for State administration; included army aviation cadets)	42,800,000
June 21, 1944	— Conference report (2½% for State administration; included army aviation cadets)	42,800,000
June 22, 1944	— House agreed to Conference report	42,800,000
June 22, 1944	— Senate agreed to Conference report	42,800,000
June 26, 1944	— Act approved (2½% for State administration; included army aviation cadets)	42,800,000

6. Supplemental Appropriation Fiscal Year 1945

May 14, 1945	— Children's Bureau expressed need for	2,547,965
May 22, 1945	— Approved and sent to Congress	2,300,000
June 5, 1945	— H. J. Res. 212 reported	2,200,000
June 6, 1945	— House passed	2,200,000
June 7, 1945	— Senate Committee reported	2,200,000
June 8, 1945	— Senate passed	2,200,000
June 12, 1945	— Act approved	2,200,000

7. Fiscal Year 1946

Oct. 7, 1944	— Children's Bureau expressed need for	44,189,500
Jan. 9, 1945	— Approved and sent to Congress (2½%, or $1,104,737.50 for State administration)	44,189,500
May 14, 1945	— House bill reported	44,189,500
May 17, 1945	— House passed	44,189,500
June 23, 1945	— Senate Committee reported	44,189,500
July 3, 1945	— Act approved	44,189,500

8. Fiscal Year 1946—Reductions in Wartime Appropriations, including EMIC

Aug. 28, 1945	— Children's Bureau report to House Appropriation Committee indicated need for retaining all	44,189,500
Sept. 15, 1945	— President sent to Congress H. Doc. 280 recommending reductions in certain wartime appropriations but not in EMIC.	
Oct. 2, 1945	— Children's Bureau stated at hearing before House Appropriation Committee that appropriation could be reduced by $8,113,-600 leaving available $36,075,900 (including 2½%, or $1,104,737 for State administration)	
Oct. 17, 1945	— House reported showing subsequent rescission recommended (H. R. 4407)	8,113,600
Oct. 19, 1945	— House passed reduction	8,113,600
Nov. 14, 1945	— Senate Appropriations Committee reported with reduction (H. R. 4407)	8,113,600
Nov. 20, 1945	— Senate passed reduction	8,113,600
Dec. 22, 1945	— President vetoed H. R. 4407 and announced transfer to unexpendable reserves rescission amounts of	8,113,600
Feb. 18, 1946	— Act approved reducing 1946 appropriation by	8,113,600

9. Supplemental Appropriation Fiscal Year 1946

Apr. 26, 1946	— Children's Bureau expressed need for	2,148,800
May 3, 1946	— Approved and sent to Congress (H. Doc. 554)	2,148,800
	— House bill reported	1,974,000
	— House passed	1,974,000
	— Senate passed	1,974,000
June 21, 1946	— Act approved	1,974,000

10. Fiscal Year 1947

Oct. 8, 1945	— Children's Bureau expressed need for	18,548,400
Nov. 6, 1945	— Revised estimate by Children's Bureau on date of hearing for	17,593,000
	— President sent to Congress (3.7%, or $649,000 for State administration)	17,593,000
Mar. 4, 1946	— Estimate by Children's Bureau for study of experience under EMIC program	974,893
Apr. 29, 1946	— President sent to Congress request for amending grants language to provide $929,000 of $17,593,000 for study of EMIC experience (H. Doc. 534)	
July 26, 1946	— Act approved ($649,000 for State administration; no appropriation for study)	16,664,000

Minimum Requirements for Hospitals Participating in the EMIC Program

The following represent minimum requirements that will be used by the Children's Bureau in reviewing State plans for approval. A State health department may use them as a basis for preliminary approval of hospitals for obstetric care, but they should not be construed as establishing even minimum *standards* for such hospitals.

Since in the various States wide differences will be found in hospital facilities available, some State health departments will be able to establish higher requirements than others. Each should develop a set of requirements that are as high as are practicable under existing conditions, and should consider the possibility of raising the requirements as soon as possible.

Since in some States it will be practicable to establish minimum requirements that could not be met by many of the hospitals in other States, those requirements which should be considered absolutely minimum for emergency approval under any conditions have been indicated by one star (*), and those which should be established as minimum when conditions permit, either at the time of approval or later, have been indicated by two stars (**).

A. BUILDINGS.

*Obstetric care shall be authorized only in buildings that meet State or local rules and regulations for fire protection and sanitation.

*Buildings shall be adequately screened to give protection against flies and mosquitoes.

*Every room in which maternity patients or newborn infants are cared for shall have at least one window to provide light and ventilation (unless forced ventilation is provided).

There is evidence that sunlight passing through ordinary window glass has some bactericidal action. Change of air content of rooms by admitting outdoor air tends to reduce the bacterial content of the air and adds to the patient's comfort.

*In every room used in the care of maternity patients and newborn infants there shall be artificial lighting adequate for the purposes for which the room is used.

*There shall be provision for adequately heating the building in cold weather, with maintenance of a fairly uniform temperature in delivery rooms and nurseries.

The shock of labor and delivery for mother and infant makes provision of suitable environmental conditions essential. The new born infant's need for artifical heat after leaving the protection of the uterus is obvious, and chilling may be fatal, especially to premature infants.

B. MATERNITY UNIT.

*Maternity patients and newborn infants shall be cared for only in wards or rooms completely separated from other wards or rooms in which patients with communicable diseases or septic conditions are cared for.

The special susceptibility of parturient women and newborn infants to various types of infection is well known. The danger of cross-infection will be less the greater the degree of separation of these patients from all other patients, that is, in a separate wing, a separate floor, or a room or rooms separated by a partition from that section of the hospital in which patients with septic conditions or communicable diseases are cared for.

**Maternity patients shall be cared for only in a part of the hospital in which complete separation from all other patients is possible.

1. FACILITIES FOR DELIVERY.

*If there is no delivery room separate from the general operating room, patients shall be delivered in their own rooms, except in case of Cesarean section. There shall be conveniently located facilities for the attendants at delivery to scrub their hands.

Since the parturient woman is especially susceptible to infection, it is unwise to deliver her in a room used for septic cases regardless of the care with which cleaning of the room is carried out. Hand-scrubbing facilities are essential to the use of aseptic technique.

**There shall be a properly equipped delivery room used exclusively for the delivery of noninfectious patients. There shall be running water in this room or adjacent to it.

*There shall be suitable facilities for administering general anesthesia.

*There shall be suitable apparatus for administering oxygen to infants.

*A reliable method of identifying each infant shall be applied in the delivery room.

2. NURSING SERVICES.

*A graduate registered nurse shall be responsible at all times for nursing care of both maternity patients and newborn infants.

**At least one graduate registered nurse shall be on duty at all times to supervise the care of both maternity patients and newborn infants.

Every parturient woman and newborn infant needs skilled nursing care. This is essential not only for the normal needs, but because of the potential danger to both from infection and hemorrhage, and the danger to the infant from asphyxiation.

In addition, the nurse is the person who is responsible throughout the 24 hours and will often be required to make decisions vital to the patients' safety (both mother and infant) in the absence of the physician.

3. CARE OF UTENSILS AND LINEN.

*There shall be facilities for disinfection or, preferably, sterilization of bedpans.

Contaminated bedpans may be a source of cross-infection.

*There shall be adequate and suitable receptacles for soiled linen (bed linen, gowns, and diapers).

Soiled linen, if not kept in closed containers, may be a source for spread of infection.

**There shall be a utility room used for maternity patients only.

4. LABORATORY AND CLINICAL FACILITIES.

*There shall be facilities *in the hospital*, or *available in the community*, for laboratory examinations, including blood counting, hemoglobin determinations, and urinalyses.

**A separate room shall be provided in the hospital for a laboratory.

*There shall be facilities in the hospital always ready for intravenous therapy.

**There shall be serum available in the hospital for blood-matching for transfusions.

*The hospital shall provide adequate facilities for sterilization of equipment, supplies, and instruments.

5. RECORDS.

*A clinical record shall be kept for each patient, mother and infant separately.

6. ACCOMODATIONS FOR PATIENTS.

a. For the mothers.

*Rooms or wards in which maternity patients are cared for shall provide average space equal to at least 60 square feet per patient.

To provide for adequate ventilation, for space for bedside care of the patient, and for separation of the patients sufficient to minimize respiratory cross-infections.

**Rooms or wards in which maternity patients are cared for shall provide average space equal to at least 80 square feet per patient.

*There shall be a separate bed for each patient.

**There shall be a separate thermometer and a bedpan for each patient.

(1) Hand-washing facilities.

*Running water shall be conveniently available to every room in which maternity patients are cared for.

To facilitate hand washing by staff (medical and nursing) before and after caring for each patient. Hand washing is one of the important measures for prevention of infection. The more convenient the facility the more likely it is that the hand scrubbing will be done.

**Running water shall be available in each room or ward.

(2) Isolation facilities.

*A room shall be available at all times in which a maternity patient who has an infection may be isolated.

Prevention of spread of infection from one patient to another depends upon separation of the patient who is suspected of having an infection from non-infected patients and upon maintaining rigid separate isolation of the infected patient until cured or, preferably, until discharged from the hospital.

**Space shall be available at all times for isolation of at least one patient for every 25 obstetric beds or fraction thereof.

(3) Dietary department.

*Food adequate for the needs of the parturient women shall be prepared and served under sanitary conditions.

**If the food service is not under the direction of a qualified dietitian, consultation should be obtained from a dietitian or nutritionist available to the community.

b. For the infants.

(1) Nursery facilities.

*If newborn infants are not kept in their mothers' rooms, a separate nursery shall be provided for them, which is used for no purpose other than the care of such infants.

*Provision shall be made to exclude visitors from contact with infants. If infants are kept in their mothers' rooms a separate room must be made available in which to place them during visiting hours.

To prevent respiratory infections in newborn infants they should be isolated from visitors.

*Each infant shall have a separate bassinet.

In order to minimize the danger of cross-infection, two infants should never occupy the same bassinet, even if they are twins.

*Individual bassinets shall be separated by at least 6 inches.

Separation of bassinets is required (1) so that bedclothes from one bassinet will be less likely to come in contact with those on either side and (2) to facilitate bedside care of each infant.

**Individual bassinets shall be separated by at least 12 inches.

*Nurseries shall be large enough to provide an average of at least 16 square feet of floor space per infant.

This is the minimum space that will permit proper spacing of beds (6 inches from walls and 6 inches between beds) and that will provide space for the nurse to care for the infant.

**Nurseries shall be large enough to provide an average of at least 20 square feet of floor space per infant.

*There shall be provided for premature infants at least 1 incubator or some type of heated bed for each 20 bassinets for full-term infants, or any fraction thereof.

*There shall be provided in the nursery facilities for washing or disinfecting the hands.

To avoid carrying infection to infants the hands must be carefully washed both before and after caring for each infant.

(2) Isolation for infants.

*There shall always be available a room in which infants who have or who are suspected of having infections may be strictly isolated from the well infants and from each other.

To prevent spread of infection, there should be provision for immediate isolation of any infants suspected of having an infection.

(3) Clinical facilities for infants.

*There shall always be available facilities for oxygen administration suitable for use with infants.

Newborn infants, especially premature infants, are prone to respiratory difficulties. Oxygen administration is essential for combating these difficulties.

*There shall always be available either in the hospital or in the community sterile sets for intravenous or subcutaneous administration of blood or other fluid to infants.

(4) Facilities for preparation of milk mixtures.

*There shall be suitable space and adequate equipment for preparation of mild mixtures (formulas) and for their sterilization and refrigeration.

**There shall be a separate room used exclusively for the preparation of sterile milk mixtures.

Statement of Total Expenses and Calculation of Reimbursable Cost of In-Patient Service Per Patient Day and of Out-Patient Service Per Visit*

For the accounting year ended________________194__

by________________hospital,________________address.

For hospitals cooperating with official State agencies administering programs for maternal and child health (including emergency maternity and infant care) and for crippled children.

A. Total amount of expenses per books[1] .... ________

B. Less the following items if included in item A.[2]

1. Research expense and medical education .... ________
2. Cost of gift shops, lunch counters, etc. .... ________
3. Cost of guest meals or meals paid for by employees .... ________
4. Cost of telephone and telegraph charges paid for by patients, guests or employees .... ________
5. Cost of drugs or supplies that are purchased by individuals not admitted as in-patients or out-patients .... ________
6. Provision for depreciation of buildings and equipment .... ________
7. Bad debts or provision therefor .... ________
8. Estimated value of donated or voluntary services .... ________

* Effective July 1, 1944.

1 The amount to be entered should be as follows:

If Reporting on the—	*Amount to be Entered*
(a) Accrual basis	(a) Total expenses
(b) Cash basis	(b) Total cash disbursements
(c) Modified cash basis	(c) Total cash disbursements after giving effect to adjustments.

Do not include in the total amount (item A) expenditures for land, buildings, and permanent improvements and equipment, whether replacements or additions.

2 If the "total amount of expenses" as shown on the statement prepared and certified to by a public accountant does not include any of the items listed under item B, then no entries would be made for item B, and entries would be made only for items A and C.

9. Interest expense ________ ________
10. Real estate taxes and income taxes ________
11. Rent expense ________ ________
12. Other (specify) ________ ________
13. Total of items B 1 to B 12 ________ ________.

C. Total amount of operating expenses applicable to in-patient and out-patient services (item A minus item B 13) ________ ________

List here material or services not provided by the hospital, such as appliances for crippled children, blood for transfusion, anesthesia, X-ray, special nursing, services of physical therapists, etc.

D. Operating expenses for calculating reimbursable costs.[3] [4]

	Total	In-Patient Service	Out-Patient Service
(1)	(2)	(3)	(4)
1. Administration	________	________	________
2. Dietary	________	________	________
3. Laundry	________	________	________
4. Housekeeping	________	________	________
5. Heat, light, power and water	________	________	________
6. Maintenance and repairs	________	________	________
7. Motor service	________	________	________
8. Medical and surgical service	________	________	________
9. Nursing service and nursing education	________	________	________
10. Medical records and library	________	________	________
11. Social service	________	________	________

3 A hospital having a total of 25 available beds or fewer (bed complement) may elect to submit a statement of operating expenses in accordance with the classification per books of the hospital in lieu of item D. These hospitals should also complete items A, B, and C.

4 The manual entitled "Hospital Accounting and Statistics", which can be obtained from the American Hospital Association, 18 E. Division St., Chicago, Ill., gives more detailed instructions on expenses to be included under each of the headings listed under item D, and a method for allocating in-patient and out-patient operating expenses. If a hospital is unable to segregate in-patient and out-patient expenses by this or a comparable method, it may obtain the amount to be entered in item D 17, col. 4, an estimate of the cost of out-patient operating expense, by multiplying the number of visits in item G 2 by $1.50. Item D 17, col. 3, will be item D 17, col. 2, minus item D 17, col. 4.

Maintenance of student nurses and of members of religious orders who serve in the hospital may be included in the appropriate items under item D.

12. X-ray[5] [6] .... ______ ______ ______
13. Laboratories[5] [6] .... ______ ______ ______
14. Pharmacy .... ______ ______ ______
15. Physical therapy[6] .... ______ ______ ______
16. Other special services[7] .... ______ ______ ______
    (Specify) ______
17. Total .... ______ ______ ______

(Equal to item C)

E. Calculation of reimbursable cost of in-patient service.

1. Total amount of operating expenses for in-patient service (from item D 17, col. 3) .... ______
2. Less: Income from Federal or State public health agencies for nursing education, including income for maintenance, uniforms, supplies, etc.[8] .... ______
3. Balance (E 1 minus E 2) .... ______
4. Number of in-patient days (excluding newborn infant days) (item F 2, col. 2)[9] .... ______
5. Average computed per diem reimbursable cost (E 3 divided by E 4) .... ______

[5] If the hospital acts as the billing and collection agency for individuals not employed by the hospital but who are providing service in these departments, the amounts so collected and paid to these individuals is not to be included in the statement of operating expenses.

[6] If the following information is known, please make entries here:

(a) Total number of films used............, fluoroscopic examinations made............, and treatments given during the year by the X-ray department............
(b) Total number of tests and examinations made during the year by the laboratory............
(c) Total number of physical-therapy treatments given during the year ....

[7] This may include salary and maintenance of a chaplain, and maintenance of chapel.

[8] The amount chargeable to Federal or State public health agencies during the accounting year covered by the statement should be entered, not the amount of cash received.

[9] Newborn infant days are counted only for the days when the infants' mothers are patients in the hospital; thus the count of days for a prematurely born infant remaining in the hospital after its mother is discharged, or an infant delivered at home and later admitted to the hospital, or an infant admitted for an illness is included in the total number of patient days. This definition is in accordance with the recommendation that State agencies pay for newborn infant days while the mother is not in the hospital at the reimbursable rate as calculated in item E 8.

6. Supplementary allowance for depreciation of buildings and equipment, rent, interest, etc. (10 percent of item E 5) .... ________
7. Total (E 5 plus E 6) .... ________
8. Reimbursable cost of in-patient service per patient day under maternal and child health (including emergency maternity and infant care) and crippled children's programs (85 percent of E 7)[10] .... ________

NOTE: Hospitals having more than 70 percent of all patient days in rooms with two or more beds (see F 3, col. 4) should use instead of 85 percent of E 7, the percent applicable as determined from table I under F.

F. Occupancy statistics.

(1)	Total (2)	In Rooms With Only One Bed (3)	In Rooms With Two or More Beds (4)
1. Beds available (bassinets excluded)	________	________	________
2. Number of in-patient days during accounting year[11] excluding newborn infant days	________	________	________
3. Percent	100%	%[12]	%[13]

TABLE I

Percent of patient days in rooms with *two or more beds* to total patient days in all accommodations (excluding newborn infant days). (item F 3, col. 4)		Percent to be used in computing reimbursable cost of in-patient service per patient day. (item E 8)
More than	*Not more than*	*Percent*
98	100	100
96	98	99
94	96	98

[10] Subject to the maximum rate established by the State agency.

[11] In counting patient days, the day of admission or the day of discharge may be used, but not both.

[12] Item F 2, col. 3, divided by item F 2, col. 2.

[13] Item F 2, col. 4, divided by item F 2, col. 2.

92	94	97
90	92	96
88	90	95
86	88	94
84	86	93
82	84	92
80	82	91
78	80	90
76	78	89
74	76	88
72	74	87
70	72	86
0	70	85

G. Calculation of reimbursable cost of out-patient visit.

1. Total amount of operating expenses (from item D 17, col. 4) ________
2. Number of out-patient visits[14] ________
3. Average cost per visit (G 1 divided by G 2) ________
4. Supplementary allowance for depreciation of buildings and equipment, rent, interest, etc. (10 percent of item G 3) ________
5. Reimbursable cost per visit (G 3 plus G 4)[15] ________

14 Including visits of patients admitted to out-patient clinics and of individuals not admitted to in-patient service or out-patient clinics who receive services in emergency rooms, X-ray, laboratory, or other similar departments.

15 Subject to the maximum rate established by the State agency.

ADMINISTRATIVE POLICIES

Emergency Maternity and Infant Care Program

Subject to amendments that may be issued after the meeting of the State and Territorial Health Officers' Association on April 12, 1945

The following statement of administrative policies, as revised in March 1945, has been prepared by the Children's Bureau for the information of the State health agencies administering the emergency maternity and infant-care program and is issued in mimeographed form only. It will be reissued after the conference of the State and Territorial Health Officers' Association on April 12, 1945 with such additional amendments as may be adopted following that meeting and any modifications that may be necessary after the passage of the Act of Congress making appropriations for this program for the fiscal year 1946. The State health agencies will be notified immediately of any amendments to these policies. This statement of policies supersedes EMIC Information Circular No. 1, issued December 1943, and amendments 1 through 11 to that Circular. Certain minor changes in content have been made in line with recommendations based on the experience of the States in administering the program, and certain items have been rewritten for greater clarity. For brevity and convenience in handling, the material in fine print labeled "Discussion" in various sections of EMIC Information Circular No. 1, issued December 1943, and in the amendments to it has been omitted from this revision. It should be understood, however, that the content of this material, as it relates to general and specific policies of the program, continues in effect. Minimum requirements for hospitals participating in the program are unchanged to date but have been omitted from this revision. They will be issued as a separate bulletin in the near future.

One major change in policy is indicated in section I, "Individuals For Whom EMIC Services May Be Authorized." Up to this time, the eligibility of an infant whose mother was given maternity care under the EMIC program was established after birth, on the basis of a separate application for care. The new policy provides that the infant born during an authorized period of maternity care may be given care during its first year of life under a joint application for the mother and infant. Several changes have been made in section III, "Application and Authorization for Care," to bring the section into conformity with this policy.

The Children's Bureau will use this statement of policies, with such amendments as may be made following the conference with the State and Territorial Health Officers' Association, as the basis for approval of the related portions of State emergency maternity and infant-care plans for fiscal year 1946, and as the basis for approval of revisions, amendments, or supplements to emergency maternity and infant-care plans received during the remainder of fiscal year 1945.

I. Individuals for Whom EMIC Services May Be Authorized.

1. A woman applying for maternity care whose husband, at the time of initial application, was in the fourth, fifth, sixth, or seventh pay grade of the United States Army, Navy, Marine Corps or Coast Guard or was an Army aviation cadet (including men in these grades and Army aviation cadets who are deceased or missing in action).

2. An infant under 1 year of age for whose care the mother made application as a part of her application for maternity care and who was born during the authorized period of maternity care.

3. An infant under 1 year of age not included in category 2 above, whose father at the time of application was in the fourth, fifth, sixth, or seventh pay grade of the United States Army, Navy, Marine Crops, or Coast Guard or was an Army aviation cadet (including men in these grades and Army aviation cadets who are deceased or missing in action).

The effective date of *eligibility* is ordinarily the date upon which an initial application was executed by the prospective mother. But when an initial application executed by the applicant is not received by the State agency until 2 months or more after the date of its execution by the prospective mother, the State agency should require her to give satisfactory evidence that her husband was not promoted above the lowest four pay grades during the interim between execution and receipt of the application. If such promotion has occurred, the wife should not be considered eligible for care under the program. The pay grade of a serviceman can be ascertained by the applicant, or the State agency, by addressing the Adjutant General, War Department, Washington 25, D. C.

If an enlisted man in one of the four lowest pay grades, or an Army aviation cadet, for whose wife or infant application for care has been made, is discharged or promoted after the date of application, or if his wife or infant moves to another State or changes physicians, his wife or infant can continue to receive services available under the plan.

II. Conditions Under Which Services May Be Authorized.

1. The individual for whom services are authorized is the wife or infant of a serviceman in the fourth, fifth, sixth, or seventh pay grade of the armed forces of the United States or of an Army aviation cadet.

2. There shall be no financial investigation or means test to determine eligibility as a condition of receiving any service provided under the EMIC program.

3. Similar service is not readily available (without financial investigation and without cost to the patient) from the medical personnel or hospitals of the United States Army, Navy, Public Health Service, or from clinics or conferences or other services provided by or through State or local public-health agencies or services available under State crippled children's programs.

4. The wife of an enlisted man may have free choice under the program of all types of available facilities and services, including private practitioners, clinics, hospitals, and other health facilities that meet the standards established under a State plan for each type of service or facility.

5. The attending physician has the qualifications and the hospital meets the standards established under the State plan.

6. The attending physican or clinic has agreed to accept payment only from the State health agency for whatever medical or surgical services he renders during pregnancy, labor and 6 weeks postpartum, or for the care of an infant, for which authorization has been issued under the State program. (See section IV for types of service that may be authorized.)

7. The hospital, if hospital care is requested, has agreed to accept payment only from the State health agency for services rendered during a period of authorized hospital care under the program, and will agree to provide at least 10 days' care following delivery if accommodations are available and if the patient wishes to remain in the hospital.

8. The hospital will provide whatever accommodations are indicated by the patient's medical condition at the per diem rate paid by the State health agency.

9. Physicians' services will not be authorized if the patient or someone in behalf of the patient is to pay for hospital care; and hospital care will not be authorized if the patient or someone in behalf of the patient is to pay the physician for medical care.

10. The cost of medical services in a clinic and/or hospital,

including maintenance and salaries, where such medical service is provided by staff physicians (such as interns, resident staff, and attending physicians employed full time or part time by the clinic or hospital or other physicians supervising or assisting interns or resident physicians) must be included in the cost per clinic visit and the hospital cost per patient day, as outlined in the Children's Bureau memorandum of April 15, 1944, Purchase of Hospital Care Under Programs for Maternal and Child Health and Crippled Children.

11. Individuals accepted for care under the program will be referred routinely to local public-health agencies for the provision of public-health-nursing services that can be made available.

12. Arrangements will be made to utilize community facilities, including appropriate social and health agencies, to meet the needs of mothers and infants that cannot be provided under the EMIC program.

III. Application and Authorization for Care.

A. APPLICATION FOR CARE.

1. *Maternity care:* Since the wife is entitled, under the program, to complete maternity care, application for care should be made by her or in her behalf, *as early in pregnancy as possible,* directly to the State or local health agency on forms provided for the purpose, or, in an emergency, by letter or telephone.

2. *Infant care:* Similarly, application for care of the infant should be made by the mother, or other person in behalf of the infant, directly to the State or local health agency, either as a part of the application for maternity care or as a separate application, if the mother has not received care under the EMIC program.

If the mother has not received care under the program, application for care of the infant may be made (1) at birth or (2) at the time medical care or health supervision is first requested from physician, clinic, or hospital.

The wife, or other person acting in behalf of the wife or infant, should enter on the application form[1] the date when care is requested to begin, ordinarily the date when the applicant first received care as the eligible wife or infant of a serviceman in the four lowest pay grades or of an aviation cadet, or a later date as requested in the application by the wife and physician. The wife should also

[1] The wife (with assistance, if necessary, from the agency distributing the forms) or the physician should send the completed form immediately to the State or local health agency.

enter the husband's name, address, serial number, and rank or rating on the date when care is requested to begin.

B. AUTHORIZATION FOR CARE.

Authorization for care is the action taken by the State health agency giving a physician, hospital, or other agency the authority to render the service or care specified in the request for authorization. It constitutes an agreement on the part of the State health agency to pay for the care authorized, upon receipt of a report that such care has been rendered.

The physician's statement on the application form constitutes a request for authorization to provide the necessary medical services indicated by him on the form and an agreement to accept payment only from the State health agency for such services. This statement is to be signed by the attending physician, or, when care is sought by the patient in a hospital or clinic, by an official of the hospital or clinic.

The State health agency shall authorize all maternity or infant care in accordance with rates and conditions established under the State EMIC plan. Payment to physicians, hospitals, and others providing service, facilities, or supplies shall be made only when such service, facilities, or supplies have been duly authorized. Except as specified below, authorization for care should be given in advance.

Verification of data identifying military status.

The physician or agency that assists the wife or mother in filling out the application form or the State health agency after receiving the form, should verify the data identifying the military status of the husband or father as entered by the wife or mother. The wife should be asked (1) to state her husband's present rank or rating and (2) to show evidence of such rank or rating through an envelope or V-mail letter from her husband, her allowance card, or other official communication. *Such evidence must be dated not more than 2 months prior to the date the application form is signed by the physician or clinic official.* If the wife has no such evidence of her husband's present rating, she should state the reason, such as, recent entry into the service or change in grade since the last letter or allowance card was received. The portion of the application form to be filled out and signed by the physician or clinic official must state the rank or rating of the husband as given by the wife and the nature of the evidence confirming such rank or rating.

If the wife's statement concerning the rank or rating of the husband has not been confirmed by the physician from the evidence described above, or if the wife does not know her husband's rank or rating, the State or local health agency must ascertain it in one of the following ways:

By requesting the wife to submit, in person or by mail, an envelope or V-mail letterhead from her husband, her allowance card, or other official communication. *The evidence submitted must be dated not more than 2 months prior to the date the physician signs the application*, or if he has not signed, not more than 2 months prior to the date the application is received in the office of the health agency.

By verifying with an official letter or statement from the armed forces. Such a statement may be obtained, if not already available, from the Adjutant General's Office, War Department, Washington 25, D. C., Attention: Enlisted Branch; or the Bureau of Records, U. S. Navy, Room 3004, Arlington Annex, Arlington, Va.; or the Commandant, Commandant Headquarters, U. S. Coast Guard, Washington 25, D. C. To these offices should be sent the husband's name, his serial number, and his address, with a request for a statement concerning his rank as of the month the application was signed by the wife.

In cases in which the physician has not been able to furnish satisfactory information concerning the husband's rank or rating, care should be authorized pending verification of eligibility by the State health agency. If it is later found that the applicant is ineligible because the husband was not in the four lowest pay grades or an Army aviation cadet as of the date of application, the authorization should be terminated when such information is received, but the care provided prior to the time the patient, physician, or hospital is notified of termination of the authorization should be paid for.

Period covered by application and authorization.

Authorization for care will be issued to physician, clinic, hospital, nurse, or others on appropriate authorization forms to cover all necessary services provided or to be provided under the program.

1. Maternity care.

(a) *The period covered by an application and authorization for maternity care* (the period for which the State health agency assumes responsibility for payment for services) shall start either on (1) the date during pregnancy when the applicant, as the wife of a serviceman in one of the four lowest grades or of an Army aviation cadet, first received care; or (2) a later date, when so requested on the application form. The period shall end 6 weeks after delivery (except as provided under section IV, A, 1, (a), paragraph 3).

(b) The State or local health agency shall approve for authorization applications for maternity care received after the date of delivery provided (1) care has been rendered in accordance with conditions established by the State agency in its EMIC plan; and (2) the application is supported by information showing a medical emergency (such as a premature delivery), lack of information about the program, misunderstanding of procedures, misinformation, or other valid reason for delayed application.

Applications meeting the conditions outlined in "(b)" received on or after July 1, 1944, for maternity care that is *not yet completed*, i. e., delivery has taken place but postpartum care was still being rendered on July 1, shall be accepted. Applications received on or after July 1, 1944, for that that was *completed* prior to that date may be accepted at the option of the State agency.

2. Infant care.

(a) *The period covered by an application* for care of an infant[2] may start (1) at birth, (2) on the date care was first received, or (3) on a later date, when so requested on the application form, and continues through the first year of the infant's life.

The initial authorization for care of a sick infant by a physician may be for a period up to 3 weeks, at which time the authorization should be renewed, if necessary. Authorization for care of a sick infant should be requested by the physician for each illness; the date when care was begun should be given in the request.

Authorization for office medical care or health supervision (see section IV, B, 5 and 6) may be for longer periods, up to 1 year.

(b) An application for care of an infant received by the State or local health agency more than 3 weeks after the date from which care was requested shall be approved for authorization provided care has been rendered in accordance with conditions established by the State agency in its EMIC plan, and provided the application is supported by information showing a medical emergency, lack of information about the program, misunderstanding of procedures, misinformation, or other valid reasons for delayed application.

Applications meeting the conditions outlined "(b)" received on or after July 1, 1944, for care of a sick infant that is *not yet completed*, i. e., a physician or hospital was still providing care on July 1, shall be accepted. Applications received on or after July 1, 1944, for care that was *completed* prior to that date may be accepted at the option of the State agency.

3. Emergency care.

In case of emergency, authorization for care of wife or infant

[2] Other than the care provided for newborn infants during the first 2 weeks of life by the attending physician as part of complete maternity care.

may be given, *provided* request for authorization of such services is received by letter, telephone, or telegraph within a reasonable interval of time, as defined by the State health agency, after the occurrence of the emergency.

IV. Services That May Be Authorized by State or Local Health Agencies and Rates of Payment.

A. For the Wife.

1. Medical and surgical services provided by physicians in private practice.

This includes services to a patient who has sought and received care in the private office of a physician during the prenatal period. For this type of care payment is to be made by the State health agency, directly to the physician.

It also covers services to a patient who has sought and received care in the private practice of a physician employed full time or part time by a medical school, for which payment may be made to the medical school or to the physician, depending on the customary procedure for receipt of such payments.

(a) *Complete maternity care.*

For "complete maternity care," that is, all services rendered by the attending physician (1) to the mother during pregnancy, labor, and the postpartum period from the effective date of authorization until 6 weeks after termination of pregnancy, including office treatment of intercurrent conditions whether attributable to pregnancy or not, but excluding home or hospital care of conditions not attributable to pregnancy (as outlined under (b) and (c) below), and (2) to the infant during the first 2 weeks of life: The rate of payment as established by the State health agency, but not to exceed $50.

When fewer than 5 prenatal examinations are made, when no postpartum examination is made, or when other services recognized as part of routine complete maternity care are omitted, the rate of payment for complete maternity care is to be adjusted to cover only the services actually rendered. When a physician refers an infant to a pediatrician for routine care during the first 2 weeks of life, no reduction need be made in the rate of payment to the physician for "complete maternity care."

In exceptional cases additional payments for attending physicians' services may be authorized by the State or local health agency for continuing care of the mother beyond 6 weeks postpartum, for a serious, acute complication resulting from pregnancy, such as puerperal infection.

(For rates of payment, see item (b) below.)

(b) *Medical care of intercurrent nonobstetric conditions.*

Additional payments for attending physicians' services for a period of 3 weeks, with review by the State or local health agency before authorizing an extension of care, may be authorized by the State or local health agency during pregnancy and 6 weeks postpartum for the home or hospital treatment of intercurrent conditions not attributable to pregnancy: At rates of payment for medical care as established by the State health agency but not to exceed $24 for the first 3 weeks of such illness, and for succeeding weeks of illness not to exceed $6 per week. The maximum rate of payment for a home visit for examination or treatment not to exceed $3 and for a hospital visit for examination or treatment not to exceed $2.

(c) *Major intermediate and minor nonobstetric intercurrent surgical operations.*

Additional payments may be authorized by the State or local health agency to attending physicians who qualify as consultants (for qualifications of consultants see section V-B) in a surgical specialty, for major, intermediate or minor nonobstetric surgical operations needed during pregnancy and 6 weeks postpartum for *conditions not attributable to pregnancy* (such as appendectomy during pregnancy): At a rate established by the State health agency but not to exceed a total of $50 for a major operation; the maximum rate established by the State agency for an intermediate operation; or $10 for a minor operation, for preoperative, operative, and postoperative care.

(d) *Prenatal care only, or spontaneous abortion.*

When only prenatal care is provided by the attending physician: At a rate of payment established by the State health agency but not to exceed $15 for care during the prenatal period. If fewer than five prenatal examinations are made, proportionate payment to be made for services rendered.

If pregnancy terminates in spontaneous abortion not requiring an operation: At a rate of payment not to exceed $15, plus proportionate payment for prenatal examinations made.

(e) *Therapeutic abortions.*

For therapeutic abortions or spontaneous abortions requiring an operation, including preoperative and postoperative care, the rate of payment will not exceed that established by the State health agency for care during labor and 6 weeks postpartum, plus proportionate payment for prenatal examinations made.

(f) *Ectopic pregnancy.*

For treatment of ectopic pregnancy, including preoperative and postoperative care when laparotomy is performed by attending physician: Rate of payment will not exceed the rate established by the State health agency for "complete maternity care."

(g) *Care of newborn infant by pediatrician.*

Routine care of newborn infant for first 2 weeks by a qualified pediatrician (see section V-C) when infant is referred by physician who does not customarily provide routine care for infants: At a rate established by the State health agency but not to exceed $6 a week. If fewer than three visits a week to the infant are made by the pediatrician, proportionate payment to be made for services rendered.

2. Hospital care during pregnancy, labor, or within 6 weeks after termination of pregnancy.

Authorization may be made for a maximum of 14 days, with extension of care authorized, when necessary, for 2-week periods, after review by the State or local health agency, with payment at the "per diem rate" established for payments to the hospital by the State health agency times the number of days' stay in the hospital, in accordance with the Children's Bureau memorandum of April 15, 1944, Purchase of Hospital Care Under Programs for Maternal and Child Health and Crippled Children.

3. Medical and surgical services provided through clinics[3] and hospitals.

When a patient has sought and received care in a clinic or hospital, the payments to the clinic or hospital will cover payment of the cost, including maintenance and salaries, of all medical services provided by interns, residents, or other physicians employed part time or full time by the clinic or hospital and by the physicians supervising or assisting the interns or resident physicians, as well as

[3] No authorization would be issued, nor payments made, for prenatal care given in prenatal clinics conducted by State or local public-health agencies. However, authorization for hospital care planned for through such a clinic would be necessary and should be requested by the physician in the clinic.

payment for all other services provided by the clinic or hospital, as follows:

(a) *For clinic services* in other than State or local health department clinics: At rates not to exceed the cost per clinic visit times the number of clinic visits and not to exceed the maximum rate established by the State health agency.

(b) *For hospital services:* The "per diem rate" established for payments to the hospital by the State health agency times the number of days' stay in the hospital, in accordance with the Children's Bureau memorandum of April 15, 1944, Purchase of Hospital Care Under Programs for Maternal and Child Health and Crippled Children.

(c) *For clinic and hospital service:* Many hospitals have an inclusive flat rate covering out-patient and in-patient medical and hospital maternity care. This flat rate may be paid if it does not exceed the total of (a) and (b) above.

4. Care of prolonged illness:

For cases of prolonged illness, the medical and hospital care and related services indicated above may be authorized for a period not to exceed 2 months. If additional care is required, extension for a maximum of 1 month may be authorized after review of the case by the State or local health agency.

B. FOR THE INFANT.

1. Medical and surgical services for sick infants provided by physicians in private practice.

This includes care that has been sought on behalf of, and received by, a sick infant in the private practice of a physician (home, hospital, or office) during the infant's first year of life. For this type of care payment is to be made directly by the State health agency to the physician. It also covers care sought on behalf of, and received by, a sick infant in the private practice of a physician employed full time or part time by a medical school, payments for which may be made to the medical school or to the physician, depending on the customary procedure for the receipt of such payments.

Medical care may be authorized for a period not to exceed 3 weeks, with review by the State health agency before authorizing extension of care.

Medical or hospital care authorized prior to an infant's first birthday may be completed even if the period covered by the authorization extends beyond the first birthday. No extension of the authorization may be issued. If it is apparent that care will be required beyond the first birthday, plans should be initiated immediately to assure continuation of care after the infant is no longer eligible for services provided under the EMIC program. Such planning will require the State health department to work closely with the family and community agencies.

(a) *Medical care:* At rates established by the State health agency but not to exceed $24 for the first 3 weeks of illness, and for succeeding weeks of illness not to exceed $6 per week. The maximum rate of payment for a home visit for examination or treatment not to exceed $3 and for an office or hospital visit for examination or treatment not to exceed $2.

Circumcision of an infant over 2 weeks of age on medical indication may be authorized at a rate of payment not to exceed $5 inclusive of aftercare, rather than payment on a visit basis, at the option of the State agency.

(b) *Major intermediate or minor surgery:* Additional payments may be authorized by the State health agency to attending physicians who qualify as consultants (for qualifications for consultants see section V-B) in a surgical specialty, for major, intermediate, or minor surgical operations performed on infants under their care, exclusive of operations for conditions that are included in State crippled children's programs: At rates of payment to be established by the State health agency but not to exceed a total of $50 for a major operation; the maximum rate established by the State agency for an intermediate operation; or $10 for a minor operation, for preoperative, operative, and postoperative care.

2. Hospital care.

Hospital care for sick infants may be authorized for *21 days* with extension of care authorized, when necessary, for *3-week* periods after review of the case by the State or local health agency: At the inclusive "per diem rate" established for payments to the hospital by the State health agency, in accordance with the Children's Bureau memorandum of April 15, 1944, Purchase of Hospital Care Under Programs for Maternal and Child Health and Crippled Children.

3. Medical and surgical services provided through clinics and hospitals.

When care of a sick infant has been sought and received in a hospital or clinic, the payments to the clinic or hospital will cover payment of the cost, including maintenance and salaries, of all medical services provided by interns, residents, and other physicians employed part time or full time by the clinic or hospital and by physicians supervising or assisting interns or resident physicians, as well as payment for all other services provided by the clinic or hospital, as follows:

(a) *For clinic services:* At a rate not to exceed the cost per clinic visits times the number of clinic visits and not to exceed the maximum rate established by the State health agency.

(b) *For hospital services:* The "per diem rate" established for payments to the hospital by the State health agency times the number of days' stay in the hospital, in accordance with the Children's Bureau memorandum of April 15, 1944, Purchase of Hospital Care under Programs for Maternal and Child Health and Crippled Children.

4. Immunizations.

In physicians' offices or at child-health conferences or immunization clinics not conducted by State or local health agencies:[4] At rates established by the State health agency but not to exceed $6 total for immunization for smallpox, diphtheria, and whooping cough, plus the cost of biologicals in States where these biologicals are not provided without cost by the State or local health agencies. These immunizations usually will require, during the first year of life, one procedure for smallpox, two or three for diphtheria, and three for whooping cough. If immunizations for all three diseases are not completed, proportionate payment to be made for services rendered.

5. Office medical care of infants including immunizations, on an annual basis.

(a) Office medical care may be provided on an annual basis by physicians with qualifications outlined in section V, B, paragraph 1 (general pracitioners). Office medical care under this plan shall include office care of infants when sick, immunizations (as in section IV, B, 4), and general advice on care of infant. This office medical service may be provided at rates not to exceed $16 a year with appropriate reductions on an equitable basis when the minimum services required by the State agency have not been provided. If health

[4]No authorization would be issued, nor payment made, for immunizations at child-health conferences or immunization clinics conducted by State or local public-health agencies.

supervision, including immunization, is provided at a child-health conference, the rate for office medical care shall not exceed $10 a year.

(b) The State plan shall include a statement of minimum services to be provided by physicians in private offices and in clinics and the method of reporting services rendered. When this service is undertaken in physicians' offices, the State agency should recognize its responsibility to supply advice, materials, consultation, or postgraduate instruction with a view to improving and protecting the standards of care given.

(c) The period covered by an application by the mother or other person in behalf of an infant for office medical care of an infant, including immunizations, may start (1) at birth or (2) at any office visit as requested on the application form, and continues through the first year of an infant's life. Authorization for care by the physician shall be made quarterly, semiannualy, or annually. If authorization is made annually, a quarterly or semiannual report from the physician shall be required so that encumbered funds may be released if no further care is to be given.

(d) Provisions for home visits by public-health nurses of either public or voluntary agencies shall be included in the plan for infant-health services whenever they are available or can be arranged in the community.

This plan for payment for *office* medical care of infants on an annual basis would be an alternative to the method of paying for office care provided for in section IV, B, 1, (a), that requires a new authorization every 3 weeks. It provides a simple method of paying for office medical care, for which authorization would be requested by the physician only on a quarterly or semiannual basis, and reports and payments made on the same basis. For the physician who is caring for a number of infants under the program this plan would result in much less "paper work."

This plan for paying for office medical care would not replace paying for medical care of a sick infant in the home or hospital as outlined in section IV, B, 1, (a), nor would it prevent the application of section IV, E, providing for individually adjusted payments for exceptional cases.

6. Health supervision of infants.

Health supervision of infants (including immunization) may be provided for infants under the EMIC program in child-health conferences and in the offices of qualified physicians under plans developed by State health agencies and in accordance with the following general policies of the Children's Bureau:

(a) *Health supervision of infants (including immunization) in child-health conferences:*

(1) In a community where conferences are maintained through public funds or by voluntary agencies or both, the mothers shall be allowed free choice of this service.

(2) Additional child-health conferences may be established with the use of EMIC funds, provided full use has been made of existing facilities under public health or voluntary health agencies and of all other resources for the establishment of such conferences through the use of funds under title V, part 1, of the Social Security Act.

Physicians conducting child-health conferences shall be paid in accordance with the schedule established for such services in the State's approved MCH plan.

(3) Health supervision may be purchased through EMIC funds for infants under the program from voluntary health agencies conducting child-health conferences. The rate per visit shall be established by the State agency, or care may be provided on an annual basis. Maximum payment for such health supervision (including immunizations and nursing service in homes) during the first year of life shall not exceed $15.

(4) The State plan shall include a statement of minimum services (medical, nursing, and other) that will be provided in child-health conferences, administered by either public or private agencies, and the extent of home visits by public-health nurses that are part of the child-health services rendered.

(b) *Health supervision of infants in physicians' offices and office medical care of sick infants:*

(1) Health supervision of infants may be provided on an annual basis by qualified physicians in their offices (see section V, C). (Wherever possible, child-health conferences should also be made available in order that the mother may have free choice.) When included in a State plan, this service shall cover complete health supervision, including immunization (section IV, B, 4) and office medical care of sick infants. It may be provided at rates not to exceed $24 a year with appropriate reductions on an equitable prorata basis when the minimum services required by the State agencies have not been provided.

(2) The State plan shall include a statement of minimum services to be provided by physicians in private offices and the method of reporting services rendered.

(3) The period covered by an application by the mother or other persons in behalf of an infant for health supervision may start (1) at birth or (2) at any office visit as requested on the application form and continues through the first year of an infant's life.

(c) *Public-health-nursing services.*

(1) Provisions for home visits by public-health nurses of either public or voluntary agencies shall be included in the plan for infant-health services whenever they are available or can be arranged in the community.

This plan for including office medical care of a sick infant in the plan for health supervision on an annual basis would be an alternative to the method of paying for office care provided for in section IV, B, 1, (a), that requires a new authorization every 3 weeks. It provides a simple method of paying for office medical care, under which authorization would be requested by the physicians only on a quarterly or semiannual basis, with report and payments on the same basis. For the physician who is caring for a number of infants under the program this plan would result in much less "paper work."

Under this plan of health supervision, medical care of a sick infant in the home or hospital would still be paid for in accordance with the provisions outlined in section IV, B, 1, (a). It would not prevent the application of section IV, D, providing for differential rates of payment for specialists, nor section IV, E, providing for individually adjusted payments for exceptional cases.

7. Care of prolonged illness.

For cases of prolonged illness, the medical and hospital care and related services indicated above may be authorized for a period not to exceed 2 months. If additional care is required, extension for a maximum of 1 month may be authorized after review of the case by the State or local health agency.

C. FOR THE WIFE OR INFANT.

1. *Consultation services requested by attending physician* from consultants on list approved by the State health agency.

(a) *Long distance telephone consultation*: The actual cost of the call.

(b) *Bedside or office consultation:* At the rate of payment established by the State health agency but not to exceed $10 per consultation.

(c) *Consultation which includes performance of a major, intermediate, or minor surgical operation by the consultant and for the preoperative and postoperative care provided by the consultant*: At the rate of payment established by the State health agency but not to exceed $50 for a major operation; the maximum rate established by the State agency for an intermediate operation, or $10 for a minor operation.

2. *Bedside nursing service when requested by attending physician.*

(a) *In a hospital or in the home by graduate nurses on a per diem basis*: Special nursing services during a period of critical illness either in the home or in a hospital when such nursing services cannot be provided by nurses employed by the hospital, and when no expenditures for special nursing service have been included in the hospital's annual statement of operating expenses, may be authorized for a period not to exceed 6 days, with review by State or local health agency before authorizing extension of care, at prevailing local per diem rates not to exceed the maximum rate established by the State health agency.

(b) *In the home by nursing staff of a voluntary public-health or visiting-nurse agency or by other graduate nurses on a visit or hourly basis* (when such nursing services cannot be made available by State or local public-health agencies): Visits for care of mother and infant while the mother is receiving bed care during the puerperium, visits for care of a sick mother or infant, or visits for care of a patient who has complications in order to carry out specific orders by the physician, such as determining blood pressure, urinalysis, or giving special treatment or medications, may be authorized not to exceed 6 visits, with review by State or local health agency before authorizing extension of care, at prevailing local rates per visit, but not to exceed the maximum rate established by the State health agency.

(c) *In the home throughout the period of labor and delivery*: Nursing care through this period may be authorized at prevailing local rates but not to exceed the maximum rate established by the State health agency.

3. *Blood for transfusions:* May be authorized at the customary

minimum rate paid by the hospital but not to exceed the maximum rate established by the State health agency.

4. *Ambulance service*: When requested by attending physician or hospital, ambulance service may be authorized at prevailing local rates but not to exceed the maximum rate established by the State health agency.

5. *Additional payment for time in travel and for cost of travel to attending physician or consultant:* May be authorized for attending seriously ill patients or for home or hospital deliveries and after-care outside of city limits of physician's residence, at rates established by the State health agency but not to exceed 25 cents per mile each way traveled outside of the city limits, with a maximum payment of $25 to a physician for travel for any one case.

6. *Additional payment for cost of travel of graduate nurse* not employed by a public or voluntary health agency to the home of a patient may be allowed at the cost of transportation outside of city limits on a public carrier or at the usual rate for mileage established for State employees.

7. *Payment to a physician assisting the surgeon* in the performance of a major or intermediate surgical operation in hospitals without a resident staff may be authorized at a rate not to exceed $10 per operation.

8. *X-ray and laboratory services.* If the attending physician does not have office facilities for taking X-rays or for providing special laboratory services, the patient may be referred to another physician or to a hospital or to a private laboratory for such services. In such instances, the physician or hospital or laboratory to whom the patient was referred may be paid at rates established by the State agency.

9. *Anesthesia.* If the patient is hospitalized in a hospital that does not have provisions for giving anesthesia or if the patient is delivered at home, services of an anesthetist may be authorized at a rate not to exceed $10.

10. *Drugs.* Drugs prescribed by the attending physician for patients not hospitalized may be purchased under the EMIC program at the option of the State agency, and under policies and procedures established by the State agency.

D. RATES OF PAYMENT FOR SPECIALISTS.

1. Rates of payment for specialists for care confined to their specialty may be established, at the option of the State health agency,

that shall not exceed by more than 50 percent the maximum rates adopted by the State agency in accordance with policies established in section IV, A, 1 and 4; IV, B, 1, 4, 5, 6 and 7; and IV, C, 1, (b) and (c), but in no case shall such rates of payment exceed those customarily received by such specialists.

E. INDIVIDUALLY ADJUSTED PAYMENTS FOR EXCEPTIONAL CASES.

A State health agency may make provision under its State EMIC plan for adjusting, on an individual case basis, payments to physicians for extraordinarily severe cases that require an exceptional amount of care by the attending physician within a period of time covered by a single authorization for care of a sick infant or a non-obstetric intercurrent condition in a maternity patient. Criteria and standards shall be set forth in the State plan that will limit the selection of such exceptional cases to those requiring an extraordinary number of visits or unusual care. The State plan shall show the maximum rate established by the State agency for each authorization period of exceptional medical care for which payment would be made under section IV, A, 1, (b) and (c); B, 1, (a) and (b).

V. Qualifications for Physicians and Nurses Participating in the Program.

A. FOR OBSTETRIC SERVICES.

Qualifications required of practitioners performing obstetric services under the program shall be established by each State health agency.

Specialists in obstetrics: If differential rates of payment for specialists in obstetrics are established, the State health agency shall determine the qualifications for specialists in obstetrics and shall set forth in its State EMIC plan the method to be adopted and the criteria to be employed by the State in differentiating between specialists and general practitioners and shall show that the group of physicians identified as specialists in obstetrics under the State plan includes only physicians who have had superior training and customarily receive higher fees than general practitioners and shall show that the group of physicians identified as specialists in obstetrics under the State plan includes only physicians who have had superior training and customarily receive higher fees than general practitioners for rendering regular obstetric service.[5]

[5] It is suggested that State agencies consider designating as specialists only those physicians who are entitled under the State EMIC plan to render obstetric service and are certified by a recognized board of obstetrics established for the purpose of such certification, or who are qualified to meet the requirements of training and experience for admission to the examinations of such boards.

B. FOR MEDICAL SERVICES OTHER THAN OBSTETRIC.

Graduates of medical schools approved, at the time of graduation or subsequent to graduation, by the Council on Medical Education and Hospitals of the American Medical Association. Individual exceptions may be made when a person with the degree of Doctor of Medicine who is not a graduate of a medical school approved, at time of graduation or subsequent to graduation, by the Council on Medical Education and Hospitals of the American Medical Association has completed postgraduate training which, in the opinion of the State health officer and his technical advisory committee, makes him competent to participate in this program.

Additional qualifications for consultants: Specialists who are certified by their respective American boards of medical specialties, or whose training and experience meet the requirements of training and experience for admission to the examinations of such boards, should be designated as consultants by the State health departments and, whenever possible, made available for bedside consultation, or telephone consultation when bedside consultation is not feasible, with physicians participating in the plan. Physicians who have had at least 1 year of graduate training in a residency in their specialty approved by the Council on Medical Education and Hospitals of the American Medical Association and at least 1 year's experience limited to the practice of the specialty may be designated as assistant consultants.

For areas where consultants with the training and experience as set forth in the above paragraph are not available, a State technical advisory committee, appointed by the State health agency for this program, should recommend to the State health agency a plan for providing consultation to patients living in such areas.

Lists of physicians approved by the State health agency as consultants in the various specialties should be made available to all physicians participating in the program.

Specialists: If differential rates of payment for specialists are established by the State health agency, a specialist shall be defined as a physician who is a graduate of a medical school approved, at the time of graduation or subsequent to graduation, by the Council on Medical Education and Hospitals of the American Medical Association and who has been certified by the American Board of his medical specialty or has the training and experience for admission to the examinations of such board.

C. FOR PEDIATRIC SERVICES TO NEWBORN INFANTS AND HEALTH SUPERVISION OF INFANTS IN THE PHYSICIAN'S OFFICE.

Diplomates of the American Board of Pediatrics or physicians who have completed at least 1 year of graduate training in a pediatric residency approved by the Council on Medical Education and Hospitals of the American Medical Association.

Exception: When a physician has had experience in rendering supervised service in a child-health conference that in the opinion of the State agency qualifies him to provide health supervision in his office, he may be designated to provide health supervision to infants in his office even though his training in pediatrics is less than here defined.

D. FOR NURSING SERVICE PURCHASED ON A CASE BASIS.

Graduate nurses registered or eligible for registration by meeting requirements of the State board of nurse examiners and having had training and experience in maternity and/or pediatric nursing as required by the State health agency.

CHILDREN AND YOUTH
Social Problems and Social Policy

An Arno Press Collection

Abt, Henry Edward. **The Care, Cure and Education of the Crippled Child.** 1924

Addams, Jane. **My Friend, Julia Lathrop.** 1935

American Academy of Pediatrics. **Child Health Services and Pediatric Education:** Report of the Committee for the Study of Child Health Services. 1949

American Association for the Study and Prevention of Infant Mortality. **Transactions of the First Annual Meeting of the American Association for the Study and Prevention of Infant Mortality.** 1910

Baker, S. Josephine. **Fighting For Life.** 1939

Bell, Howard M. **Youth Tell Their Story:** A Study of the Conditions and Attitudes of Young People in Maryland Between the Ages of 16 and 24. 1938

Bossard, James H. S. and Eleanor S. Boll, editors. **Adolescents in Wartime.** 1944

Bossard, James H. S., editor. **Children in a Depression Decade.** 1940

Brunner, Edmund DeS. **Working With Rural Youth.** 1942

Care of Dependent Children in the Late Nineteenth and Early Twentieth Centuries. Introduction by Robert H. Bremner. 1974

Care of Handicapped Children. Introduction by Robert H. Bremner. 1974

[Chenery, William L. and Ella A. Merritt, editors]. **Standards of Child Welfare:** A Report of the Children's Bureau Conferences, May and June, 1919. 1919

The Child Labor Bulletin, 1912, 1913. 1974

Children In Confinement. Introduction by Robert M. Mennel. 1974

Children's Bureau Studies. Introduction by William M. Schmidt. 1974

Clopper, Edward N. **Child Labor in City Streets.** 1912

David, Paul T. **Barriers To Youth Employment.** 1942

Deutsch, Albert. **Our Rejected Children.** 1950

Drucker, Saul and Maurice Beck Hexter. **Children Astray.** 1923

Duffus, R[obert] L[uther] and L. Emmett Holt, Jr. **L. Emmett Holt:** Pioneer of a Children's Century. 1940

Fuller, Raymond G. **Child Labor and the Constitution.** 1923

Holland, Kenneth and Frank Ernest Hill. **Youth in the CCC.** 1942

Jacoby, George Paul. **Catholic Child Care in Nineteenth Century New York:** With a Correlated Summary of Public and Protestant Child Welfare. 1941

Johnson, Palmer O. and Oswald L. Harvey. **The National Youth Administration.** 1938

The Juvenile Court. Introduction by Robert M. Mennel. 1974

Klein, Earl E. **Work Accidents to Minors in Illinois.** 1938

Lane, Francis E. **American Charities and the Child of the Immigrant:** A Study of Typical Child Caring Institutions in New York and Massachusetts Between the Years 1845 and 1880. 1932

The Legal Rights of Children. Introduction by Sanford N. Katz. 1974

Letchworth, William P[ryor]. **Homes of Homeless Children:** A Report on Orphan Asylums and Other Institutions for the Care of Children. [1903]

Lorwin, Lewis. **Youth Work Programs:** Problems and Policies. 1941

Lundberg, Emma O[ctavia] and Katharine F. Lenroot. **Illegitimacy As A Child-Welfare Problem, Parts 1 and 2.** 1920/1921

New York State Commission on Relief for Widowed Mothers. **Report of the New York State Commission on Relief for Widowed Mothers.** 1914

Otey, Elizabeth Lewis. **The Beginnings of Child Labor Legislation in Certain States;** A Comparative Study. 1910

Phillips, Wilbur C. **Adventuring For Democracy.** 1940

Polier, Justine Wise. **Everyone's Children, Nobody's Child:** A Judge Looks At Underprivileged Children in the United States. 1941

Proceedings of the Annual Meeting of the National Child Labor Committee, 1905, 1906. 1974

Rainey, Homer P. **How Fare American Youth?** 1940

Reeder, Rudolph R. **How Two Hundred Children Live and Learn.** 1910

Security and Services For Children. 1974

Sinai, Nathan and Odin W. Anderson. **EMIC (Emergency Maternity and Infant Care):** A Study of Administrative Experience. 1948

Slingerland, W. H. **Child-Placing in Families:** A Manual For Students and Social Workers. 1919

[Solenberger], Edith Reeves. **Care and Education of Crippled Children in the United States.** 1914

Spencer, Anna Garlin and Charles Wesley Birtwell, editors. **The Care of Dependent, Neglected and Wayward Children:** Being a Report of the Second Section of the International Congress of Charities, Correction and Philanthropy, Chicago, June, 1893. 1894

Theis, Sophie Van Senden. **How Foster Children Turn Out.** 1924

Thurston, Henry W. **The Dependent Child:** A Story of Changing Aims and Methods in the Care of Dependent Children. 1930

U.S. Advisory Committee on Education. **Report of the Committee, February, 1938.** 1938

The United States Children's Bureau, 1912-1972. 1974

White House Conference on Child Health and Protection. **Dependent and Neglected Children:** Report of the Committee on Socially Handicapped — Dependency and Neglect. 1933

White House Conference on Child Health and Protection. **Organization for the Care of Handicapped Children, National, State, Local.** 1932

White House Conference on Children in a Democracy. **Final Report of the White House Conference on Children in A Democracy.** [1942]

Wilson, Otto. **Fifty Years' Work With Girls, 1883-1933:** A Story of the Florence Crittenton Homes. 1933

Wrenn, C. Gilbert and D. L. Harley. **Time On Their Hands:** A Report on Leisure, Recreation, and Young People. 1941